Aging Thoughtfully

Aging Thoughtfully

Conversations about Retirement, Romance, Wrinkles, and Regret

MARTHA C. NUSSBAUM
SAUL LEVMORE

OXFORD
UNIVERSITY PRESS

OXFORD
UNIVERSITY PRESS

Oxford University Press is a department of the University of Oxford. It furthers
the University's objective of excellence in research, scholarship, and education
by publishing worldwide. Oxford is a registered trade mark of Oxford University
Press in the UK and in certain other countries.

Published in the United States of America by Oxford University Press
198 Madison Avenue, New York, NY 10016, United States of America.

CIP data is on file at the Library of Congress
ISBN 978–0–19–060023–5

9 8 7 6 5 4 3 2 1
Printed by Edwards Brothers Malloy, United States of America

To Rachel, Nathaniel, and Eliot

Contents

Acknowledgments

WE WOULD LIKE, most of all, to thank the University of Chicago Law School for creating an ideal environment for work and for critical conversations that have helped us greatly. At the penultimate stage of the manuscript's development we were fortunate to have extensive written comments from Douglas Baird, William Birdthistle, and Emily Dupree, who generously poured over the entire book. For written comments on specific chapters we would like to thank Brian Leiter and Lior Strahilevitz. And we had expert research assistance from Emily Dupree, Nethanel Lipshitz, and Alex Weber.

Introduction

THIS BOOK IS about living thoughtfully, and certainly not about dying, gracefully or otherwise. To age is to experience, to gain wisdom, to love and to lose, and to grow more comfortable in one's own skin, however much it might be loosening. Aging is many other things. For some people, it might be about regretting, worrying, hoarding, and needing. It can also be about volunteering, comprehending, guiding, rediscovering, forgiving, and, with increasing frequency, forgetting. For the financially fortunate, it can be about retiring and bequeathing and, in turn, saving and spending in the preceding years. Many of these tendencies also pertain to people who do not yet think of themselves as aging. But these young friends, relatives, and colleagues often regard their elders as storehouses of wisdom, as well as walking warnings. This quest, to find the good, or even just the wisdom, in the wrinkles, is at least as old as Cicero, whose work is as relevant in our fast-changing world as it was two thousand years ago.

If, unlike other species, we learn, record, and widely communicate our errors and successes, and do so in ways that have expanded the frontiers of the human experience and improved the lives of succeeding generations, then perhaps we can also expect progress in the personal realm. We have made advances in agriculture, manufacturing, and aviation. It is less clear that we have done so with respect to partnering, parenting, and choosing political leaders, and perhaps this is because the problems in these realms are moving targets that are not conquered over time through incremental scientific progress. Aging falls between these scientific and interpersonal challenges. On average we live longer and more comfortably than our predecessors. We have more choices, and this book is about these choices.

If we accept that aging is a time of life, then it follows that it is something we have in common. Each of us ages in his or her own way, but we can learn from others' experiences. As people age, their interests, behaviors, and preferences may change—often in ways that confirm the shared experience. As we age, are we more or less competitive? Spiritual? Frugal? Needy? Envious? Tolerant? Generous? We may need friends to help us recognize these changes, and to think through their desirability. When an isolated individual observes and contemplates, it is hard to discern whether one has become more self-absorbed, more accepting of criticism, more frightening to others, or more unreasonable in making demands on family members. Self-knowledge might therefore require friendships and conversations, and in this book we hope to set an example in this regard.

We offer different perspectives on topics related to aging, with the aim of continuing the conversation with each other and our readers. Some of our chapters are designed to help families have meaningful conversations about matters they ought to discuss before disability or death intervenes. We encourage thoughtfulness and communication about topics that are often regarded as awkward or private. Few people talk with outsiders about the problems they face in passing on property to their children, especially when children are in disparate financial circumstances, have been difficult, or are embedded in fractured families. Similarly, few people talk seriously about philosophical questions, such as the nature of one's longing for perpetual influence. Finally, most people are quite aware of physical changes as they age, and yet are uncomfortable talking about their bodies. This may have something to do with the nature of rekindled love and new romance among mature partners. We engage with such topics in these chapters. One of us approaches these topics as a philosopher and the other as a lawyer-economist inclined to think in terms of incentives, but we share a conviction that an academic perspective on these topics bears practical fruit.

Other topics are easy to broach, and for these we try to provide broad, philosophical, and policy-oriented perspectives. We talk about the all-too-common problem of wanting to manage things one cannot completely control, including other people. We see aging as a time of life, just like childhood, young adulthood, and middle age. It has its own puzzles in need of reflection. It has unique pleasures and joys, as well as pains. But, perhaps because people are disinclined to think of aging as an opportunity, few works of reflection treat the puzzles that belong to this time of life. Our goal is to investigate some of the complicated and fascinating questions that arise in this time of life; the questions are about living more than about ending.

The form of our book is inspired by Cicero's *De Senectute* (*On Aging*). Written in 45 B.C.E., the work is framed as a conversation with Cicero's best friend, Atticus, to whom he addressed thousands of surviving letters. The two were in their sixties, and Cicero, dedicating the work to Atticus in a preface, says that even though they are not all that old yet (Romans were a very healthy lot), they really ought to think ahead to what life has in store for them. The work is intended as a diversion, Cicero says, because both of them are worried about politics and about family issues.

Cicero invents a little dialogue in which a truly aged man, Cato, age eighty-three at the dramatic date of the dialogue—healthy, active, still a leader in politics, a famous host and friend, and an avid farmer—talks to two men in their thirties who press him for information about that time of life. Since they have heard all sorts of negative things about aging, they would like to know how he would reply to some charges commonly made against that period of life: that it lacks creativity, that the body can't accomplish anything, that there is no pleasure, that death is a constant fearful presence. Even though young, they say, they know that they are heading to where Cato currently is—if they are lucky enough to get there—and ask for his insider's view of their common destination. Cato happily accepts, because one of the great pleasures of age, he says, is conversation with younger people. Cicero, through his Cato, always has his eye on a larger audience—on conversation on many topics with readers of different ages, and, as it has turned out, in many different times and places.

Our book, like Cicero's, is prompted by a series of conversations between friends in their sixties about a part of the life cycle that we are entering. We too have found that talking about aging is pleasant and helpful, and that the topic can really use philosophical, legal, and economic reflection. We offer pairs of essays about different aspects of this time of life, showing how analysis and argument can entertain and offer insight. We are lucky enough to have a two-sided correspondence, with divergent personalities and disciplinary approaches. Each chapter has two essays; one either replies to the other or offers a different approach to a particular topic. Like Cicero, we hope to engage readers of various ages in a many-sided conversation.

OUR OPENING ESSAYS are motivated by Act I of Shakespeare's *King Lear*, in which the aging king makes a series of bad decisions about retirement, inheritance, and family relationships. It is a work that no discussion of aging can easily avoid. Recent productions have tended to emphasize the theme of aging, and in a reaction to one such production Martha argues that it is a mistake to see the work as a commentary on dementia or any other universal, individuality-effacing feature of aging. It is instead about the aging of a very particular type of person, one accustomed to dominating and enjoying control. Such people are easily knocked off course by aging, unless they have planned ahead and introspected. In a companion essay, Saul picks up the theme of control, and explores the ways in which people use their aging to control others, to encourage or measure love and care, with their promises about distributing property.

Chapter 2 turns to the more mundane topic of retirement. The United States is nearly exceptional in making mandatory retirement and age discrimination illegal. Saul argues for something of a return to freedom of contract, as he makes contrarian arguments against the dominant American view. The argument takes us through a history of pension plans and the history of a falling, and now rising, average retirement age. The essay explains why political forces are likely to prevent desirable changes, except perhaps some extra taxation of affluent, older workers. Martha has grave doubts about all this. She argues that the current system gives aging people more dignity. It also makes both younger and aging people expect productivity and involvement from people as they age, and these habits and expectations have good effects on the mental well-being of aging people and on intergenerational relations.

We have said that our literary model is Cicero, and we turn in chapter 3 to his two essays, *On Aging* and *On Friendship*. Martha finds them perceptive on both topics, as well as their intersection, but discovers even more insight in the letters Cicero exchanges with his best friend, Atticus, containing the daily texture of a real friendship. In response, Saul turns to Cicero's account of the way friendship contributes to life at different ages, and offers his own assessment of some of the difficult questions that arise. When should a friend do something ethically dubious or personally risky because of friendship? And when should a friend tell a friend that it is time to withdraw from active professional life?

The aging body is stigmatized, and aging people themselves often feel ashamed of their bodies. Once upon a time, Martha observes in chapter 4, the baby-boomer generation stood courageously against bodily disgust and shame. The classic manual *Our Bodies, Ourselves* urged women not to hide from their bodies, but to get to know them without shame, and even maybe to love them. Where has that bold challenge to convention gone? And doesn't it make sense to pursue the same radical antishame project once again, in a different context? Saul agrees, for once, suggesting that wrinkles and baldness might even be glamorous. He explores cosmetic surgery, the popularity of various antiaging procedures, and the likelihood that the rate of surgical interventions might depend on the communities in which we live as we age.

Aging is naturally a retrospective time, a time when we examine and reassess past life both for our own purposes and because younger people think we have some wisdom to offer. Sometimes this backward look brings regret. In chapter 5, Martha addresses the topic of backward-looking emotions, and the relationship between regret and its relatives, grief and anger. In general, such emotions seem futile, since one cannot change the past. She draws on Eugene O'Neill's *Long Day's Journey into Night* and Michel Butor's *L'Emploi du temps* (*Passing Time*) to emphasize the danger of allowing the past to determine one's life. And yet, a "presentist" approach to life, with hedonistic fervor and no introspection, is also unattractive. Martha sees a presentist flavor in many retirement communities. Saul rises to the defense of these communities but suggests that they will undergo changes in succeeding generations. More generally, he doubts that most people who are prisoners of the past can learn to be forward-looking.

What about love among the aging? Some people, and especially young ones, think of aging as a time when people do not fall in love, but they are surely wrong. Martha pursues this topic in chapter 6, beginning with Strauss's opera *Der Rosenkavalier* and then returning to Shakespeare, whose *Romeo and Juliet* and *Antony and Cleopatra* offer an illuminating contrast between young and aging love. In the opera, a mature and lonely woman finds sexual pleasure with a seventeen-year-old boy. This coupling presents an opportunity to think about misconceptions about the love life of mature women. For good measure, and to bring the discussion down from the heights of classical poetry to daily reality, Martha looks at a few recent films, including *The Hundred-Foot Journey*, starring the sixty-eight-year-old Helen Mirren, and *It's Complicated*, in which Meryl Streep and Alec Baldwin rediscover their former attraction as aging lovers (with Steve Martin playing a less significant, though ultimately successful, romantic role). Saul carries the conversation forward with a more extensive discussion of "gap couples," where there is a significant age difference between partners. He draws lessons from celebrity couples of this description, and argues that we can view romantic rejection as a good thing even as we celebrate durable couples. The chapter ends with some speculation about the future of couples like those found in the Strauss opera, where the woman is significantly older than the man.

Much of this book is about people who are affluent enough to think about retiring at the right age, leaving wealth to children in disparate financial circumstances, and improving physical appearances with injections and surgery, but there are many aging people who struggle to survive. Chapter 7 deals head on with the reality of grave wealth inequality. Saul assesses the scope of the problem with respect to the elderly poor. He is concerned for all the people who have not saved for retirement and offers a serious plan for building a larger forced savings component into Social Security. Martha's approach has less to do with what is politically feasible and more to do with political philosophy. She draws on her own "capabilities approach" to sketch what a just society ought to offer the elderly. In the process, she offers a critical comparison of the Finnish and American approaches (and their shortcomings) with regard to the elderly.

Finally, chapter 8 turns to the legacies we might like to leave behind. Saul explores two paradoxes. The first concerns the question of whether to give away money as soon as one can afford to do so or to defer philanthropy in order to learn more about potential beneficiaries. The discussion explains pieces of modern option theory and also draws on his experience as a fundraiser. The second paradox returns to the question of whether to provide for loved ones evenhandedly or to take their financial circumstances into account. The chapter offers a novel strategy for those eager to break the convention of equal distribution, but fearful of starting family squabbles. Martha finishes with thoughts about altruism and ways to perpetuate oneself. She asks and answers the enormous question of how to think about our contribution to the life of an ongoing world.

THESE SIXTEEN ESSAYS are meant to provoke rather than exhaust discussion of how we might all age thoughtfully. We hope that our readers enjoy, as we do, the different perspective that comes from aging. Subjects such as King Lear's bequests, compulsory retirement, plastic surgery, philanthropy, and romance where there is a significant age gap simply look very different when one is a half-century or so past the point where these issues were first encountered. We have tried to bring fresh approaches to these and other subjects, and to show that thinking and arguing about them is not only practical, but also one of the great pleasures of aging.

Chapter 1

Learning from King Lear

WHAT IS THE nature of Lear's vulnerability and why is he so unhappy about it? What should we learn from Lear's error in choosing among his daughters, and should he have chosen better or treated them equally? When is it a good idea to withhold expected inheritances? How does one learn to cede control?

Aging and Control in *King Lear*— and the Danger of Generalization

Martha

PRODUCTIONS OF *KING LEAR* these days are obsessively concerned with the theme of aging. Just as the postwar period saw an emphasis on emptiness, loss of meaning, and utter devastation (in Peter Brook's memorable production starring Paul Scofield, but also in countless others after that), so in our time it is the age theme that has become popular, and that may even account in part for the play's recent surge in popularity. Productions follow the preoccupations of their intended audience. Today, many or even most audience members for a Shakespeare production are personally anxious about aging, are currently caring for an aging relative, or both. We should mention also the legions of long-lived excellent actors who want to play the role, and are not deterred by its extreme physical demands. Laurence Olivier (76 when he played the role), Ian McKellen (68), Stacy Keach (68), Christopher Plummer (72), Sam Waterston (71), John Lithgow (69), Frank Langella (76), Derek Jacobi (72), and, most recently, Glenda Jackson (80). We are clearly a long way from Shakespeare's own Lear, Richard Burbage, who played the role at 39, and further yet from Gielgud, at 29. (Scofield, by the way, was only 40, but it didn't matter, because that production did not emphasize aging.)

A masterpiece yields new insights when produced with a new emphasis, and *Lear* is no exception. So I do not criticize directors for choosing to emphasize the theme of aging. And the play, in which Lear asks for expressions of love and then divides his kingdom between the two daughters (Goneril and Regan) who fawn on him and disinherits the one (Cordelia) who really loves him, investigates themes of dispossession, loss, and eventual madness that Shakespeare does connect clearly with Lear's advancing age. Still, there is something amiss with one common way this emphasis is realized: some directorial choices lead us away from the insights about aging that the play actually offers. Let's start with a representative example.

A much-lauded Chicago production of *King Lear* in 2014 begins like this.[1] Actor Larry Yando, playing the king in a vaguely modern setting, as an aging tycoon in his elegant bedroom suite, wearing a high-end dressing gown, tries out some Frank Sinatra songs on his fancy stereo. With the petulance of a child throwing away boring toys, he rejects "That's Life," "My Way," and "Witchcraft"—each time smashing a plastic remote in frustration and getting another from the attentive servants who surround him. (The repeated gratuitous destruction sounds a false note: tycoons—unlike hereditary monarchs—get where they are by not being wasteful, and he could so easily change the band without smashing the remote.) Finally he arrives at "I've Got the World on a String." Satisfied, he dances around delightedly, partnering only himself, but with great agility. As *Chicago Tribune* critic Chris Jones notes, this is "a cheap choice because those who actually need to believe they have the world on a string, like Lear, so rarely expose themselves with so obvious a lyrical preference."[2] But Lear is happy, and aside from a certain manic anxiety in his whole demeanor, shows no signs of aging. Apart from the heavy-handed choice of songs, it's a riveting performance of an unloving, captious man, aging but still very fit, wrapped up in his own power, used to having his own way with everything and everyone.

Just a few moments later, however, Lear has difficulty remembering the names of his sons-in-law—and as he searches for the words that won't come, there's a look of terror on his face, as the devastation of incipient dementia reveals itself. It's a stunning moment. But is it a convincing interpretation of the play? Director Barbara Gaines informs us in the program that Lear is about all of us who either are aging ourselves, or have an aging relative—or both. In act 4, scene 7, Lear indeed describes himself as "four score and upward," thus pinpointing the age rather precisely. Yando, however, told the *Chicago Sun-Times* that he is playing Lear "as my age, not 80." Yando is currently fifty-eight. So apparently what we are seeing is extremely early-onset dementia. (This fits badly with the way Yando moves in later acts, with the shuffle of a very old man, but never mind—right now I'm just talking about the first act.) So: is *Lear* plausibly or revealingly staged as about early-onset dementia?[3]

It has become almost a cliché to do what Gaines and Yando do, writing the decline and the mental frailty into the play's very opening. In fact the device of forgetting the names was already used by Plummer, although I don't know whether he invented it. Indeed R. A. Foakes, editor of the Arden edition of the play, finds that senior decline, inserted into the play's very opening, is a hallmark of productions in the 1990s: Lear is likely to appear as "an increasingly pathetic senior citizen trapped in a violent and hostile environment."[4] The popularity of the aging theme, so emphasized, has led to a glut of productions of the play, as audiences, more than a bit narcissistic, like to focus on their own future, near or far. *Los Angeles Times* critic Charles McNulty, in an eloquent article, doubts the wisdom of this whole trend, which he plausibly attributes to the graying of the baby boomers. He declares that it may be time for a moratorium on attempts to stage the play at all.[5]

So what's wrong with Yando's memory lapse? One obvious problem is that it is not in the text at all. It is not until he is out on the heath that Lear shows mental imbalance, and even then, it's some sort of "madness," but it surely doesn't fit the all-too-familiar cliché of Alzheimer's disease, given his verbal eloquence and his insights into the nature of human beings and their world. Indeed, a more pertinent criticism of Gaines—for of course directors can and should insert things not directly in the text if they illuminate the work—putting Lear into the box of Alzheimer's from the start makes it pretty hard to relate the Lear of the opening to the Lear, deranged but deeply insightful, who emerges later—one reason that Yando's performance of those later scenes has impressed audiences and critics less than his work in the opening.

In act 1—and my discussion in this essay is limited to act 1—it is Goneril and Regan, not the most trustworthy witnesses, who refer to Lear's aging—and in a way that does not in the least suggest dementia of the Alzheimer's sort. The former says, "You see how full of changes his age is" (1.1.190)—but she is referring to his emotionally capricious disinheriting of Cordelia, which is hardly due to dementia, whatever we think does cause it. The latter replies: "'Tis the infirmity of his age, yet he hath ever but slenderly known himself" (294–95), thus immediately qualifying the reference to age with allusion to a long-term problem—and getting to the heart of the matter, as we shall see. Even they, then, do not suggest that he is suffering from dementia or mental weakness: at most emotional inconstancy, and that, they suggest, has probably been caused all along by his character.

To see why this is the right place to look, consider Lear's human relationships heretofore, as act 1 reveals them. With his daughters—even

Cordelia, whom he appears to favor—he is formal, cold, domineering, manipulative. He wants set speeches that exemplify subordination. What he surely does not want is any part in reciprocal affection.[6] As for friendship, there's nothing even close. He has no wife, nor does he recall the one he must at some point have had. With Kent—both before and after his fall—Lear is the commanding ruler, determined to punish disobedience, though (later) willing to accept a loyal subordinate. His only relationship of potential friendship and reciprocity is with the Fool, who (unlike most real-life court jesters) doesn't care about royal power—and the maturation of that relationship, as the play goes on, tracks or even helps to cause Lear's emergence as a human being.

Aging, Control, and Self-Knowledge

The deepest problem with an Alzheimer's-demented Lear in act 1, scene 1, is that such a performance prevents us from understanding one of the play's most powerful themes: the effect of sudden powerlessness on a person who has been totally hooked on his own power and fantasized invulnerability. For Regan is right: Lear has not known himself, and has not had even a basic understanding of his own humanity. He has thought that, as king, he is a kind of god, able to control everyone and everything. So he is simply unprepared for aging, which involves loss of control and the need for care. It's bad for your progress through this world to believe that you are a king, and if you are one, it's very likely that you will slenderly know yourself, meaning that you will not understand that you are a dependent and vulnerable human being.

Janet Adelman, insightful here as always, says that what's horrifying to Lear, when he suddenly recognizes that his daughters have power over him, is "to recognize not only his terrifying dependence on female forces outside himself but also an equally terrifying femaleness within himself."[7] By femaleness she means passivity, noncontrol, and above all, a need for others. As the Fool shortly says, Lear has made "thy daughters thy mothers (1.4.163)—and yet is utterly unprepared to be, or to admit that he is, a needy child.

It's far too cheap to make Alzheimer's the problem. That's a force that strikes from outside the personality. It could happen to anybody, and it happens to everyone in pretty much the same way. It has nothing to do with the way you led your life heretofore, and it eclipses your identity quickly. Lear's problem is that, while still being himself, a captious and

sometimes violent man used to having no relationships that are not relationships of control, he suddenly finds the tables turned—and is utterly
unprepared for powerlessness. But control is his very identity, and that
is why the sudden failure of those around him to revere and serve him
strikes at the heart of the person he thinks he is. "Does any here know
me?" he asks (after Goneril's tough-minded objection to his retinue). He
means that to know him is to acknowledge his total power and his right
to do as he likes. But he is no longer using the royal "we"—thus tacitly
acknowledging that he has lost authority. "Why this is not Lear," he continues. "Who is it that can tell me who I am?" (1.4.217–21). In the intervening
lines he does say of himself, "Either his notion weakens, or his discern-
ings are lethargied," but commentators plausibly interpret these lines to
mean that he is trying to reassure himself that all this disrespectful and
disobedient behavior might be a dream—"Ha! Sleeping or waking? Sure
'tis not so." All too soon, however, he finds out that disregard and disre-
spect are no dream but reality.

None of us is really prepared for powerlessness, and powerlessness
comes to us all in varying forms as we age. (Perhaps the least afflicted are
those who really do suffer from Alzheimer's, since they soon fail to notice
what they lack.) But to those who define their identity around control
of others, powerlessness comes with a more devastating jolt. You can't
be what was the core of who you were, and then you have to figure out
some other identity, some other way to go on. Yando's superb opening
sequence shows a man who could have played this drama in a subtle and
revealing way, showing a loss of power that leads to a new sort of search
for the self. The second half of the play shows the beginning of such a
search—but only after Lear is driven partly mad by the collapse of his old
identity.

Yando indeed showed such an agonized search when he played Roy
Cohn, a not dissimilar character, in the 2012 Chicago production of
Angels in America, for which he won, deservedly, Chicago's top acting
award. In Yando's Roy Cohn, a more successful overall performance, and
one with no preachy message to spoon-feed to the audience, we saw how
gradual physical decline and impending death affect a man used to total
power (power to seduce or destroy others, power to create and uncre-
ate the truth, a sheer physical joy in his own destructiveness)—and the
results were deeply fascinating, as we saw terror, viciousness, and eventually even a glimmer of compassion swirling around in the psyche of a
vicious man with no self-knowledge.

I wish Gaines had allowed Yando to play Lear as Roy Cohn. Then we would have learned something about aging, rather than seeing a sentimentalized and generalized image of aging that makes aging pitiable and anodyne, rather than the moral mirror and moral challenge that it clearly is.

Use and Abuse of Philosophical Generalization

This is a good place for me to face up to a problem with my profession, philosophy. Philosophers are fond, and often much too fond, of universal generalizations. Now of course if we didn't generalize we would never be able to learn or teach others. If the past ever serves as a guide for the future, or one person's experience for another's, it is because some types of generalizing are useful. Nietzsche noted that a species who could not generalize would quickly die out: they wouldn't run away from the new predator because they would not see it as like a previous one. All science, furthermore, has a deep commitment to generalizing—though also to testing again and again to see which of the many factors present in any real case actually explain the result.

Our enjoyment of great works of literature such as *King Lear* also depends upon generalizing. If we thought that Lear's story was just an odd thing that actually happened, it would not resonate with us the way it does. As Aristotle says, poetry is "more philosophical" than history, because history just tells us that this or that event actually happened, whereas dramatic poetry shows us "things such as might happen" in a human life.[8] Our interest in Lear is an interest in studying the general shape of human possibilities, so we want to see patterns that might recur in lives we care about.

We know all too well, however, that some forms of generalizing obscure reality and block progress. Stereotyping of women, racial minorities, Muslims, Jews, and other disadvantaged social groups has typically been a major way of keeping them subordinated. In 1873, an Illinois law that forbade women to practice law (which they were already doing in Iowa) was challenged by Myra Bradwell, who had already completed legal training and apprenticeship and was in effect practicing law but was denied admission to the Illinois bar. The Supreme Court, upholding the law banning women, offered some stereotypes, backed up with religious piety: "The natural and proper timidity and delicacy which belongs to the female sex evidently unfits it for many of the occupations of civil life. . . .

[T]he paramount destiny and mission of woman are to fulfill the noble and benign offices of wife and mother. This is the law of the Creator."[9] Justice Bradley went on to acknowledge that many women are unmarried and therefore might be seen as exceptions to this general rule. (Myra Bradwell was married.) But he concluded that law must "be adapted to the general constitution of things, and cannot be based upon exceptional cases."

This sort of thing happens all the time, particularly to less powerful groups. A descriptive generalization is put forward, without evidence, and indeed in the presence of strong counterevidence—and then is used as a pretext to enforce conformity. Aging people, long the victims of denigrating stereotypes, as I discuss in another chapter, should be especially wary of generalizing. Especially when we know so little about what is exceptional and what is not, and when our knowledge is shifting all the time, it seems prudent to be humbly specific.

What is a philosopher to do? First, we ought to distinguish *normative generalizing* from *descriptive generalizing*. In talking about Lear I have been engaging in normative generalizing of a type familiar in moral philosophy ever since Plato and Aristotle. These patterns of life are virtuous and other types vicious. These lives are flourishing and these less so. People who like to control others, a trait problematic in itself, are especially likely to encounter unpleasant surprises as they age. And these surprises, such as loss of love and connection, are humanly important—giving us all some reasons, albeit so far defeasible, not to try to live like that.

All of this seems fine so long as arrogance does not take the place of dialogue. We all need ideals and goals, and normative generalizing is crucial when we think about what possibilities and opportunities are really important for people. A theory of human rights or constitutional liberties is highly general, a form of normative generalizing, but that seems fine, since people are not dragooned into conformity by rights, but, instead, given certain protected opportunities. That is the way I shall reason in chapter 7 when dealing with economic inequality and aging. I shall argue that certain "capabilities"—substantive opportunities—are so important for all citizens that they should have the status of constitutional guarantees.

We should, however, beware when the normative theory is grounded in *descriptive generalizing* of an excessive or dubious kind, and it is in the area of descriptive generalizing that stigma and discrimination are especially likely to warp judgment. Justice Bradley came to the normative conclusion that it was a bad thing for women to practice law because he was convinced already of certain highly general descriptive claims, such as: Only a few women can practice law. Most women want to be wives and mothers. Wives and mothers can't be lawyers. Learning to argue like a lawyer makes women mannish and bad at their family tasks. Each of these claims is false, as we know by now.

But what is most especially false, as we now see, is the very fact of the singular "way" that is charted out for women. *This* is a woman's life, *this* is her narrative. Never mind that you, Myra Bradwell, married lawyer, are doing something different, we brush that aside. No, we simply assert that being a wife and mother, and only that, is the correct description of women's role. In that case, insistence on descriptive singularity is hardly innocent of hidden or not-so-hidden normative ideas: this is how we (men) want women to be, this is how we intend to *make* them be.

Even in a benign and utterly nonnormative form, such a singular "way" comes across as a preposterous lie, once women assert the right to choose their own destinies and to be individuals. I recently attended a performance of the haunting Schumann song cycle, *Frauenliebe und Leben* (*Women's Love and Life*). The story of "women" is a singular and simple one: she falls in love, she receives a proposal of marriage, she accepts it, she gets married, she is at first scared by sex and then happy, she has a baby, and she then experiences deep grief at the death of her husband (since a romantic song cycle has to end sadly). The story seems preposterous today, albeit touching. But at the performance I attended there was also the very interesting fact that the songs, atypically, were being sung by a baritone. (In the lieder world, women typically have transgender privileges and men have none: a soprano can sing "Winterreise" or "Songs of a Wayfarer," but men basically never sing this "female" cycle.) And this male singer, moreover, without so much as a pause, segued right into the equally canonical male narrative, singing Schumann's "Dichterliebe" ("Poet's Love"). As in more than one other romantic song cycle, the male story is also singular and simple, albeit different from the female story: he falls in love, he wins her love, but her parents object because he is poor, so they marry her off to a wealthy husband, and she goes along with their choice; so he goes off and wanders and eventually dies. What Matthias Goerne's daring two-gendered performance made us ask is: whose story is whose? Is either of these stories anybody's? Aren't both symmetrical lies, albeit of great beauty? Nobody in that audience was being duped by the descriptive stereotypes, and we were invited to contemplate them as two stories of their place and time, but surely true of basically nobody, then or

now. (Even Schumann had a happy life, until he died prematurely of com-
plications of an untreated bipolar disorder; his beloved wife Clara was one
of history's most gifted female pianists and composers, and a competent
businesswoman, who was the family's main breadwinner and skillfully
managed her own concert tours. The only thing the women's cycle gets
right is that she outlived him—by forty years!)

The trouble with stories of aging, so far, is that there are too few of
them to show us the extent of variety within aging, thus too few to make
us as suspicious as we should be of the partial truths. Aristotle's idea of
tragedy was not that one tragedy shows us all the human possibilities.
How could it? It is, instead, that each tragedy shows us some human
possibilities, so if we keep experiencing tragedies (as the Greeks did, quite
a lot of them every year), we will expand our grasp of human possibilities
and see the variety of possible interactions between character types and
circumstances. We need to keep searching for stories of aging in order to
expand our grasp.

But most of us basically get this, when we deal with works of literature.
Lear tempts people to unwise generalizing just because it is Shakespeare
and because there are relatively few great literary works about aging.
However, when someone like me says, "Hold on: Lear is no more an
Everyman than Cleopatra an Everywoman," readers are likely to agree,
remembering how in most cases we do recognize great variety within literary classes of people—women, men, adolescents, kings, and so forth.
For example, we easily recognize a central fact of Shakespeare's history
plays, a fact that any citizen of a hereditary monarchy knows: that kings
experience and enact kingship in very different ways, with large consequences for millions.

When we turn to works of philosophy, we run into a much more difficult problem. The problem is that philosophers are not creative artists,
writing one story after another. Nor are they historians, writing about the
varied events that actually occurred. They are generalizers through and
through. We are not surprised that Cicero wrote just one work called *On
Aging*, that Simone de Beauvoir (1908–1986) also wrote just one book
about aging, albeit a much longer one. Philosophers certainly revisit
themes, but they usually do not write text after text with the simple aim of
showing the human variety within a topic. This singularity of statement
can be a virtue, clarifying and classifying, but it can also be a danger.

Aging is clearly a topic on which generalizing is fraught with peril.
First of all, to a considerably greater degree, even, than with childhood

or adolescence, there are so many different life stories. Some people are healthy into their nineties; others encounter serious or fatal illness far earlier. Some never experience dementia, even though they live to be over one hundred. Others experience dementia as early as their fifties. There are also many different types of dementia. Some people can do intellectual work but not find their way from one place to another. For others, the decline of cognition is more global. Then there are so many characterological differences, as Lear's case shows. And as we shall see, economic and social circumstances (poverty or affluence, forced retirement or continued work) have a large impact on health, emotions, and general productivity. In this book Saul and I try to make these different paths evident to our readers, since both individuals and societies have choices to make, as populations age.

Second, as we'll say often, aging is the subject of widespread, indeed virtually universal, social stigma. The social story about aging is laden with stereotypes, most of which denigrate aging people by imputing ugliness, incompetence, and uselessness. These stereotypes invade aging people themselves, skewing self-perception and self-evaluation. Think about Myra Bradwell. In her time, most people, including most women, believed that women could not be lawyers, and certainly not married women. Today virtually all middle-class white and Asian women think that women, including married women, can certainly be lawyers if they work hard and have an academic bent, and virtually all law schools and law firms agree. To the extent that African American and Latina women do not share that self-perception, the difference is attributable to false racial stereotypes, which are gradually vanishing from the hiring community, and somewhat less rapidly from the mentality of potential aspirants. Since modern societies have barely begun to re-evaluate their pictures of aging, how could any generalization be free of the influence of stereotypes?

Finally, one of the most baneful of all stereotypes about aging people is that they have no agency; they are just victims of fate. Of course fate is there somewhere, and usually we don't know where or when. But there is a lot of room for active choosing too, as Lear's story, with its bad choices and their worse consequences, reminds us. To rob aging people of agency and choice in the way one describes them is to dehumanize and objectify in a particularly insulting manner.

How should a book on aging confront the problem of unwise descriptive generalizing, if not through the creation of a kaleidoscopic multiplicity of works? One way would be to use literature and history (and empirical data where those exist) to provide a range of examples that could then be studied for whatever commonalities they might afford. Another would be to write in dialogue form, so that the conclusions would be those of a specific character or characters, not necessarily attributable to the author. The temptation of the premature generalization, however, haunts both of the works I've mentioned, the only two significant philosophical treatises on our topic in the Western tradition.

I'll study the Cicero text in chapter 3. Cicero sees the problem and confronts it, up to a point, very well. *On Aging* is full of lively discussion of the variety of responses to aging, and it does use the dialogue form to comment on the limits of the generalities it expresses: Cato is gently mocked for some of his obsessions (e.g. with the healthful influence of gardening). But I'll argue that Cicero's letters show us a great deal more of the real substance and variety of aging, complexities that the treatise, all too tidy, keeps from view.

As my central exhibit of the danger of philosophical generalizing, however, let me now turn to Beauvoir's *La Vieillesse* (misleadingly translated as *The Coming of Age*, when it just means *Old Age*).[10] The book was published in 1970. It was followed, in 1974, by the conversations that were ultimately published as *Les Adieux*, a series of dialogues with Jean-Paul Sartre (1905–1980) (translated into English as *Adieux: A Farewell to Sartre*).[11]

La Vieillesse is a very long book: 585 pages in the English version, as contrasted with Cicero's concise text of some 50 pages. As in *The Second Sex*, Beauvoir is fond of collecting all sort of examples from literature and history, which she does not particularly sort out, and which can give a chaotic impression. But as in that famous book, she provides, as well, a lot of useful data. The first part of the book is valuable for the empirical information it sets out about the actual lives of aging men and women in France, particularly those who are not affluent, and especially about grim conditions in nursing homes.

In the second half of the book, Beauvoir turns to the subjective experience of aging.[12] As Finnish philosopher Sara Heinämaa points out, in a convincing and sympathetic interpretive article, she closely follows Edmund Husserl's phenomenological method, which directs the philosopher to introspect in search of essential generalizations. Indebtedness, however, is no excuse. Husserl's method may illuminate some phenomena very well, but it still must be asked whether it proves its worth in the area of aging, a veritable minefield of dangers. I shall announce my conclusion ahead of time: this is among the most preposterous famous works of philosophy that I have ever encountered, and it is preposterous for all the three reasons I have mentioned: it rides roughshod over variety, it validates contingent and derogatory stereotypes, and it deprives aging people of agency.

Here is what Beauvoir has to say about who I am. (She doesn't specify what age she is talking about very precisely, but the analysis in Part I appears to begin with age sixty-five, the age of canonical mandatory retirement.) Aging is not gradual or progressive: It arrives as a sudden realization. The basic content of this "surprise" (292), or "metamorphosis" (283), or "revelation" is that the way one used to be experienced by others, a way that has become a part of one's own subjective identity, has suddenly altered dramatically for the worse. At one level one may feel young within, but seeing the sudden scorn of society, one experiences a dramatic subjective shift, since that being-seen is also a part of who one subjectively is.

Let's stop there. Where does the suddenness come from? Perhaps she is thinking of compulsory retirement, which can certainly alter a person's social meaning in a sudden way, but that is a contingent phenomenon, hardly one that gives us the essence of anything. And why, I would like to know, should I permit a French philosopher seven years younger than I currently am (sixty-nine) to tell me the meaning of my life as a philosopher in the twenty-first century? I don't recognize my own experience at all, nor that of my friends of similar age. It's partly that many things have changed as we develop better understanding of health and nutrition. But it's also that there has always been great variety. Beauvoir makes an essential claim, attempting to bully me into saying, "Oh dear, that is how I must be feeling, whether I realize it or not." Sorry, no. I feel quite sorry that she is not happy, but why doesn't she just say, "I have the following unhappy experiences?" As for me, I feel healthy and vigorous, and probably never more admired than now, although I have to say that I do not feel as attached to honor from others as Beauvoir tells me I essentially must be.

Justice Bradley would say, "But Martha, Hillary, and a few others are the exceptional cases, and we cannot make law about exceptions." I'm sorry, I totally reject that. Most of the people my age I know are vigorous and in the midst of engrossing life-activities, whether of my sort or not. Of course some have been stricken by disease, but that can happen at any age, as Cicero rightly notes. Beauvoir's essentializing doesn't just betray an annoying French propensity to tell other people what the correct way of being this or that (a woman, a citizen) is.[13] It has a deeper problem. It just happens to correspond all too neatly to familiar derogatory social stereotypes, and by now, with enough aging people contesting those stereotypes, we're beginning to see them for what they are. There's strength in numbers, and baby boomers have simply refused to be defined by the fictions of yesteryear.

So I read her book as worse than preposterous: I see it as an act of collaboration with social stigma and injustice. It's as if a Jew were to write a book saying that the essence of Jews is that they experience life as beings who are physically weak, unheroic, incapable of creativity, capable only of base scheming, and not of deep insight. But wait: that book has already been written—by Otto Weininger! Weininger's *Sex and Character* (1903) was once the bible of the European intelligentsia, and no doubt the fact that he was himself a Jew made many people believe him when he told them about the essence of Jews. But it's a grotesque piece of propaganda nonetheless. One could also imagine a book by some African American saying that African Americans experience themselves as essentially violent beings, ready to rape and kill. Wait again: that book, too, has already been at least partially written, in the section of Justice Clarence Thomas's autobiography in which he admits to identification with Richard Wright's violent hero Bigger Thomas.[14] In short, we should not believe generalizations simply because their author is a member of the stigmatized group: such descriptions can be marred by "adaptive preferences" or even self-hatred.

The third and greatest problem with Beauvoir's essentializing claims is their grim fatalism, which gives the aging person no credit for agency of any kind. Age arrives as a metamorphosis. It just happens to you. Cicero's interlocutor Cato is much shrewder: he understands that you make your own fate in some measure, by your discipline, your exercise regime, your diet, your practices of reading, conversation, and friendship. Even the aging body is not just given: it is a set of possibilities that one can actualize in many different ways. As people age, they may have to work out more regularly to keep the same level of muscular fitness. But that idea, which was already Cato's, is utterly different from Beauvoir's idea of a uniform fate toward which everyone is passive. Obviously one cannot make oneself immortal, but one can do a huge amount to feel happier and to be stronger and more active.

The denial of agency may express a peculiarly European take on life, just as my emphasis on work and exercise is very American. But that observation, too, gives the lie to this mendacious book. If she had just said, "As a Frenchwoman of a particular era, I have been schooled to think thus and so," I could hardly fault her—although even in France I note that women of my age no longer appear to have such attitudes. As for me I am glad to be in a country where, when one goes to physical therapy with a minor runner's injury, one is told not, "You are too old to run," but, rather, "You are not doing enough core exercises, and what about more ankle strengthening?" Still, had she attributed her experience to an unjust background culture, I could hardly complain. When, however, she purports to tell me who I am and how I experience my life, I have to take a page out of the book of those Muslims who protested terrorists acts, and reply, "Not in my name."

Beauvoir does see one narrow avenue for agency—but only for some people. "There is only one solution if old age is not to be a derisory parody of our former existence, and that is to go on pursuing ends that give our life a meaning—devotion to individuals, to collectives, to causes, social, political, intellectual or creative work" (540–41). This qualification appears to allow most people, indeed all who don't suffer from severe dementia, a way of exercising agency. And she adds that one way of having a future is by contributing to future generations. However, in *La Vieillesse* there are already hints that she believes this escape route possible only for exceptional people such as artists and thinkers. "The majority of old people live barren, deserted lives in isolation, repetition, and boredom."[15] Her position becomes yet clearer in *Adieux*. Sartre takes the position that people may contribute to future generations through any type of cooperative activity, political or social. (He denies that artists and intellectuals contribute in this way: their works, he asserts, are directed at personal, not communal, ends.) Beauvoir insists that a transgenerational future is possible only for exceptional individuals such as artists and intellectuals.[16]

I would say that both are guilty of irresponsible generalizing: Beauvoir from the personal importance she attaches to intellectual work, Sartre from his attachment to political action. Both, in their mandarin and bohemian way, are myopic. Neither thinks that contributing to the rearing of children and grandchildren is a meaningful way of contributing to the world. (She dismisses the idea brusquely, he doesn't even mention it.) And what about transgenerational friendships, with younger colleagues, with students, other people's children and grandchildren? What about care for the planet and for nonhuman animals? What about the work that nonsplashy people routinely do for all sorts of valuable things they believe in: volunteer work, financial donations during life, bequests after death. I'll discuss altruism in chapter 8, but it seems extraordinary that they don't consider these cases. Maybe it just seemed too capitalist to have a death-bed conversation about money.

What do we learn from these sad texts, which outrageously tell readers (with no sign of uncertainty or irony) that it is our essence to be sad? And which, in the process, insult so many average people? I guess I would say that we learn, we philosophers, to give ourselves the following speech before writing, especially about aging: Remember, philosopher, that your experience is just yours. So learn. Be curious about other people of many different kinds. Ask them how they experience life before you lecture them on how they essentially must experience life. Be prepared to see meaningfulness in lives that are unlike your own. Respect diversity.

And also: be on your guard lest your own generalizations may be deformed by societal prejudice and stigma—including the prejudice of the academic subculture against nonintellectuals and moneymakers.

Humility helps. So does a sense of humor. Beware of philosophers who lack these traits, even, and especially, when they tell you they are important enough to tell you how you ought to feel. Isn't that all too like King Lear, scripting his daughters' love?

Notes

1. The production was at the Chicago Shakespeare Theater and was directed by Barbara Gaines.
2. September 18, 2014.
3. Jones is typical in describing his illness this way. One should note that forgetting names is a separate problem and not typically linked with a more global dementia, so there's haste in the medical depiction.
4. R. A. Foakes, ed., *King Lear*, Arden Shakespeare (New York: Bloomsbury, first published 1997), introduction, 27.
5. Charles McNulty, "With Age, the Wisdom of Staging *Lear* Becomes Less Clear," *Los Angeles Times*, August 13, 2014.
6. See Stanley Cavell, "The Avoidance of Love: A Reading of *King Lear*," in *Must We Mean What We Say?*, updated ed. (New York: Cambridge University Press, 2002).
7. Janet Adelman, *Suffocating Mothers: Fantasies of Maternal Origin in Shakespeare, "Hamlet" to "The Tempest"* (New York: Routledge, 1992), 104.
8. Aristotle, *Poetics*, chapter 9.
9. *Bradwell v. Illinois*, 83 U.S. 130 (1873).

10. *La Vieillesse* (Paris: Gallimard, 1996); English translation by Patrick O'Brien, *The Coming of Age* (New York: Norton, 1996).
11. French edition Gallimard 1981, but the conversations took place in 1974; the English edition, again translated by O'Brien, was published by Pantheon in 1984.
12. I have found very useful Sara Heinämaa's article "Transformations of Old Age," in *Simone de Beauvoir's Philosophy of Old Age*, ed. Silvia Stoller (Bloomington: Indiana University Press, 2014), 167–89.
13. See Joan Scott, *The Politics of the Veil* (Princeton, NJ: Princeton University Press, 2007).
14. See Justin Driver, "Justice Thomas and Bigger Thomas," in *Fatal Fictions: Crime and Investigation in Law and Literature*, ed. Alison LaCroix, Richard McAdams, and Martha C. Nussbaum (New York: Oxford University Press, 2016).
15. Heinämaa, "Transformations of Old Age," 182, summarizing.
16. See Heinämaa, "Transformations of Old Age," 185–86.

Distributing, Disinheriting, and Paying for Care since *Lear*

Saul

THE TRAGEDY OF KING LEAR begins with aging and moves quickly to dividing, disinheriting, and then regretting. Leaving one's assets to others can be fraught with emotion and misgivings, and choosing to give over one's material goods to family members in disproportionate fashion even more so. The parent or other benefactor is likely to obsess over the decision, and how it will be construed. The various beneficiaries, whether accepting or resentful, must live with repercussions. These are important topics for the aging, and especially for those fortunate enough to be in positions to distribute or receive wealth. Lear was neither the first nor the last fictional or real person to think that love, or even expressions of love, should be part of the calculus of distribution. He has wealth and power to distribute, and these are assets that are not easily divided. Moreover, Lear has one unmarried daughter, and two others married to men who hunger for power. In modern times, this aspect of the distribution problem has shifted from children in disparate family situations to offspring in dissimilar economic circumstances, not to mention those in blended families. Sometimes the differences feed off one another because unequal numbers of grandchildren bring about varying economic circumstances. A grandparent might want to help pay for college tuition, but grown children might think it unfair that a sibling who has chosen to have many children thereby enjoys the bulk of their potential inheritance. Others might resent the dissipation of wealth in favor of step-grandchildren included in transfers or bequests. The same is true for career choices, and for decisions about ownership and employment opportunities in a family business. When economic circumstances are traced to choices rather than to happenstance, there is often serious friction, much as Lear and his family were turned inside out after he made his daughters' economic circumstances depend on their responses to his challenge that they express their love for him. Unlike Lear, most of us approach in-family distribution decisions with an egalitarian mindset.

A modern, post-*Lear* belief that one ought to love one's children equally and show no favoritism in the distribution of material goods often conflicts with strong intuitions about egalitarian outcomes and individual needs. Among affluent people this tension can be exacerbated by the prospect, or alternative, of philanthropy. We might think of our own responsibility to nonfamily causes as comparable to Lear's obligations to his countrymen. Lear can be faulted for not considering the well-being of his subjects. At least superficially, he gives no thought to which of his children will govern best or to how a division of one kind or another will promote political stability or prosperity.[1] Most of us can do much better. Shakespeare focuses on Lear's vanity and on his failure to understand himself, familial affection, and his own future in retirement. These are important things for all of us to consider—but they are not the only things.

Estate planning is an important subject for a book on aging, as it is for an essay on *King Lear*, but it is not the place to begin. A better starting point is Martha Nussbaum's essay on the vulnerability of Lear. I wonder how Martha would have advised Lear. How do we know whether we are prepared for retirement, and for the reality of needing others? And if we sense that we are not quite prepared for frailty, what can we do about it? Retiring people are often told to take on new challenges, and there is evidence that happiness comes to those who continue to learn and try new things. "Triumphs of experience" are surely superior to, and more fun than, lamentations of lost youth.[2] Similarly, we know that an aging individual, as well as the healthcare system, is better off if assisted living does not infantilize the person, but allows control and decision-making to remain in the hands of the individual whenever possible. Lear left himself with little to do, as he wandered from daughter to daughter in his quest for respect. Being mortal, as we all are, requires conversations about expectations and responsibilities, and Lear's tragedy is a reminder to think ahead.

ALONG SEVERAL DIMENSIONS, *Lear* is too easy a cautionary tale. When it comes to distributing, it seems obvious that one should not give over assets in proportion to professions of love. Every theatergoer can see immediately that the challenge, or love test, Lear administers is a mistake. Perhaps we are meant to see that Lear's foolishness is not so different from other vanities that might influence our decisions. We know, for example, that we want charities to thank us for our gifts, but it would be foolish to be most generous to those that best gush over us. Lear's vanity is distracting; even if he could see through his daughters' responses, it is surely unwise for him to distribute according to their actual affections. In lieu of the original beginning, imagine an opening scene in which Lear overhears his daughters discussing their sentiments, and he is confident that the scene has not been staged for his benefit. He might understandably be wounded if one daughter, Cordelia, expressed indifference or uncertainty about the future to him. In act 1, scene 1, Cordelia's villainous sisters, Goneril and Regan, flatter their father, while Cordelia resists Lear's request that she profess her love for him and says that she loves her father, the king, "according to my bond; nor more nor less." She proceeds to treat love as finite and notes that "when I shall wed, that lord whose hand must take my plight shall carry half my love with him, half my care and duty." Imagine instead that she, in keeping with her character, had said:

> I know not how good a father he has been,
> Having never had another.
> I cannot heave my heart into my mouth.
> I love him according to my bond
> And even that may be glib and oily art.
> When I wed, half my love will go to my new lord,
> Who may object to old pledges of duty and care.

Cordelia does not utter most of these lines; they are a modified and twisted version of the words Shakespeare gives her. If she had expressed these cool, rationalist thoughts, Lear might have exploded in anger and then decided to disinherit her and to give his possessions and kingdom to the others. He might have preferred pledges of future affection and support— even though these are mere promises—to Cordelia's reasoned hesitation.

If Shakespeare had pushed Lear along, and then into the wilderness, with this alternative beginning, Lear would have seemed a bit less foolish, for he would have acted on better evidence of affection, rather than on what Cordelia calls mere "glib and oily art." And yet his disinheriting of Cordelia would have been no less vain. It would have been more obvious that Lear's duty was to leave his kingdom in good hands, so that famine and war would not consume its inhabitants. And what if, before giving up the throne, he had solicited or overheard his daughters' plans for him after he retired? Perhaps one would promise a large retinue of knights and joint rule, while another honestly imagined frequent companionship, even as Cordelia remained agnostic or noncommittal. We are spared some of this uncertainty in our own retirements because we have stable institutions and lawyers to whom we can turn. We can contract for a place in a retirement community or manage our assets without the intervention of people we do not fully trust. But there is a limit to such self-reliance, and we all resemble Lear, like it or not, in looking for signals about how we will be treated in our old age when we are likely to require care.

It is a shame that Shakespeare encourages us to feel for Lear rather than for Cordelia. She is a straight shooter who even returns in act 4 to care for her father. It is too late; she suffers and is killed. Lear brings about his own unhappiness, and he deteriorates with his subjects, whose welfare, I will again emphasize, does not seem to figure in his retirement and succession planning. If Lear had divided his kingdom in equal parts and said that he wished to retire and give up control, knowing that he might be tormented by, rather than find great pleasure in, watching his daughters govern, then we might feel for him as they battle and destabilize their lands. Perhaps the tragic lesson of Lear would simply be that if we retire, we are forced to observe the performances of those who succeed us. Some people might prefer not to know.

Alternatively, Lear may have been determined to keep the kingdom intact and to identify a single heir. Shakespeare probably deployed daughters rather than sons because, with males in the picture, the audience would have expected a single male heir, likely the eldest, to be selected for the throne. Lear might have calculated on the involvement of foreign powers and the formation of alliances, but the audience would be thinking about a unified, rather than divided, England. As it is, the play ignores or detours around royal succession rules. In Shakespeare's time, the audience would probably have regarded monarchical succession as a fairy tale or as completely beyond their own daily lives, but a modern reader can think of Lear's decision as one we must all face, even if we do not have a kingdom to pass on. Inheritance law tracked royal succession rules for some time, but the modern reader expects a kingdom to be kept whole, even though most of us do not plan on leaving our estates, intact, to one heir. It is a bit mysterious why Lear was in a rush to divide his kingdom when Cordelia, ostensibly his favorite, had not yet wed. Perhaps he thought that his test for affections would showcase Cordelia and make it easier to give her the largest share. The modern reader might find the scene provocative if one child loved Lear best while another was more fit to rule, but Lear's blindness turns the story into a warning about the vulnerability of the aged rather than a primer on the strategy and ethics of bequests.

There are reasons to keep kingdoms and even family businesses intact, but history is full of examples of bad and even murderous behavior in the shadow of plans to pass on estates—regardless of the plan of succession. Primogeniture has generated murders, and audiences familiar with British history and literature tend to think that it is primogeniture that puts a target on the back of the firstborn, or next heir in line. But it is hard to avoid this problem; even an equal-division scheme can cause beneficiaries to shove competitors out of the way. Every formula creates some dangerous incentives. In some systems the throne is passed on with a discretionary factor; the sovereign might choose among his children, or a group of high-ranking elders is entrusted with electing the next ruler. Suspicions of foul play might reduce one's chances of selection, so perhaps these systems emerge because they reduce the murder rate. On the other hand, constant competition among potential heirs may not be good, and may cause the eventual losers in the process to misinvest in their training.

King Lear reminds us that the danger of misbehavior does not end when the ruler plans for succession. Whether or not divided into parts, a kingdom or business may simply be the battlefield for subsequent skirmishes among the heirs. And if it is divided, every plan has its dangers. Three is a dangerous number, as many children know; two can gang up on one, and, for various reasons, three is an unstable number. But slicing a country or business in two can also lead to instability and strife. Lear's vanity proved costly, but it could have been just as bad if he had left an intact kingdom to the single best flatterer or divided it into three, in proportion to professions of love.

Lear's problem began long before he made his bequests. His two older daughters are now beyond repair, and perhaps Lear suffers because he did not raise and educate them thoughtfully. Alternatively, the problem may be older than Lear; his forebears needed to set a pattern that their successors would have trouble breaking. Some societies develop strong expectations about democratic succession or one hereditary pattern or the other, making it difficult for a misbehaving and disappointed aspirant to do much harm. If nobles and laymen had come to expect peaceful succession with an identifiable heir, then it is unlikely that instability would have followed Lear's leaving. Stability can follow many plans of succession, but it is noteworthy that it seems to require a plan or tradition that keeps the kingdom intact. Dividing a kingdom in order to give equal shares to each of the ruler's offspring is not a sustainable strategy. An interesting marker of modernity, and the growth of the merchant class, is the separation of inheritance conventions practiced by the population from those applied to the seat of power. I can leave my property to my children in equal parts and they can do the same for theirs one day, and in the long run this might be a stable practice. This is not the case for most monarchs, and might not have been the case for any person of means until the seventeenth century or so. Royal succession may have been a model for some propertied families in the years between Shakespeare and our times, but it no longer occurs to us that the transfer of power in Washington, in Buckingham Palace, or in Riyadh has anything at all to do with the patterns we ought to follow when transferring wealth within our own families. Still, we can look to *Lear* for lessons about love and inheritance.

If Lear had expected to convey the throne to Cordelia, then, after she infuriated him, he ought to have chosen between the other two based on their suitability to rule or, more selfishly, the credibility of their commitments to be devoted caregivers. One interpretation that is flattering to Lear is that he wished to retire and to transfer the throne while his wits were still about him, but he was handicapped by Cordelia's unmarried status. Another version is that Lear was engineering an arrangement among sovereign powers, including his daughters and their present and future spouses. We do not know whether Cordelia on her own would have been acceptable as a ruler, and it is plausible that the audience would imagine that a formidable couple was required to govern and fend off the ambitious sisters and their spouses.

LET US NOW separate Lear's inclination to distribute in proportion to love from his strategy of relying on *expressions* of love. The latter revealed his vanity and amounted to a tragic misstep. But if we imagine Lear as practical rather than vain, we find that Lear faces a choice not unlike one on the minds of many nonfictional citizens of means in our own time. We may not have kingdoms to bestow, but many of us understand that inasmuch as we can leave wealth, there is an opportunity to (or danger that we will) control those who are likely to survive us.

Lear, like most of us, values gratitude. There is a simple and egocentric version of this preference, but also an equally understandable, less selfish

view. Few of us want to give substantial gifts to recipients who are unap-
preciative, manipulative, or incapable of recognizing that some sacrifice
has normally made their good fortune possible. The inclination is similar
to an employer's belief that a job applicant who says "thank you" after an
interview is more likely to be a good employee than one who does not,
and who simply regards the interview as an exchange of information, or
as likely to benefit the employer as herself. Similarly, a benefactor might
favor grateful recipients, not because the benefactor is vain but because
gratitude is associated with good character.

A benefactor might also wish to be remembered after death, and this
desire may also promote the social good. It might not be completely
rational, or philosophically compatible with the idea of death as an end-
point, but many humans have a desire to be remembered that strength-
ens as death nears. Professional fundraisers know that many wealthy
people would like to attach their names to buildings or other lasting
projects. Often a donor is satisfied if his or her name will be associated
with something for fifty years or so—enough time for the donor's own
children and grandchildren to have occasions to remember their fore-
bear. Most of us do not try to imagine being "remembered" by great-
great-grandchildren or other citizens we have never met. The human
urge may be less about immortality or evolutionary survival than about
being remembered by, or having some influence on, known or easily
imagined people. Put differently, the apparent vanity or mortal vulnerability that is observed might be understood as a strategy for inspiring
others to do good deeds.

There is more to be said about the desire to be remembered and the
inclination to try to influence the future, but I defer these topics, as well
as the convention of treating children equally, to chapter 8, where both
philosophical and incentive arguments are explored. For now, it is enough
to see that beneficiaries' gratitude might play a substantial role in benefactors' distribution decisions.

Gratitude can be a proxy for reliability, as I observed in the case of an
employer who likes to hear expressions of thanks from job applicants, but
there might be other explanations for the employer's preference. Perhaps
people who express thanks are well brought up and then also inclined to
be neat, to avoid unnecessary confrontations, or to be secure. A preference
for gratitude can be associated with the quest for reliability. Lear needs to
relinquish control, but he also wants some respect and care. He hopes
to have a retinue of knights, and he surely hopes for a roof over his head

and a kitchen to feed him and his entourage. In the days before retirement communities, much less individual retirement accounts, how is he to do this? Some parents might think that if their children profess eternal affection, and make public promises, they will be secure in their elderly and vulnerable years. Even if a child were inclined to renege, or simply to underestimate the sacrifice that will be required, the promise will be kept because of family and community pressure. Other potential caregivers (and beneficiaries) might swear on a sacred item or in some other way try to make the promise seem reliable in order to gain favors or wealth from the aging person, or simply to calm any fears. It is interesting that no daughter of Lear invokes the supernatural as a means of enhancing the value of her statement of affection.

At some cost, a parent can draft a trust instrument or other document that rewards a child who cares for the aging parent. I will continue to describe this as a parent-child matter, but of course the anxiety is yet greater if the aging person has no children, or none in a position to provide care. In these situations, explicit offers and promises can be even more important, because it will be less obvious which distant relative ought to provide care, and more likely that none will suffer shame if the aging person is frail, lonely, and abandoned. But contracting for care by a family member may be even more difficult than it is callous. Among other reasons, it will often be the case that in the end someone must make a subjective judgment about the care that is provided. If a parent moves into a child's home, the parent can provide for suitable rent payments and can probably do so in a way that does not offend other children, who are accustomed to an egalitarian norm, or who might begin to believe that the host-sibling is influencing the parent in an untoward way. There are physical and legal institutions that Lear could not imagine but that we can deploy. A nice thing about these mechanisms is that their use does not insult the younger generation. At a minimum, it should be easy to ask a reliable family member, friend, or formal trustee to take charge of a fund and use it to reimburse family members for the expenses they undertake on the aging person's behalf. A safe version of this plan involves the use of an annuity, which is to say a financial instrument that pays income for the life of the annuitant. Annuities are sometimes described as the reverse of life insurance policies, because they insure against the "risk" of long life. I can invest in an annuity and have the annual payments come my way, but direct that payments go to a family member or other person once I am incapable of managing my affairs, or after a certain age. I can make explicit that the annual payments are to be used for my expenses. The payments will continue as long as I live, and the annuity will provide larger annual payments, for the same initial investment, the shorter my life expectancy at the time of purchase. Annuities can be purchased long in advance, with deferred start dates, so that they amount to a relatively low-cost hedge against the expenses associated with a very long life. As a practical matter, it is terribly important to choose an annuity provider with very low fees, whether hidden or buried in the contract. With a little effort—if done long before any decline in judgment or financial acumen—one can find low-cost providers without paying any fees to financial advisers or brokers who serve as (well-paid) intermediaries.

Something more is needed if we hope to guarantee, rather than merely reimburse, care undertaken on our behalf. Like Lear, we find the attention we hope to get from others more palatable if we can believe that it is provided with love, or at least out of an attractive conception of duty. Some people have no doubt that such care will be forthcoming. Each generation provides unwavering support for its children, and so when these beneficiaries age, it seems right that they should care for those who brought them into the world and supported them. But families can be dysfunctional, hyperrational, or quarrelsome. Children can misremember their own upbringing, sometimes with the help of a spouse who does not feel accepted by his or her in-laws. We are often unsure whether our families will carry forward as we might like. For this reason, many people resort to a device that is common and worth examination. They withhold money, either by deferring the writing of a will, by threatening to change a will, or simply by not revealing the will's provisions. Alternatively, an affluent person can make it obvious that as she ages, she distributes substantial gifts that will exhaust her estate and leaves little to be apportioned by the will she has written. Deliberately or otherwise, people withhold distributions in order to motivate behavior that they would rather not, or cannot, influence in explicit fashion. In turn, potential beneficiaries cater to wealthy individuals, and in my experience they sometimes do so to the point of pandering as these potential benefactors age.

I wish I could say that this convention of "deferred distribution decisions" is attractive or efficient. If it causes children to be nice to their parents, the argument goes, then what is so bad about the idea that children might be motivated by some combination of affection, gratitude, and financial self-interest? But there are several problems. First, the parent's (or other benefactor's) old age becomes filled with unnecessary stress or cynicism; both parent and child are busy second-guessing instead of being themselves. Every visit and kindness is marred just a bit by the thought that money rather than love is in play. Pandering and paranoia can be strangely symbiotic. There is the constant wish that affection would outweigh mere duty, but the withholding distributor must also wonder whether the strategy of delayed distribution is working all too well. Any introspective or skeptical person who has been a boss knows this feeling. Employees have every reason to pander; their good wishes and friendly remarks are less valuable than those arriving from other quarters. The aging person of means puts herself in a similar situation if she too rewards good behavior. Some people would rather have knowledge than comfort, but others would prefer not to know. Perhaps Lear was better off seeing for himself how his daughters treated him once he had nothing material left to offer them. Most of us do not want insight at this price.

Another problem with deferring distribution decisions in order to ensure care is that it is difficult to compensate affection with any accuracy. It is likely that benefactors overvalue, or only remember, recent kindnesses and slights, so that transfers do not amount to an accurate system of payment for care and affection. If I revise my distribution plan every year until death, it is likely that in the final round I will put too much weight on my recent experiences. A small slight received in the last year of life might cause me to disfavor someone who was a loving caregiver—or simply a reasonable and independent child—for many years before that. The danger is exacerbated by the likely decline in my ability to pick up signals or to coordinate short-term and long-term memories as I did through most of life. As we age we are likely to lose our ability to control these complex emotions and reactions. In turn, those whom we seek to motivate may tire or lose faith in the reward system. And if withholding makes any sense at all, potential beneficiaries must believe that they will be rewarded for their efforts. It is possible that they will be eager to please because they will treat every year as the potential final year of care. But it is just as likely that they will distance themselves so as not to offend the potential benefactor. They might figure that the chance of the distributor's death in any given year is modest, and that it is sensible to wait until it appears that death will come within a year or two. At that time the strategic person will arrive on the scene and be as loving and helpful as possible—as he or she gambles with the pander-paranoia helix. I have heard some very affluent people portray family life in this way, and inasmuch as the behavior they describe is not irrational, it is worth contemplating.

A very wealthy benefactor might avoid some of this difficulty with periodic gifts. If the benefactor is prepared to give unequal birthday or Christmas presents, for example, then good behavior can be recompensed, with enough left over to reward behavior in future years as well. But this is difficult to do, and it runs the danger of alienating beneficiaries who would otherwise provide care and affection. Once a parent openly prefers one child to another, for example, it is unlikely that the spurned child will behave as the parent desires. In practice, then, the benefactor withholds and only makes unequal distributions at death—after which there is no opportunity to observe the resentment (or gratitude) that has been created.

I have tried with this harsh and cold analysis to suggest that it is dangerous to withhold in order to assess or encourage effort and affection. And yet it is also dangerous to imitate Lear and give everything away in order to see affection in an unfiltered light. For my own part, I plan to hold on to resources in order to have sufficient income to pay for my own needs. If I require care, then I hope to be able to reimburse the caregiver as a matter of course. I do not think I want to know who would provide care and even who would laugh at my old jokes if financial burdens accompanied caregiving and visits, and if there were not the prospect of reward.

WE MUST UNDERSTAND that if our children are involved in caring for us, there is a chance that hard feelings will develop. In my own case, I am lucky to have generous and considerate siblings, who lived closer to my parents than did I, and who have provided care for our parents under difficult circumstances. They, in turn, have generous and supportive spouses. About all I can do is be grateful. I trust my siblings to take resources as necessary in order to offset financial strains, but in our case these seem small compared to the investments of time and emotional energy. However, I have observed other families where things are more difficult and where family members have lost trust in one another, often beginning with some genuine disagreement about important caregiving decisions. Caregiving is rarely shared equally, and if a family directs resources to the one who expends great effort, others may come to think they were pressured by that recipient or may think that their more modest efforts were also deserving. If we do not reward the leading caregiver, then that person (or his or her immediate family) may be resentful and feel that other family members were insufficiently appreciative. If, for example, grateful siblings offer money of their own, the caregiving sibling may resent the implication that money rather than love, or a sense of duty, is the motivating force. It is not possible to commodify affection and familial duties; unequal effort is unavoidable, and every asymmetry in effort is rife with potential for resentment. Out-of-pocket expenses should, of course, be paid from the parent's estate, and surely able siblings ought to share the costs of a parent's care. But none of this is much help when it comes to care that is provided by the family members themselves. If we have raised our children well, or have simply been lucky, none of this need concern us, but there are thousands of unhappy Lears, and resentful siblings, to warn us to be wary.

Nor is resentment unknown along the parent-child axis. It is not uncommon to observe emotionally and financially charged interactions between an aging person and that person's children. Thus, an adult child might leave the workforce to care for a parent, but the family may have failed to discuss the financial implications of this sacrifice, or expression of love or filial duty. The parent may have written a will dividing wealth equally among several children, but now one child has sacrificed financially and feels entitled to material recognition. A child might sacrifice by moving into the parent's home, but the parent may regard this child as enjoying free rent. I will try hard to compensate my caregivers for financial sacrifices, and perhaps I will involve other family members in the decision-making. I would rather no child (or in-law) of mine leave the workforce to care for me, and I think I have communicated that to my children. But should that somehow come to pass, I would ask the other child to help me calculate the financial sacrifice so that the caregiver can be reimbursed with as little resentment as possible.

If Lear erred by not thinking of his countrymen, then we do the same if we do not think about philanthropic decisions as we plan for our own declining years. The average, rational affluent person will die with an estate because she does not know the date of her own death. I cannot give all my money away to good causes, after deciding how much to leave to my children, because I do not know how much I will need for myself. We have already seen that it is reckless to give it all away, and then to count on one's beneficiaries to provide care. This is especially true when one has multiple children. With a single, reliable child I might discuss the situation and trust the child to take control of all my resources and then care for me in my old age. We have also seen that one can invest in an annuity in order to guarantee an annual income for life. I should add that it is easy for a couple to buy an annuity that pays until the death of the second person to die. But the annuity strategy does not really solve the philanthropy issues because most of us will not spend all the income from the annuity in each year, so there will again be a surplus and the question is whether to give it away, or leave it to children or others to hold or distribute. I have promised to return to this issue later, and do so in chapter 8.

It should be plain that charities can also pander for distributions. A vain or lonely person who wants visitors with their hands outstretched should withhold resources in order to encourage attention. The best selfish strategy might be to make some gifts to specific charities and suggest that these favorite charities are likely to get more upon one's death. The less selfish benefactor can try to interest her children in common causes. The charity might succeed by convincing a donor that a substantial gift in her lifetime would be a good example to the donor's children or would be enjoyable to witness. In general, these gifts or bequests do not present the problems discussed earlier, because it should matter little if the charity has exaggerated and been false with its affections. It will be painful to discover that one's child is a Goneril, but so long as one's alma mater really gives out scholarships or the local hospital actually provides good emergency care, it should not matter if the president of that organization snubs the donor at the next annual dinner in favor of another, as yet uncommitted, benefactor. I should not really want the president's affection, but rather want him to succeed in fundraising and then in putting resources to good use. The only reason to withhold from such a beneficiary is if one is really uncertain about the resources necessary for self-support. But philanthropic strategies deserve a conversation of their own. For now, it is sufficient to conclude that there is much to learn from Lear's errors. But the lesson of Lear should not be to withhold resources from good causes and all children.

Notes

1. The opposite view is taken in the remarkable essay by Harry V. Jaffa, "The Limits of Politics: An Interpretation of *King Lear*, Act 1, Scene 1," *American Political Science Review* 51 (1957), 405–27. Unfortunately, Jaffe assumes (without suitable explanation) that a division into three is inherently more stable than a division into two parts. Modern public choice theory encourages us to disagree, as do various Bible stories. In any event, this is not an essay about Lear so much as how we might think about distributions and care in our later years.

2. The reference is to *Triumphs of Experience: The Men of the Harvard Grant Study*, by George E. Vaillant (Cambridge, MA: Belknap Press of Harvard University Press, 2012), an excellent book about the longest longitudinal study of human development. The title refers to the author's observation that many of the subjects came to have satisfying lives in their later years, even when earlier signs seemed ominous.

   Being Mortal: Medicine and What Matters in the End, by Atul Gawande (New York: Metropolitan Books, 2014) is the intended reference in the subsequent text. This too is an important, not to mention best-selling, book on aging. It encourages readers to think well of hospice care and to share the author's conclusion that doctors err by intervening to solve medical issues, without thoroughly considering the likely effects on aging patients.

Chapter 2

Retirement Policy

THE UNITED STATES bans age discrimination, including compulsory retirement, but is this wise? How can we ensure that employment opportunities for people who are happy and productive at work, even when their cohort has long since retired, will not disappear? Who gains and who loses from forced retirement terms in employment contracts? Why do so many people retire before age sixty, and why is the median retirement age rising?

Must We Retire?

Saul

IT IS UNLIKELY that I will be as good at my job at age seventy-five as I was at age fifty-five, and yet my employer might be stuck with me. An employer cannot require an employee to retire, even at a respectable age such as sixty-eight; mandating a retirement age as a condition of employment will be regarded as engaging in age discrimination, even if the employee was hired at a young age and even if the employer applies the policy even-handedly to all workers as they reach the stated age. The exceptions—including pilots, law enforcement officers, state court judges, law firm and investment bank partners (because they are not employees), and Catholic bishops—are few. Although a great majority of workers do retire by age sixty-eight, the fact that they need not do so surely causes employers to hesitate to hire middle-aged and older workers because they fear that these employees will not retire if and when their productivity begins to drop. Moreover, in many jobs, compensation rises with seniority even if productivity falls. Not only am I likely to be less useful to my employer at seventy-five than I was at fifty-five, but also my compensation at the older age will greatly exceed what I earned at fifty-five. Employers correctly fear that if they decrease or even flatten the salaries of aging employees, they will trigger age discrimination suits. In this chapter, I want to build an argument in favor of dismantling the part of our legal system that effectively bars retirement at a set age, even if agreed upon. Along the way, there is opportunity to think about perceptions of aging people in the workplace.

As we will see, current law and practices constitute something of an accident, or product of self-interested short-run thinking by lawmakers, as well as unrelated developments in tax and regulatory law. I argue that, within limits, employers and employees should be able to contract as they like, even if this means that some workers will be required to retire at a specified age. If aging workers are sorry they entered into these contracts many years earlier, there will be other, younger workers who will be happy to apply for jobs that have finally opened up. Moreover, employers might be more willing to hire older job applicants if it is permissible to set their terms of employment. I recognize that most of us like options in our favor; it is nice to be able to continue work as long as one wants, and to be the master of one's own timing. More important, some people live life to the fullest by working rather than retiring. I think I am one of those people. But that does not mean that an employer should be prohibited from structuring work so that other citizens, or even people with preferences like mine, agree to "mandatory" retirement, a term we must define with some care. Law might permit employers to structure wages so that they automatically decline after some age. More controversially, I suggest that affluent workers who were part of the generation that received a windfall when mandatory retirement contracts were voided by law, should now either lose that windfall or, better yet, face higher taxes if they remain in the workforce past the age at which most of their contemporaries retire. I love my job and have no plans to retire, so the argument developed here is against my own self-interest but right for society at large. There is good reason to allow retirement by contract. I do not, however, build to that conclusion. Instead, I explain why it is doubtful that law will do the sensible thing.

STRICT MANDATORY RETIREMENT IS, and always has been, unusual in the United States. Some states require their judges to retire at a specified age, such as seventy in New Hampshire. Federal law, as well as the law of many other nations, presently requires commercial airline pilots to retire at age sixty-five. But forced retirement of this kind is rare. On the other hand, *permissive* mandatory retirement, brought about by private, contractual arrangement, was once common. It is presently unusual because statutory prohibitions allow it only where the workers are partners rather than employees, or where they are public safety officers, high executives, or clergy. Age discrimination law in the United States prohibits an employer from requiring the involuntary retirement of employees, even if that requirement had been part of a long-standing contract, and even if the employee had a choice and received higher compensation in return for agreed-upon retirement. (To be fair, I have never heard of such an explicit choice.) Nevertheless, an employer can legally encourage retirement in ways that make the pattern of employment and retirement quite predictable. The employer is motivated not only by the advantages of predictability but also by the opportunity to avoid the substantial cost of meeting law's requirement that an aging employee was let go for a *very* good reason relating to the employee's misbehavior or failure to perform work duties; subpar performance is an insufficient cause. The most effective method has been to design retirement plans that encourage voluntary departure from the workforce, and the discussion here therefore begins with pension plans that encourage retirement.

THE GREAT MAJORITY of working Americans retire, voluntarily, before reaching age seventy. The median retirement age declined to a low of fifty-seven in the early 1990s; it was seventy-four in 1910 (!), when expected life at birth was about fifty, and when there was neither Social Security nor tax-favored private pension plans. People died young, by today's standards, but those who lived on kept on working. Retirement was an unknown concept, or one that applied only to small business owners who sold their firms and then had nothing else to do. Most people worked because they needed to do so or because it was expected of them; there were few (several hundred) employer-provided pension plans, few people had accumulated savings, and there were no retirement communities. If they could not work, or not get to work in an era before accommodations at the workplace and on public transportation were widespread, many seniors probably retreated to the privacy of family homes. This practice is common in many less affluent countries today; senior citizens can be invisible even where life expectancy is sixty-five or seventy. In any event, a substantial fraction of people worked until death; most left work months or several years—rather than decades—before death.

Voluntary retirement becomes more attractive when there is a critical mass of retirees. If only a small minority live long lives, these survivors are likely to be dispersed and integrated into family life. They are unlikely to have saved for what we now call retirement. Retirement communities in the United States seem to have started in the 1920s, when there was just such a critical mass that found it attractive to engage in leisure activities without a surrounding majority of younger, working people. Private pension plans also became popular, perhaps because they began to receive tax-favored treatment, but most of these plans provided only a modest fraction of pre-retirement income.

Dramatic increases in life expectancy, pension benefits, and overall affluence steadily *reduced* the age of most retirements throughout

the 1900s. In the last two decades, however, improved health, less strenuous jobs, and other factors increased the number of working years per
person and brought the median retirement age up to sixty-two. Voluntary
retirement is at a higher age for men than for women and, interestingly,
better health, financial status, and more education are all correlated with
later retirement. Only a small percentage of Americans—between 5 and 10
percent—works full time beyond age seventy.

Many variables affect decisions to retire, but one important factor
is the structure of pension plans. These plans, whether designed by
government or by private employers, may be constructed to influence
retirement choices, but they have unintended consequences. Pension-
plan design is a technical subject, but worth considering both because
it explains how present practices arose and because it influences reform
proposals. Its importance derives from the incentives to retire that are
built into pension plans either by law or by employment contracts.

LET US BEGIN with *defined benefit* plans, which are very common for government employees, and hardly unknown in the private sector. These
plans specify the payouts to beneficiaries or, more accurately, the formula that will determine these payouts; they are usually a function of
salary earned in the final years leading up to retirement. The benefits
are in this way "defined," in the sense of being known within a modest range and not directly affected by investment returns. An employer
offering such a plan sets aside some fraction of payroll each year in order
to invest and build up reserves to finance the promised, future benefits.
The risk associated with poor investments (or the benefit attached to
lucky ones) falls, at least initially, on the employer, as the promisor of the
defined payouts. In contrast, a *defined contribution* plan specifies inputs.
The employer or employee, or often some combination of the two, will
make periodic payments, often deducted from salary checks, and then
the benefits will depend actuarially on the size of the fund created by
these inputs plus accumulated investment returns. Taxes are normally
levied on distributions down the road, and not on annual accretions or
even the wages turned over to these retirement accounts. The investments are made with untaxed dollars, so that there is a huge deferral
advantage to this form of retirement savings. Defined contribution plans
are essentially tax-favored savings plans, while defined benefit plans are
more like tax-favored annuities with payouts depending on investment
returns.

Workers who anticipate significant pension-plan benefits from an employer-provided plan will be influenced by the combination of these benefits and Social Security. (Nearly all workers are required to participate in Social Security. The most important exception involves state employees, who were first excluded from Social Security and then, after 1950, included only if their states chose to be a part of the system. As it has turned out, this option is an important cause of the underfunded pension crisis now facing several states.) Most defined benefit plans strongly encourage "early" retirement at an age *below* that associated with the availability of Social Security benefits. They do so by capping benefits, by requiring contributions from those who continue to work, and by diminishing benefits for those who stay at work beyond the desired retirement age. In a typical plan affecting state or union employees, the most profitable retirement age from the worker's perspective is a bit below sixty. This can be sensible for the employer because the retiree is likely to draw a much larger salary than that required by his or her replacement. It can also save the employer the substantial effort associated with dismissing employees who become less productive as they age, or who would otherwise expect wages to continue to rise even as their own productivity was flat or in decline.

It should be plain that a defined benefit plan can be designed to be a near-perfect substitute for (permissive) mandatory retirement, so long as there is opportunity to reshuffle compensation in the manner desired by the employer. But why might employers prefer the early retirement, and even the forced retirement, of their workers, including some who are marvelously productive? Employers did not lobby for the end of mandatory retirement, and they did not play a dominant role in the design of Social Security. Conventional (and insightful) wisdom is that when employees receive training in their early years at a firm, they must be "overpaid" later on in order to keep them from moving to other firms that did not bear the cost of training and that will try to hire them away from the employer that provided training. The first employer might underpay during the training years, and then overpay during the employee's midcareer years in order to prevent defection. At some point, the workers might shirk or just stay on the job past their most productive years in order to continue to collect these back-loaded, high wages. To combat this problem, employers can structure wages so that they increase with seniority, but then start decreasing when the worker is mature and when diminished productivity is likely, or lateral hiring is unlikely. It might be hard to get this just right. In the modern era with laws against age discrimination, it is plain that lawsuits are to be expected by an employer that pays workers less as they age. It is possible that an employer could hire young workers and tell them that wages will initially rise over time, but then decline after thirty years. The sixty-year-old might complain, but the employer will argue that this was a bargain offered at age thirty, and thus not one that discriminates against older workers, defined by statute as forty and above. The same sort of argument might be made in favor of mandatory retirement; the employer is not requiring a sixty-eight-year-old to retire, but rather contracting for every thirty-year-old to agree to retire in thirty-eight years! Law rarely accepts such long-term waivers and, in any event, it is probably too late to introduce and test these arguments.

The important thing here is the idea that mandatory retirement is but one way of ensuring that workers do not remain with their employers too long, especially at high wages, even as employers are not discouraged from training them in the first place. The second point is that a concerned employer can structure a defined benefit pension plan to encourage retirement by shifting compensation dollars from wages to retirement benefits, and by scheduling these benefits around an ideal retirement age. If fixing a retirement date is prohibited, then employers can recreate its desirable effects with defined benefit plans. The result is especially appealing because extraordinary workers are left some choice regarding retirement.

IT MAY BE useful to point to the comparable utility of age cutoffs where very young people are concerned. Law, as well as private parties, uses age minima for driver's licenses and other rights. When we require drivers to be at least sixteen years old, and rental companies require licensed drivers to be twenty-one or twenty-five, it is because it is costly to make case-by-case determinations of maturity and other valuable characteristics. There are surely mature fourteen-year-olds, just as there are excellent eighty-year-old employees, but at both ends of the spectrum it is sometimes useful and reasonable to allow categorization. We worry less about discrimination when the group is very broad. Just as we were all young, we will all be old, and in such cases law is usually less concerned with discrimination against discrete minorities. Indeed, discrimination against young drivers is more troubling than it is against older workers, because the former group has less political power.

When compulsory retirement is forbidden, even when agreed to in a contract, employers can try to unlink compensation from seniority, as is naturally the case in industries where workers earn commissions, but I have already suggested that there are problems with paying workers less as they age, or even as their productivity declines—or simply stays constant as wages rise with seniority. The process can be demoralizing for the worker and costly for the employer. If wages are reduced for all workers above some age, and in lockstep fashion, then many workers will indeed be the victims of age discrimination. And even if an upside-down U-shaped wage curve could be agreed to in advance and found legally acceptable, it may be unattractive because the most productive older workers will be underpaid and will defect to other employers. No employer wants to be left with the least productive workers. From a social perspective, younger workers and customers develop unhealthy attitudes toward older people when they find the latter to be the least productive; hidden from view is the fact that the superior mature employees have moved to other workplaces because they were underpaid at this one.

In the era before Social Security and large-scale pension plans, employers could dismiss workers as they liked. Once union and other protections took hold, they could no longer just dismiss veteran workers, but there was a wage and pension system in place that made retirement virtually inevitable, even before the Social Security age, or the age of any mandatory retirement agreement. With these contracts, little changed when age discrimination law came into effect. Thus, steelworkers and schoolteachers have continued to retire and to begin to collect pension benefits, long before most other workers. In the case of public schoolteachers, for example, the median retirement age is fifty-eight, and most retiring teachers collect pension payments equal to 60–75 percent of their final salaries, often with a continuing cost-of-living feature. Teachers who choose to work past this point usually lose a substantial amount of the pension benefits, so that one who continues to work must do so at a fraction, as low as one-half, of the previous wage. Under these conditions, few people choose to continue to work past sixty; defined benefit plans did most of the work that had been done by mandatory retirement contracts.

Unfortunately, some employers underfunded their pension plans. Others overfunded in order to gain tax advantages. New laws were passed and defined benefit plans—though useful for managing an aging workforce, especially once age discrimination law effectively barred forced retirement—became unattractive. They remain in force for more than 80 percent of public employees, but for few—about 15 percent—private sector employees.

The steady increase in the median retirement age over the last fifteen or twenty years can in this way be traced to the shift from defined benefit plans to defined contribution plans, or to no plans at all, as many employees save for retirement on their own in tax-favored retirement accounts. From an employer perspective, it has become difficult if not impossible to encourage retirement. Law seems to tolerate "golden handshakes," or incentives offered at age sixty-two, say, to employees who agree to retire within two or three years. But it is widely thought that payments at age thirty, or upon hiring, in return for a worker's agreement to retire at age sixty-five, would amount to unlawful discrimination, or simply be voided as a matter of contract law. It is noteworthy that sophisticated workers, including partners in law firms and consulting firms, who are not employees for the purposes of these laws, continue to contract for mandatory retirement. Their partnership agreements regularly provide for termination of the partnership interest by age sixty-five. Similarly, corporate officers and university officials are often, by private contract, required to step down at a specified age. In the latter case, they cannot be required to retire from their faculty positions, but the responsibility and extra compensation associated with an administrative position come to an end at age sixty-eight or at another specified point.

These private contracts are useful reminders of the desirable features of compulsory retirement. Of course, some workers are fantastic at their jobs well past any age we could specify. There are eighty-five-year-olds who are extraordinary managers, and requiring them to retire would impose serious private and social costs. Some law firms, for example, go to great lengths to keep these few marvels on the job. But there are also many workplaces in which it is awkward or even harmful to suggest to someone that he or she ought to retire, and if workers can continue forever, then more such conversations are required. Age discrimination law requires that the firm show that the worker is no longer fit for the job, or has misbehaved, and this can be difficult, expensive, and humiliating. It is easy to see why some employers might prefer to have a rule requiring retirement at a specified age, even though the rule comes with a cost to some employees as well as to the employer. Contractual retirement of this sort also makes room for new employees and new ideas. Nothing stops the retiree from opening a business or looking for work elsewhere, because nothing requires all employers to mandate retirement; the idea is that compulsory retirement would be of the permissive, contractual, and agreeable kind.

It is plausible that such contractually forced retirement would reduce rather than encourage any stigma attached to aging. If everyone in a workplace must retire at age seventy, there is the danger that persons above seventy will be seen as over the hill, even away from the workplace. But there is the alternative and rosier possibility that retirees will be understood as having agreed to a scheme in which they benefited from the retirement of their predecessors, and they now agree to make room for their successors. A rule requiring retirement can be less of a taint than a few drawn-out and uncomfortable processes in which ineffective senior workers are shown to be liabilities and then pushed out. Where there is no mandatory retirement, older employees might be seen as the least competent because the employer cannot easily reduce their wages or let them go. If this seems far-fetched, I invite observation and introspection. Which teller do you approach at a bank? In my experience, tellers in their thirties and forties appear to be the favorites; they are sufficiently experienced to be quick and to recognize regular customers, but not so experienced as to be, well, slow. It may well be that a seventy-five-year-old teller is as proficient, but from the employer's point of view that older teller has received wage increases over the years and is surely not twice as productive as the forty-year-old.

It is likely that if law were (once again) to allow employment contracts to specify a retirement age, employers might find middle-aged and even older employees more attractive. At present, employers must not discriminate against older job applicants, but it is difficult to bring a successful lawsuit on behalf of persons *not* hired. Age discrimination lawsuits are almost all about the dismissal of older workers rather than about the failure to hire them. An employer might readily hire someone at fifty-five if that person could promise to retire at age sixty-five, but employers are advised by their attorneys that such a contract would be unenforceable and would make the firm vulnerable to age discrimination suits. If the average employee is less useful after age seventy, then the rational employer might not want to be in the business of discerning which employees should be dismissed. However, if the entire pool could be counted on to retire by age seventy, it would make more sense to hire middle-age applicants.

When law brought about the end of mandatory retirement, employees were essentially granted (free) options to stay on the job longer than originally understood by both parties. Since the end of mandatory retirement, many employees have been hired, so that if contracts with mandatory retirement ages were again permitted, law would need to decide whether these terms could be applied to existing contracts—exactly as their abolishment was applied to then-existing contracts—or could only be allowed in new contracts. Technically, employers eager for mandatory retirement could let all their employees go and then offer to rehire them under the terms of new contracts with the desired clauses. It is likely that employees, and politicians eager for their support, would block this strategy. Put differently, many present-day employees have planned to retire beyond age sixty-five or seventy, and it seems unfair to interfere with these expectations without any compensation. However unfair they might have been to employers, whose expectations about employee retirements were dashed with the imposition of law invalidating these contractual terms, it is unfair to employees—or simply politically unfeasible—to do the same to them. By and large these will not be the same employees who received windfalls when mandatory retirement provisions were effectively voided by law. An employee who was hired in 1980, as I was, was enriched when his potential work life was made infinite by legal fiat. An employer who really wants such an employee to retire at age seventy, perhaps to make room for young talent, to save the cost of salaries that had grown with seniority, or to edge out employees whose productivity has declined, must induce retirement with severance pay, subsidized healthcare, and other costly benefits. This is especially costly because it must be done across the board. Employers run the risk of lawsuits if they try to induce retirement only on the part of less productive older workers.

Indeed, many employers have developed retirement incentives that are accepted by a significant percentage of eligible employees. An employer might have a standing offer that any employee at age sixty-five can agree to retire at age sixty-eight and, in return, receive a payment equal to one year's salary or even more. If these plans remain in effect for many years then, eventually, the employees who accept or reject these payments will no longer be those who received a windfall from the elimination of compulsory retirement. It is plausible, therefore, that no great change in law is needed from the employer's perspective. Employers will simply have shifted from at-will employment contracts (allowing them to dismiss workers without fear of lawsuits) to mandatory retirement to defined benefit plans and now to severance contracts. A less optimistic story is that employers have learned to be very careful before hiring employees who can overstay their welcome, with the threat of lawsuits in the air. I will not overclaim and say that the surge of part-time workers comes as much from the inability to contract about retirement as it does from the cost of healthcare and other benefits, but there is probably some cause-and-effect relationship between the end of compulsory retirement and the bringing on of more part-time workers. In universities the substitution is dramatic. University expansion has come through hiring adjuncts rather than full-time faculty; the adjunct faculty scramble for positions and pay, while full-time, tenured professors, now enriched by the option of staying on as long as they please with almost zero risk of removal for cause, comprise less than half the teaching force and a yet smaller fraction of new appointments.

IF THE BAN on mandatory retirement contracts is costly to employers, and therefore to many employees, why do we not see pressure to change the law? Law might, for example, allow private contracts with set retirement ages. Current employees would oppose this change, and it would likely be necessary to protect them against the possibility that an employer would simply terminate them and then offer to rehire them under the terms newly permitted by law. Moreover, employees might fear that they will be terminated in order to make room for new employees who could be signed to these new, mandatory retirement contracts. But if set retirement terms are only permitted in new contracts with new employees, then there will be very little political pressure to pass such laws. Employers will have little to gain because they will not enjoy the benefits of the new law for many years; they must "pay" for law now but profit from it far in the future—assuming the law does not change back meanwhile. Some of the same myopia that brought about underfunded pension plans will bring on political malaise and a disinclination to work for freedom of contract. More important, ours is an aging population and the center of political gravity is likely to oppose anything that can be seen as limiting the options of senior citizens. This may already be evident from the inability of state and local governments to reach negotiated, political solutions to their underfunded pension plan problems. If the ban on mandatory retirement is ever to end, reform will need to come in steps that anticipate the objections of powerful groups.

One way to reduce opposition to legal reforms is to delay change, pushing the burden of change into the future. A proposal made in 2017 to allow retirement ages in employment contracts beginning in 2037 would have a decent chance of passing because most of the apparent losers are unknown and certainly not politically organized. On the other hand, job applicants who would benefit from the change are unidentifiable in 2017, and employers in favor of the change will discount the far-off benefits and not invest much in political effort.

Another strategy would be for employers to announce that compensation will follow an inverse U. One can barely imagine a state's civil service system providing that pay automatically, and without exception, decreases by 5 percent a year after thirty years of service. The employer might argue that the plan controls costs and makes room for new employees (by encouraging retirements). It is not clear that courts would allow this scheme, and inasmuch as it would almost surely be limited to new employees, so that any savings would come about after decades, such a plan is probably not worth the effort it would require to enact.

A better strategy, I think, would be for law to promise that no age discrimination suit could be brought by anyone over a specified age, such as sixty-eight. Social Security and other retirement plans would provide income for retirees, and it would be a part of the strong statutory default for retirement. Some employers might then offer employment contracts that reduced compensation by 5 percent every year after age sixty-eight. (Automatic decreases prior to that age would need to survive age discrimination suits.) Other employers might simply structure contracts so that employment ceased at age sixty-eight, perhaps the same age that maximum Social Security benefits became available, but the employer and employee could choose to negotiate a new contract for work beyond that age, and at any wage they agreed upon. In a job like mine, retirement would come at age sixty-eight, whereas there is now no retirement age, but my university could choose to offer me a job beyond that age for any number of years it liked, and at a salary that was (or was not) unrelated to earnings before age sixty-eight. In some countries, retirement is regulated in this sort of way, with the presumptive retirement age tied to the age at which retirement benefits become available. In Israel, for example, the retirement age is sixty-seven for men and sixty-two for women (though at present the government is in the process of raising these ages in steps to seventy and sixty-four, respectively). At age sixty-seven, a man's employment comes to an end, whether in public or the private sector, and he begins to receive retirement income from the state. His employer, or another employer, is free to engage him for pay beyond that age, but these contracts are rare. The same would be true in the United States, under the proposal sketched here, except that one age (sixty-eight, let us say) applies to both sexes, and there would likely be a significant minority of workers rehired beyond that age, if only because our retirement benefits are relatively less generous than those found elsewhere.

It might seem surprising that law in many countries provides retirement benefits to women at a younger age than it does to men. The typical difference is five years. This differential was introduced in the post–World War II period, but has now been eliminated in many countries. Women everywhere outlive men, but in no country is the pensionable age higher for women than for men. Women tend to retire at *younger* ages than men, even in places like the United States where retirees qualify for pensions at set ages, regardless of sex. On the other hand, because women are more likely to be caregivers, it is very common to require fewer years of contributions than are required of men. Proposals to raise the retirement age, which is to say the age at which a full pension is available, are often opposed most vociferously by women. The obvious reason for this objection is the expectation of earlier retirement, but it is also the case that lower-income workers have more to lose, in relative terms, by a postponement of the retirement age, and that women, on average, have lower incomes than men.

Another idea for easing back into a legal regime that permits retirement ages to be set by contract is to begin by taxing affluent older workers. Most voters are worried about the solvency of the Social Security system. They will also be sympathetic to seniors who have supported family members and now need to work for their own, often postponed, retirement. These workers may have relied on the absence of mandatory retirement, or simply gone through tough times. Consider, however, a proposal to limit full benefits to retirees who leave the workplace by the median retirement age, unless their annual income is under $75,000 a year after that age. Imagine that Social Security benefits are capped at $30,000 per year, and that this amount is available to someone who retires at the prevailing median retirement age of sixty-two. Under this proposal, the cap would be $27,000 for one who retired by age sixty-three, $24,000 at age sixty-four, and so forth until an affluent person (with more than $75,000 in annual income) who retired beyond age seventy-two would simply receive no Social Security benefits at all. This sort of plan amounts to a substantial tax on high earners beyond the median retirement age. Someone who retires at age seventy-three, earning more than $75,000 per year in each year between sixty-five and seventy-two, would receive no Social Security benefits at all for the remainder of his or her life. Each year of work beyond age sixty-two costs $3,000 times the number of years of expected life, though the losses are of course deferred. One who chooses to retire at age sixty-six rather than sixty-five, for instance, has an expected life of another seventeen years or so, and loses $3,000 per year because of that extra year of highly compensated earned income. With an interest rate of 5 percent, the implicit tax on that extra year of earnings is about $34,000 in present-value terms, in addition to the conventional income tax on whatever amount is earned. This is a very significant surcharge, or discouragement, for a sixty-five-year-old who earns $100,000. It probably has very little impact on an executive or doctor who enjoys a salary of $500,000.

Most present and future Social Security recipients should be expected to favor this plan because it conserves resources for a troubled system at the expense of a fairly small group. The losers are very affluent older workers—most of whom began their careers expecting a mandatory retirement age, and then received a windfall. As for younger citizens, those who expect to be well compensated might come to resent Social Security, because they might pay in to the system and then receive low or zero benefits. But this result will only be true for workers who choose to retire later than the median retirement age. The more likely impact, especially with respect to workers who earn between $75,000 and $150,000, is to encourage early or typical retirement in order to avoid the implicit and substantial tax on work done after that age. I offer a more dramatic plan for Social Security in chapter 7, but that plan addresses the problem of the elderly poor, and a generation of nonsavers; here the focus is on opening up jobs held by workers whom employers are afraid to let go.

The tax idea just sketched is pegged to the median retirement age, but it could just as well apply after thirty years of (taxed) retirement earnings. Apart from the embedded progressive feature, it is not that different from the previously mentioned scheme in which employers, by contract, promise that wages will decrease after many years of service. Both plans are designed to encourage retirement, or to match compensation to expected productivity, and both leave room for really exceptional older workers who wish to continue at work.

Note that in the absence of a plan to tax affluent Social Security recipients, current trends explain a fair amount of the inequality gap in our society between the top and the middle. Civil service workers and union workers retire at a fairly young age. Pension plans have encouraged this pattern, as we have seen, but often these jobs are trying. New, younger bosses materialize, often with trendy or idiosyncratic demands, and retirement may come as a relief. This is not the case for lucky people like professors at major universities, scientists, and various other professionals. Our jobs are often not physically demanding, and many of us enjoy going to work. But if late retirees are disproportionately highly compensated, then the lack of mandatory retirement exacerbates income inequality. I do not regard this as much of an argument for allowing mandatory retirement contracts, but it is something to think about.

The larger point here is that the ban on mandatory retirement is just the sort of thing that an interest-group-driven democracy is likely to create and then find very difficult to undo. Rules against age discrimination are appealing, and many voters will think they stand to gain from the antidiscrimination law. When the rule extends to an outright ban on mandatory retirement provisions, millions of voters immediately think they are better off. At first the law had several exceptions, so that it was difficult for opponents to point to obvious cases where aging workers were liabilities. Voters would be likely to underestimate the difficulty of proving that someone was no longer able to perform a job. Few employers would invest in efforts to oppose the ban because they could encourage retirement quite effectively with defined benefit plans. Indeed, when the ban on mandatory retirement went into effect, most employers had defined benefit plans and, therefore, their workers were retiring at ages below the focal point created by Social Security. By now things have changed; the median retirement age is rising, but the major tool for encouraging earlier retirement has been made obsolete, and partly so by law. Many workers will stay on the job well beyond the point where their productivity justifies their compensation. Employers will suffer, as will younger workers who will not be hired until these older workers retire. At the same time, the median age of the population has increased and seniors have considerable political power. Any assault against the ban on mandatory retirement, or any attempt to make it easier for employers to dismiss underachieving employees (protected by age discrimination law), will arouse the fierce opposition of this powerful group. Younger workers are unlikely to support change with matching intensity because members of this potential interest group do not really know whether they will individually gain from legal change. An identifiable group of potential losers will normally be much more active and successful in the political arena than will a group of dispersed, unidentifiable, potential winners. It is unlikely that younger workers and voters can undo the ban on compulsory retirement—even where employees voluntarily agree to such terms. If change comes, it will be because of evidence that businesses are migrating to other countries with greater freedom of contract.

No End in Sight

Martha

LIKE ALL AMERICAN academics of my generation, I have been rescued from a horrible fate by the sheer accident of time. At sixty-nine, I am still happily teaching and writing, with no plan for retirement, because the United States has done away with compulsory retirement. Luckily for me, too, the law changed long enough ago that I never even had to anticipate compulsory retirement or to think of myself as a person who would be on the shelf at sixty-five, whether I liked it or not.

Moreover, given that philosophy is a cheerfully long-lived profession, I have been able, from the angle of my profession as well, to anticipate happy productivity in my "later years." Elsewhere, following Cicero, I discuss the longevity, and the late-age productivity, of ancient Greek and Roman philosophers, and numerous leading philosophers of more recent date. My cohort grew up on such stories. Examples closer to home also nourished our hopes: the great John Rawls published only a couple of articles before the age of fifty, when *A Theory of Justice* appeared. And Hilary Putnam, who died in 2016, just shy of his ninetieth birthday, never stopped changing his mind and generating new ideas. At his eighty-fifth birthday conference, when young philosophers delivered papers for three days on every aspect of his work, from mathematical logic to the philosophy of religion, he bounced up gleefully to reply to each, and almost always said something more interesting than the speaker.

It's no accident, then, that it seems weird and horrible to me to see members of my age cohort in philosophy turned out to pasture, just because they happen to be employed in Europe or Asia, even though they are a few years younger than I am. Some have been dismissed not only from department and office but also from university housing, forced therefore to relocate, sometimes to distant isolating suburbs, too far away to interact regularly with scholarly pals or graduate students, or for any of them to see much of their former colleagues. This seems all wrong to me, and I feel so happy that I can go on until summoned by fate—or until I want to do something different.

My romance with work is part of my romantic and idealistic take on life—to which Saul, characteristically, delivers a contrarian jolt of hard-headed realism. So now I have to stop focusing on my own emotions (!) and come up with some arguments. Fortunately, I am not at a loss. (If this were email, a smiley face would appear at this point.)

A caveat: I'm talking mainly about work that the worker experiences as meaningful, not about mind-numbingly repetitive white-collar work, and certainly not about hard physical labor. For those careers, retirement is already a popular choice in the United States, and, under the right circumstances, compulsory retirement of the sort Saul envisages might do just fine. We must carefully distinguish between the age at which retirement is permitted and an age at which it is required. But notice that early retirement from boring jobs now often leads to the choice of a second career, often with more meaning attached. Recently both the rabbi and the cantor in my temple were second-career women. If those doors should close through compulsory retirement of some type, meaningful second-career options will be limited to volunteer work, available only to those with sufficient income.

Healthcare, Equality, Adaptive Preferences

But let's think further. And let's start with the best case of compulsory retirement I have encountered, in the academic world: compulsory retirement in Finland. I've spent a lot of time there, and by now many of my good friends are compulsory retirees, the age being sixty-five. (Retirement is compulsory in all walks of life; I focus on the academy for now, since I know that area best.) The climate is salubrious, and my retired friends are for the most part healthy and potentially productive. But they can't teach or go to the office. Still, nobody is complaining. To my knowledge there is no lobby group pressing for an end to the policy. My personal acquaintances by and large express satisfaction. Indeed, Finnish norms dictate no complaint, even to colleagues, even in the direst matters. The right way to face terminal illness is thought to be silence until a few days before the end. So my friends would think it bad form to complain or even to start an interest-group movement. What are their underlying attitudes?

Social norms kick in there too, I believe. I probe and ask and observe, and I really do believe that people feel satisfied. Or if they feel pangs of discontent, they also feel guilty about those feelings.

So why are philosophers in Finland apparently satisfied with something Americans by and large repudiate and disdain? Social norms and expectations, I'll argue, are the largest factor. But there are two other factors I want to explore first.

The first is health insurance. Finland has a generous and high-quality comprehensive national health insurance scheme, the same for all, and it supports a high quality of both medical and nursing care (including in-home care) whether or not one is working. People grow up used to this, so they don't get anxious about future needs for care. US elder care under Medicare and Medicaid lacks some features of the Finnish system, and aging people correspondingly feel less secure. Recently, as the Finnish system starts to be cut, and nursing care is only unevenly available (see my chapter on inequality), Finns are becoming much more worried about retirement. But they are still doing relatively well in world terms. Still, security about healthcare is not the primary issue for the group I'm talking about, the people who work because their work is meaningful to them.

More important, there's an equality issue. Finns do not regard compulsory retirement as a disparagement, because (they say) everyone is treated alike. There is no message of ranking. It's a simple calendar age, and it is imposed without exception. It does not track antecedent inequalities of status. So you don't have to hang your head in shame. With Saul's scheme, appealing in many ways though it is, there is no equal status, and those whose contracts force retirement will feel they have to hang their heads by comparison to those whose power was great enough to negotiate a desirable long-term contract ex ante. My guess is that if Americans reject the Finnish system they would be even more dissatisfied with Saul's system, because it causes invidious comparisons.

Still, I would like to ask my Finnish friends why any rational person thinks it is good "equality" when all aging people are treated equally badly. Surely we would not accept as a good type of equality the denial to all citizens of religious liberty or the freedom of speech. I shall return to that point in my next section.

If people were forced to retire when, and only when, they were true slackers, they would feel more stigmatized than they might in Saul's system, but at least, in their hearts, they would see a basis for the differential treatment. But the inequality problem in any academic scheme of negotiated retirement is not likely to be as rational as that, or based on sound academic values. We've been there before. In the old days before the end of compulsory retirement in US universities, judgments about who should retire were made in accordance with all sorts of irrelevant factors, such as fads and social prejudices. In the Harvard of my graduate school days, when the university was permitted to decree that some retired at sixty-five, some at sixty-eight, and some at seventy, choices were conspicuously not made in accordance with academic productivity or beneficial contributions to the academic community. They were more often made in keeping with fads, alumni connections, and even baneful prejudices such as class and (I am sadly convinced) anti-Semitism. (They were not based on gender simply because there were no tenured women.) In short, unequal treatment, problematic in general, is especially problematic when it gives incentives to institutions to distort the academic enterprise in ways that track existing hierarchies that are peripheral to the academic mission.

Would Saul's plan have less distortion of that sort? To some extent it would, since people would negotiate ex ante, not when they were close to retirement age. But once inequality is built in, I surely don't trust institutions to make even ex ante judgments on the basis of sound academic values. They can certainly tell ex ante whether the person fits the preferred human type or types of the day, and let's not kid ourselves that we have outgrown the prejudices that disfigured Harvard in the 1970s. We still have our prejudices, even though we may not know exactly where and what they are. More obvious still, institutions will always be full of prejudice against "irrelevant" or "useless" fields. Even ex ante, they are still all too likely to ax the philosopher. In today's climate, I fear we'd find most of our humanists on short-term contracts and more "relevant" disciplines walking away with the long-term. Nor would universities take the retirement of senior humanists as an occasion to hire more young humanists, a point frequently made in defense of compulsory retirement in Europe. They would be more likely to downsize the whole division. And without famous senior people to defend those programs, these cuts would have less opposition than they would today (a point often missed in Europe, where people often still believe that making productive and well-known philosophers retire is a way to protect the young).

To be sure, even without compulsory retirement, bad values can still lead institutions to decide against replacing people after they retire, in order to shift that slot to a more "relevant" field. But time helps. Many fads are short-lived, and institutions and people sometimes do come to their senses. I find myself wanting to hang on and speak out for the humanities until, just maybe, the trend against them might shift. If that means living for two hundred years, I would enjoy that.

Finland has avoided the equality problem in a way: all people over sixty-five are treated alike. Whether that is sufficient to give us true equality before the law is an open question, and I shall address it in my next section. But there's a further problem: the well-known problem of what social science calls "adaptive preferences." People define their sights down, altering preferences for things that their societies have put out of reach, or not forming such preferences in the first place—the phenomenon that political scientist Jon Elster called "sour grapes," after the Aesop's fable.[1] Elster's focus was feudalism: for centuries, people had gotten used to the "fact" that the world contained two classes of people with two destinies, and they didn't rebel against those destinies—until, he argues, the Industrial Revolution unleashed a productive wave of discontent. Economist Amartya Sen has used this insight to explain the self-reported satisfaction of women with their educational status, even their health status, in nations that tell them from birth that women don't deserve as much as men, that women are weaker than men, and so on. His study of widows and widowers after the Great Bengal Famine shows that the widowers were full of complaints about their health (the person who had waited on them hand and foot was no longer there). The widows, however, having been told repeatedly that they really had no right to exist any longer, reported their health status as "fair" or even "good"—when a neutral medical exam showed a range of nutritional and other problems.[2] And of course what your body feels like most of the time is your baseline. If you've never been well nourished, and if, in addition, you're told all the time that women are weaker than men, you will think you feel pretty good even if you are not doing well by objective medical criteria.

In my essay on stigma, I cite research showing that adaptive preferences are a large problem for aging people, and I study its connection with pervasive (albeit illegal) forms of age discrimination. So the good cheer of my Finnish friends is ambiguous: it might show only that people told from the cradle that they should "make room" for others at sixty-five will adjust their aspirations to that reality. The fact that Americans would clearly be unhappy with such a system may be like the Industrial Revolution in Elster's analysis. Productive discontent has been unleashed, and baby boomers are refusing to lie down and die.

Adaptive preferences have real effects. Nonetheless, despite all the social incentives to decline, aging workers are not declining as predicted. Prejudices about workplace productivity have been falsified in many studies.[3] So perhaps we ought to conclude that older workers are not only not overpaid, but actually underpaid relative to the work that they would do were they not already held back to some extent by adaptive preferences.

Unfortunately, the research we have until now does not yet enable us to study the interaction between social stigma and compulsory retirement. One would predict that having no retirement age would counterbalance, to some degree, the demeaning messages that are all around us. At least we're now getting mixed messages, not uniformly negative messages. But since the work mingles US and British data, and since Britain is itself mixed, having compulsory retirement in some fields and some places and not others, it is hard to study these interactions. What worries me about Finland is that when you are told from the cradle that productive work ends at sixty-five, you will believe it, and you will define your possibilities and projects around this. You will expect to go on the shelf and others will expect you to be on the shelf. Not to mention the absence of things like office space and research support, you won't get the invitations you are used to or the respectful treatment from younger colleagues.

And you will not protest, because, in short order, you will come to see yourself as useless. One of my retired Finnish friends was happy initially, finding that she had more time to spend with her husband (also forced into retirement) and more time for the gym. Two years on, however, she is ashamed to come to dinners after a visiting lecture by me, her friend. She feels she does not belong, and that she ought to say no, even when I invite her. This is a terrible form of psychological tyranny.

The emeritus status might conceivably be redesigned to be less stigmatizing, as when, in our law school, retired professors keep an office, are welcome at workshops and roundtable lunches, and teach if they want to. But nobody has thought this through in a convincing way across the wide span of the professions.

Now of course Saul's plan allows for a lot more individual flexibility than the Finnish plan. The very features that make it do worse on the equality problem make it do better on the adaptive preference parameter. No specific age is the age at which one is on the shelf, and people will see all around them productive people in their later years, so they won't be forced to see themselves in the light of a stigmatizing social norm. But I still worry. The United States in particular is so full of youth-worship that it is only the total removal of compulsory retirement that allows so many of us to resist society's psychological pressure, in our thought about ourselves and our worth, and to continue to lead productive, respected lives, in which we do not define our worth by a calendar number.

Sometimes it's a good idea to have a per se rule, even when flexible policies offer distinct advantages, just because one envisages a host of abuses that would likely accompany flexibility. Sexual harassment policies, for example, are utterly inflexible, even though they forbid some sexual relationships that probably are not problematic. Still, the per se rule is preferable on account of the abuses it prevents.

The Equal Protection of Law

The greatest advantage of ending compulsory retirement is the one Mill claimed for ending discrimination against women: namely, the advantage of basing central social institutions "on justice rather than injustice." There are other dividends: in particular the fact, now widely acknowledged, but seen already by Cicero, that work is very important for health and happiness. Among the important benefits of the US regime is the wonderful fact that people by now do not care how old their colleagues are. We may add the joy of looking ahead to the next day's interactions with colleagues who are themselves of varying ages, thus nourishing nonstigmatic mixed-age friendships. As I note in chapter 3, the young men visit Cato, look up to him, and enjoy his company. Cicero knew how valuable cross-generational friendships are for both older and younger, and often alludes to his own aging mentors.

Mill emphasized that all forms of domination seem "natural" to those who exercise them. Feudalism made elites think that serfs were by nature a different type of human being. It took revolution to change consciousness. Racial discrimination and discrimination against women have been similarly rationalized by a belief, no doubt sincere, that this discrimination was based upon "nature." Discrimination against people with disabilities was not recognized as the social evil it is because for a long time so-called normal people just thought it was natural that society catered to their needs (including their bodily limitations) and kept "the handicapped" outside. Discrimination on grounds of sexual orientation was wrongly rationalized as acceptable because gays and lesbians were acting "against nature." Age is the next frontier and, so far, most modern societies think that unequal treatment on the basis of age is not really discrimination, because of "nature." They are wrong. Age discrimination, of which com-pulsory retirement is a central form, is based on social stereotypes, not on any rational principle. And it is just as morally heinous as all the others.

We must now face the inevitable objection that ending compulsory retirement is simply too costly. In addition to observing that keeping peo-ple productive rather than supporting them through Social Security might be thought to be a savings, not a cost, we should reply that when it is a matter of extending to a group equal respect and the equal protection of the laws, expense cuts no legal ice. When that same argument was made against including children with disabilities in integrated public school classrooms, the courts said that the financial shortfall of the school district that was griping about including "extra" children must not be permitted to weigh more heavily on an already disadvantaged group than on the major-ity. This was the correct response.

And just imagine the response if people were to say, let's exclude women and minorities from the workplace, because there are not enough jobs—or, more pointedly, because "they" are taking "our" jobs. People of reason would rise up, objecting that the full inclusion of all qualified work-ers on a basis of equality is an urgent issue of justice. Not all people are people of reason, and this so-called argument has recently been a major political force in the United States. But fear of popular anger should not stop us from doing what is just, any more than the huge violence of the civil rights era stopped the struggle for racial equality.

The objector will reply that aging people are expensive in a special way: they require special treatment, mentally and physically. First we should make the reply made by Cicero's Cato: it all depends on your hab-its. Many do not require anything special at all. Furthermore, suppose they do. Under the Americans with Disabilities Act, employers are required to make reasonable accommodations for workers with a range of disabilities, so even the extra expense of accommodation is acknowledged as a require-ment of justice.

But suppose job-related competence really does slip badly, despite all accommodation: Employers under the US system may lure people into retirement, and outside of the academy people can be fired for cause. What is forbidden is (*a*) refusal to accommodate, and (*b*) termination sim-ply on grounds of age. This is as it ought to be, since there is such great variety among aging lives. Compulsory retirement, the leading form of age discrimination, is one of the great moral evils of our times, the next frontier of justice that any theory of justice must address.

The United States has done well to reject compulsory retirement and to adopt laws against age discrimination. All countries ought to follow this lead. Indeed it is astonishing how powerful law has been. Our country is perhaps even more youth-focused than most, and yet aging workers are treated much more justly. Such would not be the case, were law not firm and unequivocal. (And law would not have become firm and unequivocal but for the work of lobbying groups, above all the AARP.) There is a lot of work yet to be done, since age discrimination persists, albeit illegally. But I'm happy that we aging professors have no end in sight—apart from the one that awaits us all. And having some useful work is a fine way to avoid useless brooding about that one.

Notes

1. Jon Elster, "Sour Grapes," in *Utilitarianism and Beyond*, ed. Amartya Sen and Bernard Williams (Cambridge: Cambridge University Press, 1982), 219–38, and in his book of the same title (Cambridge: Cambridge University Press, 1983).

2. Sen has discussed this phenomenon and his empirical findings in many places; see, for example, his "Gender Inequality and Theories of Justice," in *Women, Culture, and Development: A Study of Human Capabilities*, ed. Martha Nussbaum and Jonathan Glover (Oxford: Clarendon Press, 1995), 259–73.

3. See Peter Warr, "Age and Work Performance," in *Work and Aging: A European Perspective* (Basingstoke: Taylor and Francis), 309–22; Casey Wunsch and Jaya Vimala Raman, "Mandatory Retirement in the United Kingdom, Canada, and the United States of America," The Age and Employment Network, London, 2010. These social scientists argue that standard economic models holding the employees are underpaid early in their career, paid close to the marginal value of their labor during midcareer, and overpaid in later years, do not fit the facts: the evidence does not suggest that older people are overpaid relative to their productivity. (For the standard view, see Edward P. Lazear, "Why Is There Mandatory Retirement?," *Journal of Political Economy* 87 (1979).) I am indebted to a very helpful research report on this topic by Emily Dupree, which discusses a wide range of further publications.

Chapter 3

Aging with Friends

WHAT CAN WE learn from Cicero's remarkable dialogues on friendship and aging, and from his correspondence, as he aged, with his real-life best friend? Do real friends offer support, tell you when you are wrong, or simply offer companionship? Is making friends a different enterprise as we age?

On Aging, on Friendship

ARGUING WITH CICERO

Martha

Even if I have nothing to write to you about, I'm writing anyway, because it makes me feel as if I'm talking to you.

—LETTER FROM CICERO TO ATTICUS IN MAY 45

(WHEN CICERO WAS SIXTY-ONE AND ATTICUS SIXTY-FOUR)

FRIENDSHIP IS HUGELY important as people age. Its presence challenges, comforts, and enlivens. Its absence makes daily life seem barren and poor. The death or decline of friends is a major source of late-life depression. So it's not surprising that the best philosophical work on aging in the Western tradition, Cicero's *On Aging* (*De Senectute*), is also about friendship, and is written in close connection to his work *On Friendship* (*De Amicitia*). Written within a year of one another,[1] both are dedicated to his close friend Atticus (then sixty-five, while Cicero himself is sixty-two). The dedication links them: "As in that other book, an aging man myself, I wrote to another aging man about aging, so in this book, with the greatest friendliness I have written to a friend about friendship" (A 5).[2]

The works are dramatically linked as well. *On Aging* is set in 150 B.C.E., when its main character, Cato the Elder, is eighty-three. The conversation is provoked by questions from two young men, then in their thirties, Scipio and Laelius, both well-known historical figures and close friends. The *De Amicitia*, set in around 129 B.C.E., shows this same Laelius, now in his fifties, mourning the recent death of his dear friend Scipio. Provoked by two young relatives, he describes the benefits of friendship. Cicero (born in 106) immediately points out that one of these young relatives, by that time an aging man, taught Cicero law and was a much-admired mentor. So the dramatic choices link the two works to one another and both to Cicero's own life; they also emphasize the themes of aging and of friendship, both between men of similar age and across generations.

Cicero introduces *On Aging* with a direct address to Atticus—but in a poetic quotation that contains an intimate joke. He cites a passage from the famous poet Ennius in which a character named Titus (Atticus's first name) is addressed by a friend: "O Titus, would it be worthwhile if I could help you and relieve the anxiety that now sears you and sticks in your heart?" It's the sort of poetic joking the two friends often engage in, teasing one another, and the joke refers to the work's announced aim: to distract Atticus from anxiety. But that stated aim is itself an intimate joke: for in fact it is always the other way round, the emotionally volatile Cicero who needs the friendly concern of the calmer Atticus (an Epicurean who seems to have practiced the detachment that he preached) to distract him from his cares, and Cicero is well aware of this.

Consider, then, the type of friendly intimacy revealed in this elaborate joke. It goes to the heart of my concern: for it reveals a type of closeness based on complementarity, longtime knowledge of difference, teasing, and sheer daily familiarity that Cicero's two philosophical works ignore or even deny. I'll investigate the two works against the background of the friendship, amply chronicled in letters, and I shall argue that Cicero's official arguments omit much about friendship and aging that his letters reveal. If friendship matters for aging, as it does, we need to ponder the whole texture of a real friendship, not just Cicero's philosophical schema, however admirable.

Cicero is a fine philosopher (as has not always been granted). But he is also real in a way no other ancient Greco-Roman philosopher is—the only one whose intimate conversations and thoughts we know, the only one whose personal correspondence, with both Atticus and scores of other acquaintances and family members, has survived.[3]

Cicero wrote the two works at a time of almost unbearable pain. The death of his beloved daughter Tullia in 45 B.C.E. (in childbirth, after the dissolution of her third marriage) cast him into a deep depression that we will have occasion to discuss later, since it is a large theme in the friendship. The impending collapse of the Republic intensified his grief and gloom as well.[4] Our two essays, written during that terrible time, are intended, he tells Atticus, as a "gift that both of us can enjoy together" (S 2). Such a book could "make aging easy and pleasant," even if it doesn't "wipe away" all its cares.

These two books have been justifiably popular over the centuries. Both have some very good ideas and arguments. But still, there is something missing. Although in form they are dialogues, they are very abstract, and they lack, therefore, a key aspect of both friendship and aging: the nuanced sensitivity to the particular that Cicero often praises under the rubric of *humanitas*. From the letters to Atticus, we get much that complicates and deepens them. So, arguing with Cicero, I shall be setting him against himself. And it seems easiest to do this in Ciceronian style, as a kind of dialogue with him, although I shall not even try to imagine the other side! For strategic reasons, I take them in reverse order.

On Friendship

Your *De Amicitia* is a justly admired analysis and encomium of long-lived friendship. Some of its good ideas are the importance of goodwill for enduring friendship (A 19); the value of intimacy, and the relief of discovering that one can talk about things that one usually conceals from others (22); the way friends make life go better by sharing both joy and adversity (22); the way that friendship nourishes hope (23). Even though these are familiar ideas, you present them with restrained eloquence.

Two sections are even better, because the insights they offer are more surprising. The first is your critique of the Stoic account of friendship, an account that was plainly very popular at this time of trouble. These men "who, I am informed, are considered sages in Greece" say something that you find quite "astonishing": namely, that we should avoid too much intimacy in friendships, so that one person doesn't become bogged down by the anxieties of others (45). Each person has enough on his own plate, and it is troublesome to be too much involved in other people's business. In short, "It is best to hold the reins of friendship as loosely as possible, so that we may either draw them up or slacken them at will; for, they say, an essential of a happy life is freedom from care, and this the soul cannot enjoy if one man is, as it were, in labor for many."[5]

You reply that this model of friendship is too self-protective: virtue is generous, and does not shrink from caring for another's pain on account of the difficulty it may bring. Besides, taking this risk-incurring generosity out of friendship would take away the "most delightful link in the chain of friendship"—love.[6] Love is generous and uncalculating (51).[7]

A second impressive contribution is your critique of another common picture of friendship, which says that we should measure our goodwill to our friends by their goodwill toward us. Friendship is an accounting game, and you should never give, or feel, more than you have received or can expect to receive (56–57). You utterly reject this way of thinking. "It surely is calling friendship to a very close and petty accounting to require it to keep an exact balance of credits and debits. I think true friendship is richer and more abundant than that and does not narrowly scan the reckoning lest it pay out more than it has received; and there need be no fear that some bit of kindness will be lost, that it will overflow the measure and spill upon the ground, or that more than is due will be poured into friendship" (58). This error is closely linked to the Stoics' error, since the behavior described here is frequently a sign of excessive self-protectiveness.

There are good arguments here, then, although the writing is too abstract and lacks vivid illustration (unlike your best philosophical works, which are rich in historical and personal examples). But there are two points on which I need to argue with you, or, rather, to set you arguing with yourself.

The first is the emphatic claim that a good friendship is characterized by harmony of beliefs and tastes, and by agreement. "For friendship is nothing else than an accord (*consensio*) in all things, human and divine, conjoined with mutual goodwill and affection" (20). Later you go even further: "There should be between them complete harmony of opinions and inclinations in everything without exception" (60).

This sounds virtuous and high-minded, but is it true? Friends probably have to share many interests and tastes, or else they would diverge too much over time, undermining the friendship. If one is a sports fan and the other loves classical music, that's all right if that's the only major divergence. They can agree to spend some time apart. But suppose they differ about everything: one loves dogs, the other hates dogs; one loves the Socialist Workers Party and the other the Tea Party; one loves elaborate meals in gourmet restaurants, the other hates pretense and prefers pizza. All of these things impose strain, especially as people age. Some strains can be negotiated, but probably not a long list of them, covering central areas of life.

But you don't go into the topic very deeply. You don't even distinguish differences of taste from differences of opinion, or both of these from differences of temperament. But large-scale differences of taste and interest probably threaten friendship a lot more than differences of opinion: one can argue about opinions, and that is fun. Some differences of temperament can function this way too, giving rise to occasions for pleasant teasing and self-teasing. Indeed, when we turn to the letters, we'll see, I think, that this sort of jousting provides major pleasures.

To go deeper, however, I now turn to your own words, hoping to discover how you and Atticus forged a bond that endured for decades and supported both of you during aging.

Exhibit A: A Total Mode of Life

On December 5, 61 B.C.E., in one of your earliest letters to Atticus, you respond to a letter in which he has been justifying his character, telling you that his concern with money above all is petty. Since Atticus is essentially a banker, he probably felt defensive on that score. You tell him that he did not need to say that, but then you continue:

> I have never felt any difference between us—apart from our overall choices of a total mode of life (*praeter voluntatem institutae vitae*). What one might call desire for glory has led me to seek political office. But a different, and unexceptionable, course of reasoning (*minime reprehendenda ratio*) has led you to seek a virtuous detachment (*honestum otium*).

You go on to list all the things in which the two of you do concur. But isn't this remarkable? The overall choice of a total mode of life! What you are discreetly alluding to is Atticus's Epicureanism, which emphasizes avoidance of risks and cares, including those of political involvement—so different from your own political philosophy, which places service to the Republic, with all its risks, at the very top of the list.[8] With such a huge difference at the beginning of a friendship, how did the friendship last and deepen?

You and Atticus confront your differences with a focus on important values that you do share—you mention honesty, integrity, conscientiousness, and, above all, love. And you also display, throughout the letters, the leavening effect of shared tastes and interests. You both are lovers of poetry, you both like relatively modest parties (Atticus was known for having at his no dancers or acrobats, only a person reading poetry!). Your constant delighted gossip contains many shared perceptions of people, and lively curiosity about human behavior. You also share a deep love of the Republic.

But things are more interesting still. For in this letter we see that you already know how to confront difference with humor, teasing, and self-teasing. The revealing sentence could be read straight, and even read this way it shows a remarkable grace of vulnerability: you're willing to admit that your motives might be impure, and to grant that his choice is understandable and even reasonable. But I think the sentence is best read as part of the joking and irony that is such a ubiquitous feature of the letters. You tease him for his apolitical life, and tease yourself for your politics.

However, here's a further complexity: this teasing, which in a way is a *consensio*, is also at the same time a temperamental *dissensio*: it depends on mutual awareness of different personality types: that Cicero is a committed public guy who wears his heart on his sleeve, that Atticus is a more retiring guy who does not like to stick his neck out. So what the correspondence so far really shows is an intimate play of difference and similarity, which becomes in the end a delighted complementarity, with vulnerability on both sides. For teasing is a very special way of being vulnerable. Especially for someone like you, so high-minded, so serious, it seems to be delightful, and rare, to allow someone to play with your highest commitments (or to encourage you to self-tease about them) in a way that only a trusted friend could.

As people age, this sort of play, which requires awareness of difference, becomes even more precious. Especially when people are well known, they become fixed in the world's mind as who they seem to be. There is a large wooden figure out there, and the real, vulnerable, often conflicted and frightened, self goes unseen and uncared for. When a child meets new people, they tend, if they are at all sensitive, to be curious about the child's interests and idiosyncrasies. But when someone meets a famous aging person, they somehow think that they know who that person is, because they have read some of that person's work, and of course you do pour a lot of yourself into your work. Then, if that person's public persona is terribly high-minded and serious, as yours is, they tend to address that serious persona and to have little curiosity about the rest of the person. Thus in all the many volumes of letters back and forth between you and other friends, we find not many who know that you are a person who likes teasing and joking. And yet, after Tullia's death, in one of the most tragic letters in the whole corpus, you warn your ex-son-in-law (who also understood this aspect of your personality) that he will shortly see a changed person: "Not that I'm so broken down that I've forgotten I am a human being, or think that one must simply submit to fortune. But all my humor and love of fun, which used to delight you more than others, has been entirely snatched away from me."[9] So, that way of connecting to people is valuable in general, but particularly valuable for, and valued by, you.

Here, then, is the underlying cement of the friendship, from early days: a complex blend of similarity and difference. Now I turn to aging itself, and the way your friendship sustains you then.

Exhibit B: Grappling with Loss

All friendships that last long enough confront loss—especially if they extend into the time of aging. Yours with Atticus was marked not only by many illnesses, but also by two huge tragedies for you, more or less simultaneous, and simultaneous with the onset of aging: the apparent death of the Republic, and the death of Tullia. Atticus had less to complain of: his health was good, and both his mother and his wife died after the correspondence stops. So you had no occasion to support him in a time of trouble.

Not so with you. Let's focus on Tullia: here we'll see again that difference of a sort, in the context of love, is extremely useful. Tullia died in mid-February 45 B.C.E. You could not stand being in your own house, so you moved in with Atticus for several weeks. Then, on March 6, you left Rome, arriving on March 7 at your villa in Astura, a lonely place on the Bay of Antium surrounded by the sea. At this point the correspondence resumes. You mention your "burning pain" that "presses and refuses to go away" (March 7). On March 8, you acknowledge a letter from Atticus that asks you to "put yourself back together from this mourning." You say that you are doing everything in your power—even writing a philosophical consolation to yourself[10]—but "grief conquers every consolation."

On March 9, your letter is short:[11]

Please make my temporary excuses to Appuleius, since a real cancellation is impossible.[12] In this lonely place I have nobody to talk to. It is as if in the morning I go into hiding in a dark dense forest, and don't come out until evening. Apart from you, I have no greater friend than solitude, where all my conversation is with books. But sometimes tears interrupt. I try to stop them as much as I can, but so far I am not up to it. I'll write back to Brutus, as you suggest. You'll have that letter tomorrow, and when you have someone to give it to, you'll give it.

On March 10, apparently responding to a concerned letter from Atticus, you write:

> I don't want you to drop your business and come to me. I'd rather come myself, if you are held up for a longish time. After all, I never would have left your company, if it hadn't been clear to me that nothing at all could help me. But if any relief were possible, it would be in you, and as soon as relief can come from anyone, it will come from you. And yet I can't be without you now. But we agreed that coming to your house won't work, and mine won't work either; and if I were somewhere closer by, I still wouldn't be with you. The same business that keeps you from me now would keep you from me then. There's nothing more appropriate for me right now than this solitude. But I fear Philippus will take it away: for he arrived yesterday evening. Writing and letters don't make me feel better; but they distract me.

On March 11, you describe your attempt to "escape the biting pain of memory," and, for the first time, describe the idea of building a shrine to Tullia, a massive project that obsesses you right up to the end of your life. On March 15, you respond to a letter in which Atticus has urged you "to disguise the intensity of my grief," adding that others criticize you for not doing this. You reply, "Can I disguise it more effectively than by spending all my days in literary composition? I do this not for the sake of concealment, but in order to ease and heal my mind. Still, even if I don't achieve very much for myself, I certainly satisfy the demand for concealment."

On March 17 you reply to a letter in which Atticus more forcefully asks you to return to Rome, saying that people really demand your presence. You express your distaste for city bustle, "with people crossing my path whom I can't see without being upset." As for the demands of others, "For a long time, you should know that I have thought more of just you than of all the others."

Soon a slight shift is noticeable: the topic of return to Rome becomes a live option. Atticus (apparently) answers, saying that, after all, the Forum and the Senate House are your home. You reply, on March 19:

> Atticus, I'm dead, I've been dead for a long time. But now I admit it, since I've lost the one link that held me to life. So I look for lonely places. But if anything does lead me back to Rome, I will try, so far

as is in my power (and it will be in my power) to prevent anyone but you from seeing my grief, and even you, if possible.

The daily letters continue, but grief is not always the main topic. However, grief swells up again, like a wave. On March 24, you respond to a letter from Atticus that urges you rather strongly to try returning to your old habits. You refuse, saying that mourning for the loss of liberties was bad enough, but Tullia was a comfort. Now you see no reason to pay any attention to what other people think. You add: "Through writing, I have diminished my active mourning (*maeror*); but the pain itself (*dolor*) I cannot diminish, nor, if I could, would I want to."

I'll stop there, although the letters go on, since Atticus's business continues to detain him (a fact that you note, impatient)—with the topic of grief becoming less central, but recurring at times. But on March 30 you announce that you are departing for Rome. It becomes clear from later letters that you spent a month at Atticus's house.

Here we see several kinds of *dissensio*, all supporting a deep agreement in affection. Most evidently, there is difference of circumstance. When someone is mourning, it's valuable to be reminded that there is a life outside of mourning. (Atticus can also help you in practical ways, making your excuses to Appuleius.) Second is difference of life-experience: you had just lost the person who (perhaps apart from Atticus) mattered most to you (your undistinguished son Marcus didn't matter nearly as much, and your relationship with your wife was rocky), and at a time of deep political bereavement. The fact that Atticus has had a smoother life helps him point you in the direction of ongoing life. It's crucial that Atticus has a lively imagination: otherwise he might have been totally unable to comprehend grief of this magnitude.

And finally there is the temperamental difference we've already seen. You allow your anxieties and sufferings to be widely seen. Indeed, you are an extreme anti-Stoic where love is concerned—for being completely immobilized and unable to appear in public for more than two months is extreme in any culture. Atticus might have telegraphed profound disapproval. Instead, always gentle and calm, he appears to have gently urged a resumption of life, and he was able to do this because, apparently, he combined love for his friend with imagination, and both with a subtly different attitude toward proper mourning. You needed that pull, as we often need a gentle pull from a friend to get out of a hole that life has put us in. Had Atticus said, "I totally agree with you, you ought to be alone for at least two years and not allow anything to console you, otherwise you would be disloyal to Tullia," he would have been less adequate as a friend.

All in all, then, the *De Amicitia* is superficial on the subject of *consensio*. We need to make more distinctions, looking at life.

What about the book's other major claim, that the best friendship, perhaps the only lasting friendship, is between people who are good? It's not as if there is nothing in your claim. Friendship can easily come apart when one or both are selfish, or cowardly. And you are surely right that a major problem for a friendship comes when one is pursuing schemes of dubious propriety, and asks the other to go along. So, let's concede: a certain level of baseline goodness is a necessary condition for friendship, at least for lasting friendship of the sort you and Atticus had, the sort that will support people as they age.

Still, necessary conditions are not sufficient conditions. There's far too little, indeed nothing at all, about the subtle particularities that make one person care for another. Many people are above a moral baseline; few become one's best friend. Who knows why? Complementarity certainly plays a role in your case, and shared tastes in what one might call the "neutral zone," that is, neither virtues nor vices, such as your shared taste for poetry and political gossip. But we find many more distant friendships in the correspondence where there are some shared literary and political tastes—and yet there's no spark, no fun. With Atticus, by contrast, there's constant enjoyment: joking, teasing, gossiping, something that fills up the day and makes it a good day. "Even if I have nothing to write to you about, I'm writing anyway, because it makes me feel as if I'm talking to you." That's not produced by virtue (though virtue helps, cementing trust). It's something more ineffable.

There is something else that complicates the simple story of goodness. The exposure involved in deep friendship means that each can see the other's flaws in ways that most of the world cannot. Good-enough people usually manage to act pretty well, but they may have all sorts of fears, conflicts, and hesitations along the way, and these are seen only by the friend—except when, as here, history permits the world to see them too. You, Cicero, do not have an unblemished record from history. People say that you are greedy, cowardly, divided in mind, and so on. But: they are able to say these things only because we can see you with an intimacy and inner exposure that we don't see any other great Roman. With others we see only the final result, the noble action. With you, we can see the backstage side of nobility: the agonized deliberations, the fears. The presence of these conflicts make you not only more human but also better: it's not admirable to charge off into danger without taking its measure fully.[13] And I would add that complicated people are simply more intriguing; the sort of exposure that friendship permits allows you to emerge as more interesting than a moral exemplar.

The pressure to do the right thing in difficult times is exhausting. One huge role for the friend is to give the other friend a rest, a safe haven for minor vice: for venting, panic, even for childish displays. You seem to agree: to friends, you say, we can say things that we usually conceal from others (22). But here we must mention complementarity again, as you do not. A close friendship between two highly strung and intensely emotional public figures is not impossible, but surely it is rare. In your case, such a friendship would not have worked well, since you are uncontrolled at times and very needy. Atticus evidently has a strongly maternal character, besides being just fun and joyful in a way that lures you back into sanity. So the ability to talk freely requires, at least sometimes, a certain lack of *consensio* in temperament.

One further point: lack of *consensio* in friendship explains how friendship can expand our horizons, leading us to understand new issues, new ways of looking at the world. This ability to deepen one's understanding of the world as one ages, while deepening the friendship itself, is precious, and is offered by very few other pursuits. (Perhaps the arts offer similar benefits.) So without understanding why your emphasis on *consensio* is inadequate, one can't really understand the benefits of friendship for aging.

On Aging

On Friendship was already about the aging process, and a companion piece to the other work. Once again: while there are many fine things in *De Senectute*, there is also something oddly abstract about it, which makes me want to object, and to use your own words against you.

The first fine thing is the very fact of such a work. I know of no good philosophical work on this topic before or after it, in the Western tradition.[14] The stigma against aging that you confront and effectively attack is so deep that philosophers simply don't confront the topic.

And it is not because philosophers are not an elderly bunch. Philosophers in the Western tradition do a high proportion of their best work above the age of sixty. The Greco-Roman tradition is particularly impressive in that regard. Your spokesman in the text, Cato the Elder, was eighty-three at the fictional time of the dialogue, and lived to be eighty-four. He mentions three other long-lived thinkers. Plato, he records (correctly), lived to be eighty and was still hard at work when he died. Isocrates lived to be ninety-nine, and wrote his most famous work when he was ninety-four. And Gorgias died at the age of 107, and was working right up to the end (13). "When someone asked him why he chose to stay alive so long, he replied, 'I have no complaint to make about old age.'" We could add others, including the remarkable Cleanthes the Stoic, who died by suicide (fasting) at one hundred.[15]

As for modern philosophers: they do a good deal worse on average, since they live in less salubrious climates and have the bad luck to know tobacco. Still: Kant lived to eighty, Bentham to eighty-four, and the amazing Bertrand Russell, living in the worst climate of all, reached ninety-eight. Do philosophers live longer than others of similar wealth and class? It's hard to say. But they certainly do appear to do a larger than average proportion of their useful work in their later years. Beginning on that note, you begin with something people need to bear in mind.

The drama of the dialogue subtly rebuts its central theme, the stigma against aging, even before Cato begins to rebut it in argument. For it depicts the two younger men seeking Cato out, taking pleasure in his company, and hoping to learn from him. They have sought him out, because, as they note, they would quite like to get to be that old, and, in case they do, they would like to know more about what that time of life is like. They feel that Cato is doing very well, so they want to know why, given the negative reputation attached to that time of life. In response, Cato gracefully, cogently, rebuts four charges commonly made (he says) against his time of life: that aging people are inactive and unproductive; that they have no physical strength; that they no longer enjoy bodily pleasures; and that the nearness of death makes them prone to debilitating anxiety.

As you use Cato to rebut the common charges, you are clearly having some fun yourself: for you portray Cato as mentally and physically impressive, but also as having at least one or two mildly annoying traits commonly associated with old age. Cato talks too much and listens too little, he is fond of long digressions about his own past, and he focuses too much on his own pet hobbies, without considering the interests of his audience. In this case, Cato, the real-life author of a very boring work about farming, *De Agri Cultura*, bores the two young men, and the reader, by long digressions about mulching and plowing, and there's an especially hilarious passage about the miraculous properties of manure. Some

Romans found these topics interesting, but we know that you did not, so the portrait is playful. On the whole, then, old age isn't perfect; but it acquits itself very well.

Now to the serious argument. In general, your Cato is dead right: there is a huge stigma against the aging. Things have not changed much, if at all. He organizes his argument around four common points made in derogation of the aging, and these charges are still made ubiquitously.

To the first charge, inactivity, part of Cato's reply is to say that the stereotype is simply untrue: hence his many examples of important contributions made by the elderly. (Notice that these people are on average at least twenty years older than you and Atticus.) Particularly lovely is the story of how the heirs of the poet Sophocles tried to get him declared incompetent so that they could get their hands on his money. They hauled him into court—where he read to the jury some speeches from the *Oedipus at Colonus*, which he had just been writing (at the age of around ninety). He then asked the jury whether they thought this the work of a mentally incompetent person. He won (23). More generally, says Cato, although some activities that require a lot of physical strength are harder for people as they age, intellectual pursuits do not diminish. One would hardly call the captain of a ship incompetent because he could not ply the oars (17).

As for politics, which all agree to be among the most important human tasks, the Roman Senate takes its very name from *senes*, aging men (20): it's meant to be a council of elders, because it's believed that aging men have experience, wisdom, and deliberative capacity. If a senator were to live to be one hundred, would he be complaining about old age? Cato asks. "No, for he would not be spending his time running and leaping, or long-distance spear-throwing, or hand-to-hand sword play; he would be engaged in using reflection, reason, and judgment," qualities in which the elderly are distinguished (19). Cato does mention the possibility of deteriorating memory and other mental faculties in aging, but he insists that use and practice can ward off this problem (21). It's interesting to ask why there is no mention of Alzheimer's disease, despite the long lives these people evidently led and the realism of the dialogue. A conjecture that appears to be supported by recent research is that environmental factors explain why Romans appear not to know of this disease.

As for strength of body: certainly there is decline, says Cato, but to a large extent decline can be lessened by vigorous regular physical activity. You just have to make the best use of the bodily resources you have. He cites many examples of people who continue long vigorous walks, horseback riding, and other exercises, even into their nineties (34). As for himself, he can't quite do what he used to do on the field of battle, but nobody has had reason to complain of his lack of stamina in his political tasks, or in entertaining guests and helping friends (32). When someone really can't do much, the failure is typically caused by ill health, and ill health can strike at any time of life (35).

Once again, it is interesting to see how far environmental and life-style factors appear to have kept people vigorous into late years. None of them had our modern sedentary lifestyle, nor did they smoke, nor did they breathe polluted air. Just listen to Cato's advice (to his audience of young men), which sounds extremely modern:

> My young friends, we should resist old age; we should compensate for its defects by watchful care; we should fight against it as we would fight against a disease; we should adopt a regimen of health; we should do regular moderate exercise; and we should eat and drink just enough to replenish our strength, not so much as to crush it. Nor, indeed, should we give our attention only to the body. Much greater care should be given to the intellect and the mental faculties. For they too, like lamps, grow dim with time, unless we keep them supplied with oil. (35–36)

We sometimes think that the "use it or lose it" philosophy about exercise, mental and physical, is a recent discovery of the baby boom generation. Not so: it was just an obvious fact for people whose lifestyle forced them to be active. If you lived in a US city today, you would have to join a gym to be healthy, and you were surely not a keen sportsman. But an ancient Roman, in addition to the constant walking, was expected to serve in the military, and you did a very good job of that as proconsul in Cilicia, storming a mountain fortress at the head of your troops at the age of fifty-seven.

Cato also reminds his audience that one very important part of the body is the voice, and that oratorical skill declines less rapidly than other physical abilities. (Remember that public speakers had no amplification, so they needed vocal equipment comparable to that of today's opera singers, the only unmiked singers we now have.) Moreover, to the extent that the voice may become less forceful, one may adopt a quieter, less bombastic and more subtle style of oratory that is currently in fashion (27–29). (Here commentators think that you may be thinking of your own delivery, which—hard though it is for your readers to imagine it, given your over-the-top writing style—was said to be subtler and less bombastic than that of others.) Finally, if you can't do any of these physical things any more, you can certainly teach them, and good rhetorical teaching is extremely important.

More generally, Cato continues, aging people often have more social influence (*auctoritas*) than younger people, and that influence itself can be a major source of agency and productivity. If the body and voice are weaker, so what, when the mere nod of an influential leader's head can achieve results (61). But of course the aging won't be so honored unless they confidently claim their due from others, refusing to be defined by stigma. "Old age is honored only on condition that it defends itself, maintains its rights, is subservient to no one, and to the last breath rules over its own domain" (46).

Accordingly, to silence the skeptics and defend his claim to respect, Cato now gives his own life as an example:

> I am now at work on the seventh volume of my *Antiquities*. I am collecting all the records of our ancient history, and at the present moment am revising all the speeches made by me in the notable causes which I conducted. I am investigating the augural, pontifical, and secular law; I also devote much of my time to Greek literature; and, in order to exercise my memory, I follow the practice of the Pythagoreans and run over in my mind every evening all that I have said, heard, or done during the day. These employments are my intellectual gymnastics, the race-courses of my mind; and while I sweat and toil with them I do not greatly feel the loss of bodily strength. I act as counsel for my friends; I frequently attend the senate, where I initiate subjects for discussion, after having pondered over them seriously and long; and there I maintain my views in debate, not with strength of body, but with force of mind . . . but . . . the fact that I can do them is due to the life that I have led. (47)

Because of good habits, his mental activity is unabated, and he has physical force enough to do what he needs to do.

Another contribution of habit, says Cato, is that good habits can also diminish the whining and complaining for which the elderly have such a bad reputation. Grumpiness is a flaw of character; it can be curbed, or even eradicated, by a disciplined practice of not complaining, which one needs to begin early! (65).

Now we reach the third charge, concerning the bodily pleasures. Cato's approach to this one is similar to his approach to physical strength: the aging have what they need, they don't miss what they don't have, and they spare themselves a lot of annoying difficulties. People who feel less sexual desire are less likely to break up families or get into trouble with the law. People who don't get drunk or overeat are healthier, have less indigestion and less insomnia (44). Thus they are better able to carry out their mental and indeed their physical tasks. Besides, they can still enjoy food and drink in moderation; and they then discover the true meaning of the word *convivium* (banquet): it means "shared life." For when people are not drunk they discover that the pleasure of conversation is much more appealing than the pleasure of getting drunk (45–46). Cato points out that he is still very fond of late-night parties, organized as serious talk-fests, with a topic appointed for discussion.

Cato then launches into that boring digression on the pleasures of agriculture. But even that has a useful point: there are many hobbies that aging people can pursue with undiminished zeal, hobbies that give them keen sensory pleasure. Music, theater, travel—all of these would be examples parallel to farming, for the person who doesn't feel its allure.

Cato's first three arguments are, then, extremely cogent, and also novel and fun to ponder. And the work as a whole is less musty and abstract than the *De Amicitia*, since Cato keeps us vividly aware of his own life and its ongoing achievements and pleasures, not to mention its struggle against stigma. Still, I am dissatisfied. If, once again, we hold the treatise up against the letters, there are two obvious omissions.

The first omission is conflict and anxiety. Much though you have repudiated Stoicism in the *De Amicitia* (and in your life), the confrontation with pain and death in this work is serene to a fault. The whole long passage on death, answering the fourth charge, assures us that it is not something to be feared, and that one should face the end with equanimity and good cheer. You did not face adversity that way, and you didn't even think you ought to. Because you died while still relatively young, we really don't know how you would have faced your eighties and nineties, but we can certainly guess, by looking at your reactions in your sixties. You are externally composed, but only because you don't let people see you until you can maintain a veneer of composure. With Atticus you are fearful, griefstricken, full of complaint. You even credit him once with stopping you from committing suicide. And there are myriad minor complaints, both to Atticus and to family members, largely about digestive problems. It's hard to believe that you would have been utterly calm and Stoic about your own death. So your spokesman, Cato, just leaves out a lot of you and your need for friendship. Cato is pretty solipsistic, despite his pleasures.

Certainly Cato is right that grumpiness and complaint are flaws of character, to be controlled where possible. And no doubt the calm demeanor he depicts could be socially helpful, a way of not inflicting a burden on others. But as to how one should really feel—and how one should let one's close friends know how one feels—what's wrong with acknowledging grief and fear? The idea of resignation that this treatise slides into at the end is repugnant to people who love one another and love life.

Now of course this work was not written as a neutral treatise, it was written to distract both Atticus and Cicero from the looming (though not yet actual) annoyances of old age. So why not err a bit in the direction of Stoic calm? Well, because it strikes a false note.

But now I come to the far odder omission. Cato talks about dinner-table conversation, but he leaves out the best friend. He does say that aging is talking, and that what fills up the day as time goes on is the fun of *convivium*, of shared conversation—a pleasure, he adds, that the young don't fully appreciate. But he portrays himself as isolated, and never mentions having close friends.

For you, by contrast, intellectual conversation is fine, but intimate friendship is where shared life really resides. At Cato's banquets there is a topic set for discussion, and everyone pursues the topic. A fine institution, but it's not the entirety of life, or of friendship. What about the pleasure of gossip? Of talking just to talk? Once again, I cite your words against you.

Exhibit A: Gossip and Affection

One could open the letters more or less at random and find an example of intimate joking, gossip, private allusions. But later ones, from the time of aging, are often incomprehensible without elaborate commentary, so I choose an earlier one that is at least decipherable. From Rome, August 59 B.C.E.:

> I believe you have never before read a letter of mine not in my own handwriting. You may gather from that how desperately busy I am. Not having a minute to spare and being obliged to take a walk to refresh my poor voice, I am dictating this while walking.
>
> First then I want you to know that our friend Sampsiceramus is bitterly unhappy about his position and longs to get back to where he stood before his fall. . . .

As for me (for I'm sure you want to know that), I take no part in political discussions, devoting myself entirely to legal business and work. . . . But our Lady Ox Eyes' nearest and dearest flings out formidable threats of wrath to come, denying this to Sampsiceramus but flaunting it ostentatiously before all else. Therefore, if you love me as much as I'm sure you do: if you are asleep, wake up! If you are standing still, walk! If you are walking, run! If you are running, fly! You cannot believe how much I rely on your advice and knowledge of the world, and, most valuable of all, your affection and loyalty. . . . Take care of your health.[16]

The intimacy of the gossip in this letter makes it hard to follow, but fortunately your jokey nicknames are often repeated. Sampsiceramus is a frequent name for Pompey. Sampsiceramus was a Syrian despot whom Pompey had installed, so it's a way of poking fun at Pompey's luxuriant ways. As for "Lady Ox Eyes": this epithet is used frequently in your letters for Clodia, the sister of your great political enemy Clodius. Here you depict Clodius as stirring up trouble once again. With "blood relative" you allude to the constant rumors of incest between Clodius and Clodia, which you never allow to die down. So it's all intimate in-references, some quite malicious, on matters both high and low. And of course the jaunty yet needy urging to Atticus to come back to Rome. The *De Senectute*'s lack of this dense foliage of friendship looks all the starker by contrast. But it's this, and not virtue, that explains why the friendship goes on into the time of aging and tragedy.

Exhibit B: Gossip about a Huge Turning Point

The snarky gossip about Clodius is petty, compared to the letter I now want to submit, which does come from the period of *De Senectute*. Sometimes friends are together when something momentous occurs, and sometimes not. This letter about a surprise visit from Julius Caesar three months before the assassination of March 44 is the stuff of tragic drama—and yet it is turned into high comedy by the sheer zest of the narration. December 19, 45 B.C.E. Italics indicate Greek in the original.[17]

What a burdensome guest—and yet: *je ne regrette rien*.[18] For it really was extremely entertaining. But when he arrived at Philippus' place on the evening of December 18, the house was so thronged by soldiers that there was hardly a spare room for Caesar himself to dine in. Two thousand men, no less! I was pretty concerned about what would happen the next day, but Cassius Barba came to my rescue and posted sentries. Camp was pitched in the open and a guard placed on the house. On the 19th he stayed with Philippus until one, admitting nobody—doing his accounts, I think, with Balbus. Then he took a walk on the shore. Around two he went to his bath... After anointing he took his place at dinner. He was taking *a course of emetics*, so he both ate and drank *fearlessly* and with pleasure. It really was a fine, well-prepared meal, and not only that, but cooked and seasoned well,

 —Good talking too, in fact a pleasant meal [from Lucilius].

His entourage moreover were lavishly entertained in three other dining rooms. The humbler freedmen and slaves had all they wanted; the spiffier ones I entertained in style. In a word, I showed him that I was a man of the world. But my guest was not the sort of person to whom one says, "Do drop in next time you are in the neighborhood." Once is enough. *Rien de sérieux* in our conversation, *mais beaucoup à propos des lettres.* All in all, he had a good time and was pleased. He said he would spend a day at Puteoli and another at Baiae.

 There you are: a visit, or should I call it *a billeting.* Annoying to me, but not horrible. I shall stay here for a little while, then to Tusculum.

This is serious stuff: the man who is killing the Republic, your bitter enemy, arrives unannounced like a conquering army, presumptuous, uncivil, simply billeting his two thousand troops in and around your country house. The superficial calm, the literary gossip, the sprinkling of Greek phrases, the meal, the bath—all this masks mortal peril, bitter opposition—and the death of institutions you love. And yet, what's so remarkable about the letter is that it is so much fun, and conveys the sense that the teller is having fun. It is narrated as high comedy, with an unusually high ratio of Greek in-jokes and poetic quotations. The big joke is that it is told as the tale of a dinner party, when it is really the stuff of tyranny and violence. Imagine you without an Atticus: these events would have been profoundly ominous, and more than a little depressing. The presence of a friend can turn the horrible into the funny. In the very act of making literature of Caesar's visit you make it an intimate gesture, therefore something positive. And of course it can be this only because you can rely on Atticus to read the letter on two levels, serious and comic, and therefore to appreciate the spirit of defiance that has turned the one into the other.

Aging brings many challenges—stretches of boredom, bitter disappointments, anxieties. Cato's solipsistic approach, despite its real merits, really does not rise to the occasion. No doubt there are people so serene that they slide through aging with their mental and physical gymnastics, their love of gardening, their carefully regulated dinner-table discussions, their Stoic detachment from death. But you are not among them, and you don't even think it good to be like that. But if one is not like Cato, then it's the daily texture of friendship—the gossip, the presumed understanding, the in-jokes, the conjuring tricks as pain becomes pleasure—that makes this stretch of life a real *convivium*.

Cato says that aging is in many ways superior to what precedes it because of the quality of the talk it contains. But he doesn't make good on that promise; your letters do. Aging is bound to contain tragedy. It is not bound to contain comedy, or understanding, or love. What supplies both of these is friendship.

Notes

1. *De Senectute* came first, and was probably written in 45 B.C.E.; *De Amicitia* was written in 44 B.C.E., and is thus among Cicero's last works. He died in 43 B.C.E., assassinated.

2. Latin *senex* covers a wide range of ages, including Cicero and Atticus, but also including the dialogue's protagonist Cato, who is eighty-three. That is why I translate "aging" rather than "aged," and the title of the work as "On Aging" rather than "On Old Age." Here and elsewhere, I give the section numbers of the shorter Arabic numeral sections, not the larger Roman numeral chapters.

3. To Atticus, 426 letters written between 68 B.C.E., when Cicero was thirty-eight and Atticus forty-one, and 44 B.C.E., when they are sixty-two and sixty-five, and a few months before Cicero's death. (Atticus lived to 32 B.C.E., when he died of colon cancer.) Of course letters cover only times when they were apart; moreover, we have only Cicero's side; but Atticus is a vivid presence. With many other friends and relations, we have both sides, ably edited by Tiro, the freedman who became a close friend of Cicero's.

4. Although he sympathized with the assassination of Julius Caesar in 44 B.C.E., he was not directly involved; but his subsequent attacks on Antony led to his death.

5. In this section of the essay, as with the later discussion of *De Senectute*, I draw on and often revise the translation by W. A. Falconer in the Loeb Classical Library, which is old-fashioned but basically correct. Elsewhere (as in my discussion of the preface), I make my own translations.

6. Although Greek has several distinct terms for different types of love, Latin has only *amor*, which in consequence covers a very large terrain, from the erotic to the familial and the friendly. But it always indicates strong affection.

7. Here Cicero may be implicitly criticizing the Epicurean view of friendship that he depicts in *De Finibus* Book I and prodding Atticus to reject that aspect of his Epicureanism.

8. Roman Epicureans are a mixed lot, and the conspirator Cassius evidently did run risks for the sake of the Republic. The focus of his Epicureanism lay in his denial of divine portents and divine influence in human affairs. See David Sedley, "The Ethics of Brutus and Cassius," *Journal of Roman Studies* 87 (1997), 41–53. Atticus, however, seems much more like the full-fledged Epicurean described by Lucretius.

9. Letter to Dolabella, April 45 B.C.E.

10. Notice how rapidly Cicero got down to writing; the self-consolation was a lauded and famous work, and the letter suggests that it took him just a day to plunge into it—after arduous travel.

11. In this section all translations are my own, though after consultation with Shackleton Bailey's version.

12. Appuleius had recently been elected augur, and Cicero was required to be present at the inauguration ceremony unless he presented a medical certificate. A temporary deferment could be achieved through a third party.

13. Here I am agreeing with Anthony Trollope's marvelous *Life of Cicero*.

14. I find Simone de Beauvoir lacking; see chapter 1.

15. The Stoics recommended suicide whenever nature's limits seem to have been attained.

16. Shackleton Bailey's translation, for the most part.

17. A combination of me and Shackleton Bailey. I try to find French equivalents for the Greek, but there is not always an apt one, so italics denote words that are Greek in the original.

18. My use of the Piaf song is precise, since "Non, je ne regrette rien" was a song of the French Foreign Legion after their defeat by de Gaulle, whom they perceived as anti-Republican.

What Are Friends For?

Saul

WHEN WE WERE VERY YOUNG, our parents urged us to "make friends," because they observed that having good friends was a valuable asset, or a characteristic of happy people. Friends learn from one another, and a good and diverse peer group is one of the best things a young person can have. Parents hope their children will attend good schools, and although these schools advertise their faculty, art centers, and facilities, the students seem to understand that the peer group matters most. Young, affluent parents try to help things along by choosing homes near other families with children, buying video game consoles that will attract the neighborhood kids, and purchasing minivans so that children's friends can be included in various activities. Many parents and schools urge their children to practice and specialize in a sport, in part because an athletic team is a ready source of friendships and a sense of belonging. Friends and teammates beget security. Most important, they help us define and improve ourselves. They open new horizons and become our partners in the adventure of life. If Martha and her friend Cicero were writing about youth, they would demolish the Stoic argument about the unnecessary burdens of friendship with a few words about the value and great pleasure of numerous and diverse friends.

Some adults never quite embrace the pleasure of friendship. They value new friends because they believe or are taught that a more extensive network of friends is a mark of success, or simply a means of finding a life partner, a better job, and ongoing business opportunities. Facebook capitalizes on, or reflects, this view by totaling each participant's friends and advertising the result to the world. Part of one's self-presentation in this domain is the number of friends one has gathered. These Facebook friends may be just what our parents ordered, but they may not be real friends, or the kind those classical authors discuss, any more than were all our schoolmates real friends. Instead, they form a pool of ready associates with whom we have something in common and can develop into friends without much introduction.

Soon enough most of us learn that one does not just go out and make friends, because the good friends one has are the product of one's personality and circumstances rather than sheer effort. It is probably valuable, not to mention enjoyable for many of us, to have numerous acquaintances, but even these probably have more to do with one's nature and opportunities than with a life plan. If quantity in friendship is valuable, it is probably because it is likely to be correlated with diversity. In contrast, Cicero values harmony and like-mindedness, and he writes as if friendship is an investment fully within one's control.

However we plan our friendships, our friends and acquaintances are, simultaneously, investing in us. Some of them gather and maintain friends with special zeal. Most people are happy with a few close friends and then 50–100 lesser friends in their network, but here and there we find unusually social, connected people with twice that number. There is probably a limit on the number of relationships we can maintain. The brain's capacity for networking was thought to set a limit of 150–200 friends, though people in tightly knit communities, with large families, seem to maintain many more close relationships than that. The power of social media to keep friends and memories at hand has increased many people's capacity for maintaining friendships. We all know well-connected people who act as nodes or controllers of networks and who never seem to tire at events where many people come together. We sense that they might be addicted to people and their (our) ups and downs. This sort of energetic friend rushes to our side when there is a crisis and shares in our joys and sorrows—especially if he or she is among the first to know of them. In our cautious moments, these superfriends might spread gossip and judgments about us, much as they provide us with information, some useful and some not, about other people in our network. It is these superfriends whom the Stoics might have had in mind when they decried the troubles that numerous friends bring on.[1]

Why do those Stoics dwell on the burdens brought on by new friends and ignore or discount the offsetting pleasures that friends bring? I think a better argument in favor of holding "the reins of friendship as loosely as possible" is that some friends will be unwanted intruders. If we value our independence and do not want to be influenced too much by the values of others, then we must be careful not to rely on friends who will regard us as wrongdoers, or as their special projects, if we do not conform.

The claim that goodwill is a precondition of friendship seems right, but it is less interesting than good faith, which is essential to successful friendship. Goodwill refers to the idea that a friend is more than an instrumental means. In turn, good faith signifies a strong presumption—perhaps an inviolable one if the friendship is to survive misfortunes, as it must in a marriage or a dangerous expedition—that one party has the other's best interests at heart. I assume the best of a good friend; I do not believe rumors that the friend has wronged me; I can ask the friend for advice without fearing that the friend will exploit information I reveal. Many generous people convey goodwill to most people they meet, but good faith is sufficiently risky that it may even define friendship. Friends are those people whom we know and care about beyond our self-interest (the goodwill thing) and whom we trust sufficiently that a presumption of good faith serves both sides well. Friendship requires this presumption to run in both directions. If this is friendship, then what could possibly be wrong with having many friends?

Trust is no small thing. A gang of criminals might trust one another because of a developed code of honor, often based on neighborhood or ethnic ties and a sense of us-against-them. Each member may believe that to violate the trust is to bring on mortal danger. Here the Stoics are surely correct. A new member of the gang poses a risk to the others, and the risk is likely greater as new members join. Criminals might need friends even more than the rest of us do. The expression "There is no honor among thieves" is wishful, insulting, and absurd.[2] The deep friendships found among criminals cast serious doubt on the claim that friends must be "good-enough" people. The more plausible claim is that, for most people, friendship is endangered when one's friend suggests an illegal or deleterious joint project to another; conventional friendships may work best with good-enough behavior simply because these risks are not introduced.

Most of us have experienced these awkward moments when friendship is imperiled by risk and moral judgment. As adolescents we can choose to join or avoid collective troublemaking, with few positive or negative repercussions. I do not feel particularly bonded to friends with whom I illicitly and repeatedly slipped into the World's Fair at age eleven, nor did I sense any lasting distance from friends whom I declined to accompany in a night of juvenile (but destructive) wilding at about that age. But once we are adults, decisions to join or decline such ventures have lasting effects. Friends who consume illicit substances together, who cheat on exams together, or who commit assaults together develop bonds that last for many years. Executives who commit fraud together develop very strong connections—and any coworker who declines to participate is often then excluded from decision-making more generally. Similarly, if one declines to smuggle something for a friend, or to lie to the police when a friend asks, the friend is likely to take the disinclination not only as a sign of risk aversion but also of moral judgment, and friendships do not often survive such assessments and fissures.

As an adult, I like to think that good friends would not ask me to do illegal or dangerous things—either because they intuit that I will decline, or sense that if I do decline, our friendship will suffer. A mere acquaintance might suggest something illegal or dangerous, but the acquaintance has little to lose. If I accept, then we may become friends because the shared risk helps us form a bond. I might not ask a friend to do something dangerous, even if it were perfectly legal. The extreme case is easy. I would not want a friend to risk his or her life in order to save mine. I might risk mine to save a younger person's; most parents would sacrifice their own lives for their children's. But it would be awful for a young person to sacrifice his life for me, and perhaps just as bad for a peer to do so. The harder question is a substantial risk, rather than a certain death. *The Diary of Anne Frank* and other reports of heroic efforts during wartime are really quite remarkable.

Imagine that a friend calls and tells you that, as a matter of life and death, he needs to hide in your home for two days and begs you not to ask any questions or tell anyone. Whether the friend is hiding from the police, a vengeful lover, a violent debt collector, or a killer, the risk to you is likely modest, especially if the friend is careful, knows how to shake a trail, and is good at disguises. If the police accuse you of harboring a criminal, you can claim that you figured that your friend was hiding from a wrongdoer. But would you ask to hide in a friend's home in similar circumstances? I would not impose a great risk on a friend, especially because there is likely to be just a small reduction in danger to myself, and so perhaps I should assume that a friend would not impose it on me.

Would you ask a good friend to hide you during a war? Would you ask for a kidney? The recipient of a kidney from a live donor has a very good chance of five or even ten years of life that is of significantly higher quality than those experienced with regular renal dialysis and no transplant. The immediate risk to the kidney donor is modest, but the donor runs the risk associated with needing that other kidney later in life. Would you give a kidney to a good friend, and are you really a good friend if you would not? I would not simply donate a kidney to an unknown stranger, unless it were part of an exchange in which my friend's child gained a kidney and a very substantial improvement in quality of life. Is my intuition motivated by a desire for gratitude or admiration? I suspect that the donation would not do the friendship much good, because it creates a severe inequality. Cicero rejects the idea that friendship is an accounting, but he may be missing the likelihood that a serious asymmetry is unlikely to be good for a friendship. In any event, declining to give a kidney would surely change the friendship. Unsurprisingly, kidney-donation websites recommend informing one's friends and family of the need, but not asking directly for a kidney.

All these examples get at the question of how to think of the instrumental character of friendship. Martha is quite the instrumentalist here, as she advertises the capacity of friendship to produce joy, comedy, and love. But is this sort of friendship a kind of insurance policy or an ongoing calculation? The question is critical as one ages, so let me begin with youthful decisions. Long-term marriage has an element of insurance. A and B agree to care for one another in sickness and health. The implication is that the relationship has many benefits, including the promise that if A is in great need, B will help, and even enjoy helping. If B knew at the outset that A would be the needy one, B might not have entered into the marriage, but it is entirely different once they are in a committed relationship, and especially so after years of partnership. If B turns around one day and says he has other opportunities, and A is looking a little wrinkled, so that it is time to move on, most of us would think that a long-term contract, or insurance policy, had been violated. Is this true of all friendships? Martha and Cicero want us to believe that friendship comes with benefits (and here I mean the joy thing), but it also comes with risks. If the fun moments are suddenly few and far between, is it permissible to abandon the friend? This is one of the great challenges of aging. Retirement communities are full of stories of friends who turned on a dime and abandoned an old friend as soon as it was clear that this person could no longer perform well at the bridge table or had a terminal illness.

This choice between a forward-looking and an in-the-moment calculation is something law does all the time. Here, the former perspective suggests that we all benefit from insurance contracts; there will be fewer friendships if friends can be abandoned when they no longer pull their weight, and we will all be worse off because friendship really does produce many benefits. But the in-the-moment perspective is also attractive. The individual only lives once, and why should the healthy and sharp ninety-year-old waste precious time sitting in the garden with an old friend who is no longer witty and who is a liability in any bridge partnership? If one gets genuine pleasure from being a good friend, then of course the question is easy. But if not, then I think friendship is a complicated kind of arrangement, perhaps something of a medium-length insurance contract, on top of all the unambiguously good things.

For me this question resembles the one about hiding in someone's house or giving up a kidney. I am all for the insurance policy, but not in the extreme. I am happy to be cared for when in need, but only when there is a reasonable prospect of recovery so that I might benefit my care-giving friend. Once I have lost my mind I do not want a friend to waste his or her time because of some implicit insurance policy that made more sense in earlier years. It feels good to write these words, because I hope my spouse and friends will live their lives to the fullest if their energy and wit outlast mine.

For those who disagree, and I think Martha is one of these, I'll go further and say that the friendship contract is a kind of agreement to maximize joint utility. If three members of a foursome exclude their declining friend from the bridge table, we can see it as an assessment that the gain to the three is much greater than the loss to the one. If I decline first, and my friend is a much better conversationalist than I, then the responsibility of friendship is to hang in there so long as the pleasure I get from our exchanges is more than what she loses from my decline. She should not abandon our friendship just because she can do better. But I want her to let go if the cost to her is great and the apparent benefit to me of the continuing friendship is rather small.

FRIENDSHIP HAS ANOTHER PURPOSE. Friends are an important source of advice, if only because their good faith can be presumed. With respect to aging, friends might need advice about healthcare, children, inheritance plans, and many other things. But rarely do these matters stress a friendship and, in fact, most people enjoy giving advice. Good leaders ask for advice not only because a few perspectives are often better than one, but also to make others feel valued and included. In contrast, consider the question of whether to give advice when it has not been requested.

Imagine that you observe or learn that a friend has so declined in the workplace that colleagues or clients are ridiculing him behind his back. The friend can retire without serious, adverse financial consequences. Assume the friend's decline does not put anyone's life in danger. The reason to proffer advice is that you are confident that your friend's pride would lead him to step down if he truly understood his current state of decline. To be sure, he may not have the same preferences he had in all those prior years, but you are not planning to force him out, simply making sure he understands that from what you know and observe, it is time to listen to a good friend's advice. If you do nothing, some humiliating event will likely occur or someone will eventually say something so painful that retirement will be inevitable and far more unpleasant. You have the ability to save your friend this pain. One problem is that your friend might be humiliated by the knowledge of your discovery of his decline, but your advice will surely include suggestions about new activities and challenges.

Chapter 2 discussed compulsory retirement but not the question of when to retire. It is obvious that a mandated retirement age can solve part of this problem of decline and humiliation, albeit at substantial cost. If most people retire because of contractual agreements or because pension plans make continued employment economically unattractive, then there will be few people who require special encouragement to retire. Colleagues and employers who find this sort of counseling very painful will be eager to put in place contracts or pensions that encourage or even require retirement at a fairly young age. But we do not have compulsory retirement in the United States and, even if we did, a friend might be the chair of a civic organization or a trustee of a university where there is no retirement age and yet where the opportunity for public humiliation is substantial. The problem of decline is therefore not limited to the conventional workplace. Positions of civic leadership are often filled with older people because they are perceived as having more wisdom, more social influence (that *auctoritas* idea, again), more time, or more name recognition—or even because they are better situated to make major gifts to the organizations in question. These last reasons add to the danger that other people in the organization will not take into account your friend's potential humiliation. Their goodwill and good faith cannot be counted on.

I must emphasize that I am not arguing for retirement as soon as someone passes the point of peak performance. Participation in work as well as in civic activities can be good for the aging participant as well as for coworkers and other beneficiaries. I argued in chapter 2 that it is a problem that compensation must often continue to increase for workers who are past their peaks, but that is not something that need concern a good friend. One role for a friend—whom we might call Cicero—is to keep an eye on his good friend's well-being and quality of life, especially when the friend, Atticus, is past his peak. Both of these are likely to be positively related to continued employment and civic engagement. At the same time, Cicero must evaluate the humiliation Atticus will suffer if the latter becomes the subject of ridicule. In part, Cicero's job is unfairly difficult because the same society that values Atticus's experience can suddenly turn on Atticus if and when Atticus's decline becomes obvious or costly. We properly encourage and celebrate the self-sufficient eighty-five-year-old who manages a substantial enterprise, enlightens us with wise observations, and counsels younger colleagues. But if that same person is in a car accident on the way home, we are quick to shake our heads at the failure of family and friends to take away the car keys.

The aging civic leader or coworker in danger of humiliation is both similar to and different from the friend in need of a place to hide. An important similarity is that no one friend has reason to think that he or she is the only one who can intervene and save the day. There may be hotel rooms or other places to hide; similarly, other observers could take the aging person aside and explain, convincingly, that it is time to swallow some pride and withdraw from an activity. But a good friend is one who acts *as if* no one else will save the day. Friends solve collective action problems for one another. For this reason, friends sometimes cooperate when intervening in the life of a third, or mutual, friend. Just as several family members or friends are often encouraged to stage an intervention in order to convince someone that it is time to enter a substance abuse rehabilitation program or give up a driver's license, so too, several colleagues might agree to sit down with someone who needs to be told that it is time to retire from a position of responsibility. When the group approach is inappropriate or yet more humiliating, a good friend needs to be prepared to have a one-on-one discussion, whether or not another friend has tried before.

Much as we might have serious conversations with family members or physicians about end-of-life medical interventions, we can communicate our preferences regarding other potential hazards and intercessions. A promise made today to give an organ or hide a friend in time of need may elicit performance many years in the future because the promisor feels a moral responsibility or sense of guilt, but it is no guarantee, and offsetting moral considerations are easily constructed by a friend who does not want to take on risk.

In contrast, imagine that Atticus, at age sixty-five, asks Cicero, to "promise to sit down and tell me when you think I have declined sufficiently that I am in danger of really embarrassing myself or greatly imposing on others at work or in volunteer activities." Atticus's request and Cicero's acceptance may also not be indicative of their real sentiments ten years later, but at least Cicero will feel compelled to talk to Atticus. Cicero will say, "I promised you that I would have a conversation with you, and much as it pains me, that time has come." Cicero is not obliged to force Atticus out of the workforce or other position, even if that were possible. But the conversation may be worth something, and it is unlikely to be worth less simply because Atticus will recognize that Cicero felt compelled by the promise rather than by observations alone. That is what friends are for.

It is, of course, not the only thing they are for. If we are lucky, or even wise, then as we age we rediscover the sheer fun of friendship. To make a new friend is to embark on a new exploration. I hope to have more friends, rather than fewer, as I age. If I retire, it will be in part to have more time for old and new friends. The very process of choosing and investing in friendship is a mark of our continuing independence. Friends may be useful when it comes to advice and other matters, but ultimately they are for sharing and enjoying the adventure of life.

Notes

1. Martha tells me that while Cicero traveled, and his friends might have been away on military service, friends might have encountered one another easily and frequently in Rome.
2. To be sure, the proverb's origin may be Cervantes's "The old proverb still holds good, thieves are never rogues among themselves," in which case the modern version is upside down.

Chapter 4

Aging Bodies

HOW DOES ONE get comfortable with an aging shell, not to mention its interior? Is the popularity of plastic surgery and other antiaging procedures a good or bad thing? Why do some bodily functions disgust us?

Can Wrinkles Be Glamorous?

Saul

BABIES ARE CUTE. We love their smooth skin and tiny parts. Our tastes may have evolved to improve the chances that we will care for the young of our species. Alternatively, we associate extreme youth with innocence, and find that attractive. We have no reason to fear babies, and no reason to think they are poised to attack or poisonous to the touch. Some adults even like changing diapers. Babies are innocent, needy, and hold the promise of a better future.

If we are hardwired to find babies adorable, and young adults in their late teens and twenties to be attractive, then what should we think of those who present with wrinkles, baldness, and other signs of age? Ideally, wrinkles would be a proxy for wisdom, humor, and companionability, rather than the end of life. We know of societies that glorify age, but ours has a strong preference for youth and therefore, individually, for bodily interventions that preserve the appearance of youth. At the same time, we have legal and social conventions against some body interventions. Can we make sense of the dividing line between improvements and mutilations, and can we perhaps improve our bodies and ourselves with age?

Acceptable and Distasteful Procedures

As we will see later in this chapter, it is pointless to argue that all body improvements are objectionable. Healthy eating, exercise, and some attention to fashion, hygiene, and makeup are normal for most well-adjusted people. It is therefore a stretch to insist that nose surgery, a Botox injection, or LASIK eye surgery is entirely different from everyday body adjustments. And yet, there is something troubling about a society with a high rate of elective surgeries. Americans now spend some $13 billion a year on cosmetic surgery—much more if we add in eye surgery, tattoos, cosmetic dental work, and hair transplants—but South Koreans avail themselves of cosmetic surgery at four times the rate found in the United States. Koreans are intense consumers of eyelid procedures that make them appear more Western. That goal is unsettling to modern, Western observers. We don't usually mind being imitated, but our political and social sensibility is for people, and especially people we have discriminated against, to be true to their identities. We like to think that our discrimination and racism is a thing of the past, so it is painful to think of Koreans' trying to look like us. If their surgeries exaggerated rather than softened their "Asian" features, it would probably not bother us at all. Similarly, a desire for white skin makes us cringe, even if the motivation has nothing to do with us. We do not speak about it much, perhaps because reduced exposure to the sun can also be motivated by a desire to reduce the risk of skin cancer. Where motives are mixed, and adult body decisions are at issue, we hesitate to regulate or even to be terribly judgmental. In our culture, many people tan themselves, but then many others protect themselves against the sun. Our standards of beauty have become sufficiently diverse that we do not take special aim at either group. Law regulates but does not outlaw eyelid surgery and suntanning in the United States, and in any event my focus thus far is about discomfort and social norms, rather than legal prohibitions.

Other interventions by discriminated-against groups similarly intrude on our comfort zones. Most white people would hesitate before suggesting that an African American woman straighten her hair or that an Asian or Native American curl her hair or otherwise do battle against genotypes. Within a minority group, the intervention is more likely to be a comfortable if not regular topic. I learned a great deal about hair interventions and politics from the best-selling novel *Americanah,* written by a Nigerian (and by now, also American) author. Many black women think that straightening helps them in the workplace or in various social situations. As with tanning salons and the coexisting preferences for lighter or darker skin, there is also demand for braiding and for shaping natural growth (and not only by black women). There is enough diversity with respect to hair fibers and follicles that by 2016 few people have strong reactions when a member of a minority group straightens her hair. I live on a street in Chicago with six (!) hair salons, all catering to African American women, and I have never heard a negative word from a white person about any attempt to shape one's image in these salons. The same is true of hair color. If a woman of Mediterranean or Semitic descent experiments with

blonde hair, we may wince if we do not like the shade or the professional-
ism of the coloring, but not because we think the person is trying to imitate a group that was or is dominant.

Nose jobs, more properly known as rhinoplasty, are a tougher call, in
part because the intervention requires surgical tools and, more impor-
tantly, because it is much less readily reversed than hair modifications.
Rhinoplasty is popular among teenagers, a group known for volatile opinions and, therefore, a magnet for legal regulation. In my adolescence, it
was common for Jewish girls I knew to have their noses altered, and certainly to speak openly about the procedure—though many would have
been startled and offended if a non-Jewish person had raised the topic. I
confess that I almost always found the result more attractive than the original, natural nose. In retrospect, the popularity of the procedure (especially
in orthodox Jewish communities) is somewhat puzzling because Jewish
law looks with disfavor on cosmetic body alterations, and some authori-
ties prohibit them unless necessary to correct "abnormalities." The more
permissive approach allows alterations in order to achieve psychological
well-being. The contradiction continues to this day; rhinoplasty and facelifts are very common in the same demographic group that completely
eschews tattoos as "mutilations" of the body. To be fair, tattoos appear to
violate an explicit biblical prohibition (Leviticus 19:28), though there is
debate regarding the meaning of the verse, but the larger issue is the idea
that humans are made in the divine image, and ought not to be violated
or "improved." Rhinoplasty among Jews may have gained popularity as an
attempt to assimilate, or avoid traumatic comments in an era when boor-
ish people would point to their own noses to signal that a college class-
mate was Jewish. Today, rhinoplasty is widely accepted but less common
than it was in an era when people worked harder to escape their ethnic
identities. Breast augmentation and other surgical interventions are now
far more common than rhinoplasty.

Before turning to procedures aimed at reversing the signs of age, consider this three-step theory regarding the acceptability of body interventions. (1) Law and social convention look favorably on allowing adults to
express themselves by making choices about their own bodies; parents are
encouraged to make choices for their minor children, at least when there
is medical necessity or another powerful reason, but law is more likely to
constrain individuals when the intervention is irreversible. (2) Mainstream
opinion is especially disinclined to tell minority groups what to do with
their bodies, though it is uncomfortable when the minority might have

been pressured to conform to the majoritarian culture. (3) Interference is allowed or even a matter of human rights when the minority group imposes irreversible alterations on subjugated subgroups or individuals.

Let me start with the best example of the theory just sketched, and then work toward interventions that relate to aging. Female circumcision is strongly disfavored and labeled as female genital mutilation (FGM). It is regarded as a violation of human rights by the United Nations, and is now outlawed in the United States, France, and Britain. It remains widely practiced in some countries, more as a matter of cultural norms than religious edict. Some anthropologists regard the objection to FGM as cultural colonialism, and they in turn are accused of moral relativism. Meanwhile, male circumcision is widely practiced, though the procedure has declined in popularity in Europe and Asia despite renewed medical evidence in its favor. Rates of circumcision remain especially high among Muslims and Jews, for whom it has great religious significance. The asymmetrical objection to female circumcision may reflect not simply the shifting sands of medical opinion about male circumcision, but the absence of any known medical advantage to female circumcision and the association, in a subset of cultures that traditionally practiced female circumcision, between circumcision and views about female modesty and sexual suppression.

In short, circumcisions are irreversible (unlike most body piercings, which usually, but not always, heal and close up after jewelry is removed) *and* we are distrustful of cultural norms that leave women worse off or mutilated. A long history of subjugation of women makes us skeptical of cultural claims in favor of female circumcision. Feminists may disagree about burkas or niqabs, even if they were first legislated by men, but the wearing of a garment is a reversible decision (leaving aside deeper psychological influences and a claim that the tradition prevents skin cancer). In contrast, if the dominant group, which is to say men over the course of history, pierces or circumcises its new members, we are much less inclined to intervene on behalf of the "victims." Consenting adults operate in an entirely different cultural space. Labiaplasty and vaginoplasty are increasingly common procedures, and my impression is that cultural and feminist objections have declined. The procedures may be done with men in mind, but the decision-makers are adults.

There is a vocal "intactivist" movement in the United States and Europe that objects to male circumcision, especially when forced on infants and minors who can hardly consent. But the fact that so many thoughtful people find female but not male circumcision abhorrent, suggests that a critical difference is that one is practiced on a group that is, at least to Western eyes, seriously constrained and subjugated by a variety of practices.

Ear piercings, at least in the United States, are inflicted (or gifted or celebrated) predominantly on girls, and so it might be surprising that mutilation of this kind is not also protested. But piercings are generally reversible, or at most leave a small scar. If they were difficult to reverse, then law would likely require children to await maturity, or even the age of majority, before being pierced. Some states come close. For example, Wisconsin requires parental approval (and physical presence) for piercings as applied to sixteen- and seventeen-year-olds. Through age fifteen, parents can consent only to ear piercings. In accord with observation (1) above, as reversibility becomes more difficult, there is more legal intervention. Similarly, many states prohibit tattooing of minors, though some states permit the procedure with parental permission.

Breast augmentation and sex reassignment surgery, as well as associated hormone therapies, are also unavailable before adulthood, except in unusual medical cases. In both instances, we can imagine strong objections based on the intuition that the demand for these interventions might be fueled by the preferences or bullying of a male-dominated society. At present the values of self-expression and self-identification overwhelm any anxiety about these interventions with respect to historically dominated groups. I suspect that if sex-reassignment surgery were overwhelmingly female-to-male (in fact there are more reassignments in the other direction), it would be vilified rather than supported (and covered by insurance) by progressive citizens. In any event, nearly all these interventions require the subject to seek treatment and consent as an adult; law has less to say about the matter than does social convention. When law is involved, it is usually a political or legal battle regarding insurance coverage rather than control over an individual's body. Cosmetic surgeries are frowned upon in some circles, but, for the most part, law stays out of the picture, unless the surgery is irreversible and the patient is a minor. Even there, if the minor and the minor's guardian are in agreement, rhinoplasties, some piercings, and other procedures are permissible. When law blocks the family's decision, it is usually because of medical concerns, as with breast augmentation before physical development is complete, or a majoritarian attempt to reduce the pressure teenagers can bring to bear on their parents, as in the case of tattoos or less conventional piercings.

Aging, but Attempting to Look Younger

Rhinoplasty and piercings are cosmetic procedures that appeal to many minors, and they are not interventions that we normally associate with aging. Breast augmentation, however, though unavailable to teenagers, is very common for women in their twenties through fifties. At present, the only cosmetic surgical procedures that are common for people over sixty-five are facelifts, necklifts, and eyelid surgery. Even these decline sharply after middle age. Nonsurgical procedures (such as injectables) also drop considerably once people are in their seventies. I am not going to claim that people in their seventies are a subjugated group, and in any event the decline almost surely comes from reduced demand, rather than from legal intervention or strong social disapproval. It is possible that the demographics of cosmetic surgery will change, because the generation that created a boom in this business will maintain these preferences and spending habits as it ages. Plastic surgeons and pharmaceutical companies can be expected to adjust their practices to meet the demand. But if the preference for body interventions in the cause of youthful appearance reliably diminishes with age, so that it continues to be the case that very few seventy-five-year-olds yearn for altered noses or breasts, then we might conclude that older people are simply more comfortable in their own skins, as presently constituted. An economist might say that these investments are less appealing as one ages, because for the same cost there are fewer years left in which to experience or benefit from the change. But that seems wrong both because aging can create a sense of urgency and because many cosmetic procedures require updating, so that the useful life of the investment is not very different for the young and the old.

There are other procedures that ought to be counted as antiaging body interventions. LASIK and other eye-correcting surgery begin at about age twenty, and their frequencies decline with advanced age, but this is largely because the problems of aging eyes are unresponsive to such surgeries. In any event, the desire to see better without corrective lenses has only an indirect connection to youthful appearance. Hair restoration, including transplants, is more obviously an antiaging procedure. As with breast augmentation, it is most popular with people in their thirties and forties, when hair loss seems to have the greatest impact on appearance for men. In all these areas—female breast augmentation, male hair transplants, and eye and dental procedures—law allows individual choice. We are free to do almost anything we want in order to look better and, yes, younger.

The fear of fraud and exploitation that drives so much regulation of cancer drugs is nearly absent where aging and cosmetic surgery is concerned. The Food and Drug Administration keeps an eye on safety, but allows consumers and their doctors to decide what is efficacious. If people in the sixty to eighty age range do not begin to dominate the market for facelifts and other cosmetic surgeries, it will be because they choose to forgo these interventions. Entertainers and politicians, male and female alike, are expected to have their faces refreshed in their sixties. In some surveys, a modest share of supporters say they would not vote for someone who had a facelift, but it is probably the case that many *more* become favorably inclined toward a candidate because of nipping and tucking.

Although the dramatic increase in cosmetic surgery is centered on young and middle-aged adults, there is also an unmistakable increase among older patients. This increase can be associated with a larger pool of seniors, increased affluence, and a more aggressive cosmetic surgery industry. There remain physicians who discourage breast augmentation in healthy eighty-year-olds, as if the surgery is more necessary for someone half that age, but demographics and economics guarantee an increase in these and other surgeries for older patients. Why might people first seek a youthful appearance, but then cease to do so? A twenty-year-old might find this question absurd because to such a person it might seem plain that older people ought to give up on the niceties of self-presentation. I have been asking college students what they think they will be like when they are three or four times their present age, and many just cannot imagine (a good answer), but some look serious and respond by saying that they will be dead by then, because life will not be worthwhile (or calamity will strike) by that point. Almost none describes new activities or adventures. Fortunately, the answers are much more positive once people enter the workforce, perhaps because it is easier for them to picture themselves in the shoes of their bosses. A twenty-year-old is likely to think that plastic surgery is a waste at age sixty, because to the very young person older people all look alike or could not possibly care much about their appearances. In fact, there is no reason to think that people care less about appearance as they age; hair salons and beauty products appeal to young and old alike.

A hyperrational economist or evolutionary biologist finds many things about self-presentation difficult to understand. We comprehend mating rituals, like peacocks' displays, as proxies for fitness. It takes effort to present plumage to an audience of peafowl and then to hold the display, and so the competition among the males makes sense, if only after the fact. If a teenage boy successfully displays a fancy sports car or rock-solid abs, we can think of him as signaling financial security, competitiveness, health, or rebelliousness, and each of these might be a desirable trait in a mate. Similarly, if a young woman has beautiful long hair, well-toned arms, or the most fashionable clothes, she might signal affluence, health, effort, or other desirable qualities. But why would people undertake these costs when they are beyond the age of reproduction? Perhaps the behavior is ingrained and not easily abandoned at an advanced age. For thoughtful people, able to overcome primitive instincts, physical attraction is a kind of door-opener. A gorgeous model must always wonder whether suitors like the inner person, or are too easily attracted to physical attributes. Whether the attraction is primitive or competitive (the suitor wants to win in the competition for attractive mates), the attractive person must be anxious that, with aging, the partner will lose interest. She (let us assume) cannot simply reason that her suitor will also take steps against the danger that he (assuming a male suitor) is overly swayed by her appearance, because he can exit the relationship and redeploy whatever qualities he had. It is youthful attraction—thick hair, firm breasts, smooth skin, and so forth—that presumably does the work, and these attributes will depreciate, while power and wealth will remain valuable to the imagined suitor.

As we age, we no longer compete for reproductive partners; if there is competition, it is for companions or even future caregivers. Virility still matters, but it is rational to look for signs of—and then to avoid—dementia and decrepitude. Antiaging procedures remain useful as a signal of health, but mobility and various life habits are increasingly important attractors. It is easy to understand why some plastic surgeries decline in importance among people over fifty, while great attention is given to hair-styling, cleanliness, and fitness. These become more important than uplifted breasts and the battle against baldness, to take one example for each sex. Hair care is especially interesting because it might be a proxy for one's ability and inclination to care for oneself, and be a ready companion rather than a burden.

Whether young or old, few people really want to be defined or paired according to how they look. We have inner selves, and, even as a practical matter, our appearances will change over time. As we age, we must hope that our friends and lovers will not turn out to have liked only our (cracking) shells. Appearance is an important way of encouraging someone to get to know you, but it is not the essential *you*. A gorgeous model should probably be more cautious before committing to a relationship; he or she needs to be sure that the other person has the right depth and values. But at any stage of life, antiaging procedures can be understood as a means of encouraging contact, and of beginning the process of getting to know someone. Once someone self-presents a certain way, it is difficult to test a developing romantic relationship by downgrading one's appearance, because to do so can seem insulting or careless. A facelift, breast augmentation, or hair transplant can do more work than subtracting five years from one's profile on an online dating site. The other person will learn the truth, whether it is age or a personality trait, when he or she might not have taken the trouble to do so if a first glance showed a less inviting glimpse. It is not irrational to open a book because of a catchy title or an elegant cover.

As we will see in chapter 6, it is not surprising that some people are attracted to much older partners or friends. They may find experienced people more interesting or more financially reliable, but it is also plausible that some people like the contrast; the younger person might feel more youthful because of the obvious comparison. From an antiaging perspective, the ideal "gap couple" (and here I mean something like sixty-five/forty-two, not forty-two/twenty-five) is comprised of an older person who feels younger when with a younger partner—and then a younger partner who feels yet younger because of the comparison with the older one. It is, therefore, plausible that plastic surgery is in greater demand where the comparison group is younger rather than similarly aged. There is probably more plastic surgery among salespeople and executives in their forties, who compete with people in their thirties, than among authors, politicians, or professional sports coaches in their forties, because these professionals rarely compete against people ten years younger.

Aging among the Aged

A visit to a town with many retirees casts some light on the effect of comparison groups on antiaging procedures. Plastic surgeons are in evidence in Sun City, Arizona, as they are in Boca Raton and The Villages in Central Florida, so that it is obvious that the demand for plastic surgery does not completely subside when competition in the workplace or mating market comes to an end. The photo galleries on these doctors' websites show face and neck work on sixty-four- to seventy-four-year-old women, but nationwide only 4 percent of surgical cosmetic procedures are performed on patients over sixty-four. Liposuctions and tummy tucks, for example, are very popular, but not, or not yet, among older people. If nonsurgical cosmetic procedures are included, the percentage of procedures involving patients over age sixty-four is higher, but it is still only 10 percent. Nationwide, more than 90 percent of cosmetic procedures are performed on women, and this is true in every age group. The places with the highest number of plastic surgeons per capita, including Beverly Hills, San Antonio, Miami, San Francisco, and Atlanta, do not have disproportionate elderly populations. Indeed, a couple of these hotspots for plastic surgery suggest that demand increases when the surrounding population is young. I should add that the 4 percent and 10 percent statistics come from the American Society of Plastic Surgeons, and thus exclude circumcisions (as not cosmetic), piercings (28 percent male), tattoos, and most labiaplasties and vaginoplasties. It is apparent that the excluded procedures are especially uncommon among older and even middle-aged people, so that people over age sixty-four constitute a very small fraction of all patients for these invasive cosmetic procedures.

Women in retirement communities seem to spend much more time on their hair and on being sociable and pleasant than they do on body interventions. Perhaps at some age it feels foolish to try to look "young," as many forty- to fifty-year-olds do. Young respondents say that tattoos make them feel sexy or rebellious—or at least as rebellious as one can feel when more than one-third of adults eighteen to forty have at least one tattoo. It would be interesting to compare the responses of older tattoo-parlor clients, except that at present they are such a small minority within their age group that the same responses might mean something entirely different. It is hard not to compare the residents of these communities with other age-specific communities, like college campuses or many workplaces. The retired group seems, at long last, comfortable in their own skin. I confess that at times I find their wrinkles glamorous. At some age, a weathered and wrinkled face seems more beautiful to me than does smooth and clear skin. The person behind the skin seems more interesting for the wrinkles and, if the eyes sparkle, I find myself engaging the person in conversation, rather than looking over the person's clothes, accessories, or body features. I want to believe that the lower rate of cosmetic surgeries within this age group reflects an increasing comfort in one's own (changing) skin. Both baby skin and aged skin are beautiful in their own ways; the former hints at promise or perfection, while the latter suggests experience and wisdom. Once we are mature adults, most of us would rather be wise than promising. Perfection would be nice, but we know it is out of reach.

AS WE AGE, we think differently of ourselves, depending on the demography of the group in which we are embedded. An attractive person can easily seem (and feel) dowdy and even misshapen in a room full of models. In a retirement community, most people look and feel quite normal; distinctions might be based on mobility or one's connection to an oxygen machine, but wrinkles, hair volume, abdominal muscles, and breast shape can seem less important to the residents than they do to comparable people who live among the population at large. Some aging people insist that they want to live in a "normal" community, where people of all ages circulate. Leaving aside economics and politics and focusing only on appearances, it becomes clear that for many people the opposite is the case, and subconscious comparisons might be key. It is not just that a retirement community offers activities and neighbors looking to play golf or cards. For some residents, these communities offer a peer group that makes it easier to feel attractive. Some seventy-five-year-olds might feel compelled to look younger if they lived in a world with people many years younger; they feel more comfortable when the comparison group is also wrinkled. This is the sort of thinking that leads to practices, or even laws, against superthin models; everyone can be better off if no one can starve herself.

The importance of the comparison group has implications for cosmetic surgery. Imagine, for example, that we found much more plastic surgery among eighty-year-olds in a retirement community than within the same age group dispersed in a city. We would have two ready explanations for the difference. First the demand for cosmetic surgery is fueled or dampened by the peer group. This group spreads information about the availability and effectiveness of something like a new skin resurfacing technique or a good doctor, and then more individuals join in or imitate the practices of their friends and neighbors. Alternatively, the peer group might bring about serious internal competition for youthful appearance. If the eighty-year-olds in a retirement community compete for status or romantic partners, then they might engage in a kind of arms race, in this case by patronizing plastic surgeons. On the other hand, if we find fewer cosmetic surgeries among residents of a retirement community, reasonable but different explanations would come to mind. Residents may be in frequent contact with one another, and not need special means of initially attracting one another in order to overcome inertia. Thus, it would not surprise me if, holding age constant, people lied about their age less in retirement communities than elsewhere. A second explanation for a lower rate of body alterations in a retirement community brings us back to the comparison group. In such a community, a seventy-year-old is relatively young, and is surrounded by people who are considerably older. It may be that when the comparison group has plenty of older-looking people, there is less demand for cosmetic procedures because it is actually easier to feel relatively young than it is when one is living on the outside, where even a seventy-year-old person can sometimes feel old. Age is in part a matter of self-perception, and it is influenced by the available comparison group.

I wish I could report that one of these arguments about the demand for cosmetic surgery in and out of retirement communities is better than the other, but in fact it is hard to get fine-grained data on cosmetic procedures. Doctors classify their patients by procedures and then by age groups and minority status, but there are no ready data by retirement communities or even by zip codes. My very inadequate and prying questions lead me to think that invasive surgeries are, unsurprisingly, more common than average in some retirement communities, and then lower than average in others. It would be nice to aggregate and then know on average whether living among peers drives the rate of cosmetic surgery up or down, but I'm afraid we just do not know. Moreover, if we did know, would we be sure that a higher rate of one antiaging strategy meant a higher rate for others? I have already suggested that cosmetic surgery and deception about one's age may be substitutes rather than complements. Similarly, a low rate of cosmetic surgery might be correlated with a *high* rate of exercise, hair transplantation, consumption of peptides and antioxidants, and so forth. And note that these antiaging strategies might be positively correlated for a community, but negatively correlated at the individual level. If Smith gets a facelift, her neighbor, Jones, might be more inclined to exercise or try a skin resurfacing procedure, whether or not Smith is also more likely to exercise or undertake a second cosmetic procedure.

During my first trip to Japan, when I was in my thirties, I found aging Japanese men to be unusually handsome. Compared to my American experience, I suddenly thought that men aged much more attractively than women, at least in Japan. These men had pronounced wrinkles, but they were very distinguished looking. It soon became apparent that one thing that had influenced my judgment is that male-pattern baldness is uncommon in Japan. Someone accustomed to seeing many older men without much hair (as I appear today) is more inclined to find the sight of all these men with full heads of very dark hair to be attractive. The slightness and absence of obesity surely helps as well. This observation makes me think that the comparison group point is more complicated. In a crowd of older people, nice eyes, smiles, and neat hair can make someone look very inviting. In a crowd of tall statuesque models, all of us mortals look distressed. And yet a subway car with many older well-coiffed men can look much better to someone accustomed to older men without hair. To me, these Japanese men looked distinguished. In lower Manhattan, where young people congregate, even a fifty-five-year-old can look out of place, and the observer's brain notices stiffness, thinning hair, and hearing aids. But in a room full of mature adults, once the observer's brain is accustomed to various qualities that are now plentiful, wrinkles begin to look interesting. My brain interprets them as signals of depth or wisdom. The same logic that causes middle-aged people who work in Silicon Valley or Hollywood to rush to plastic surgeons in order to look young might allow older people who are surrounded by contemporaries to forgo these interventions and to feel comfortable as they are.

I do not want to push the glamorous or wise wrinkles thing too far. I doubt that any sixty-year-old intentionally chooses to present himself on an online dating site as wiser by using a photo that is brushed to make him look older rather than younger. Age misrepresentation on dating websites is common—but only in the downward direction. Self-presentation is a tricky business. If a sixty-two-year-old lists herself as forty-seven, and shows pictures that were taken fifteen years earlier, she can expect her first-time date at a restaurant to turn right around and leave, after spotting her in the agreed-upon location. The self-presentation comes across as dishonesty, an undesirable trait, because the lie is too big. On the other hand, if the same person vaguely implies that she is five years younger than she is, the deception is acceptable or even typical. The presentation is aspirational and understood to mean: "I wanted you to agree to meet me and then to judge for yourself my 'true' age and qualities." People do not like to be profiled, at least when the stereotype is negative, and so we allow some room for creative expression. I wonder whether people who undergo cosmetic surgery are more likely to understate their age or claim senior discounts. Eventually, I hope they find that their deepening wrinkles are attractive and worth keeping.

Our Bodies, Ourselves

AGING, STIGMA, AND DISGUST

Martha

IN THE 1970S we women used to talk about loving our own bodies. Inspired by the generation-defining tome *Our Bodies, Ourselves*, we trained for childbirth without anesthesia, we looked at our cervixes using a speculum, and in general cultivated in ourselves the thought that our own bodies were not sticky, disgusting, and shameful, but dynamic, marvelous—and, more important, just us ourselves. Today, as we boomers age, male and female, what has happened to that love and excitement? I fear that my generation is letting disgust and shame sweep over us again, as a new set of bodily challenges beckons.

During a recent routine colonoscopy, I saw my appendix. It was pink and tiny, quite hard to see, but how interesting to be introduced to it for the first time. The colonoscopy was my fourth, on account of a family history. I refused sedation as I always do, and I had the enormous thrill of witnessing parts of myself that I carry around with me every day, but never really know or acknowledge. I chatted with my doctor about many things, including the various justices of the Supreme Court, the details of my procedure, and, not least, the whole question of sedation and anesthesia. He told me that 99 percent of his patients have either sedation or, more often now, general anesthesia, since that is increasingly urged by the hospitals. (In Europe, he said, about 40 percent of patients are not sedated.) He listed the costs of this trend: financial costs that are by now notorious; lost workdays for both patient and whoever has to drive the patient (whereas a non-sedated patient needs no caretaker and can go right back to work); lost time for nurses and other hospital staff; and, of course, the risks of sedation and the even greater risks of general anesthesia.

And, I'd add, the loss of the wonder of self-discovery. You are only this one body, it's all you are and ever will be; it won't be there forever; and why not become familiar with it, when science gives the chance. I began refusing sedation out of a work ethic; I continued through fascination.

What are the countervailing benefits of unconsciousness? Naturally someone benefits from charging the notoriously high fees, and no doubt greed is part of the explanation for why US hospitals increasingly push anesthesia. But I mean, what benefits might there be for the patient? There are no pain nerves in the colon, so any discomfort in the procedure is due to pressure (unless one has done three hundred sit-ups the previous day, and thus has inflamed abdominal muscles, a practice I have learned to avoid!), and, of course, to disgust and shame. On a scale of discomfort from 1 to 100, with childbirth way up there, colonoscopy ranks around a 5, much less uncomfortable than a facial peel, and it lasts only thirty minutes. So we must conclude that a great part of what motivates people to choose sedation, imposing great costs on society, on their loved ones, and on themselves, is disgust and shame. The way the nurses talked made it clear to me that patients are terrified if they might even fart during the procedure, and of course it is the cleanest fart in town, since the colon has already been thoroughly cleansed.

Bodily disgust and shame are winning a battle at least some of us have waged against them for decades. Why? The answer has much to do with the specific type of stigma attached to the aging body, a stigma that has both social and, very likely, evolutionary origins and that has large and pernicious effects on people's relationships to others, and, as they age, their relationship to themselves.[1] Aging is the only disgust-stigma category into which every one of us will inevitably move, if we live long enough. It seems that women, having fought toughly against the stigmas associated with misogyny, are now giving way to the very powerful stigmas associated with aging; and men, perhaps less prepared to fight a war against stigma, if they are men of the majority race and religion, now find themselves joining the stigmatized category of the aging without putting up the least resistance. Giving way to a social disgust-stigma, in this case, means finding oneself disgusting. If other forms of stigma are strongly associated with the social subordination of others, isn't this one, too, a very powerful form of socially inflicted subordination in which the aging themselves more or less willingly participate, subordinating or effacing themselves?

It seems that this can't be terribly good, and it may be very bad. So we should pause to reflect, looking at what we know about the stigma attached to the aging body, its origins, its relationship to and difference from other types of stigma, and what we know by now about its powerful effects.

Disgust: "Primary" and "Projective"

What is disgust, and why is its social role troubling? The emotion has recently been the subject of some important research by a team of US experimental psychologists, led by Paul Rozin.[2] All humans appear to share an acute discomfort when confronted by their own bodily fluids, excretions, and smells, and also by the decay of the corpse. I use the term "primary disgust" for a shrinking from contamination by such objects and by other objects that closely resemble them in smell or feel (such as insects and animals that are slimy, smelly, etc.). Primary disgust, though not present at birth, is culturally universal and is probably grounded in inherited tendencies. Although this aversive reaction may in some cases protect people from real danger (and perhaps that was its evolutionary origin), Rozin shows that its cognitive content is quite different from that of fear: it is about contamination, not danger, it is a reaction to the animality and decay of the human body, and it is both underinclusive and overinclusive for real danger. (Many dangerous things are not disgusting—think of poisonous mushrooms—and people feel disgust even when they are rationally convinced that danger is absent, as with many experiments done with sterilized cockroaches and other nondangerous but disgusting creatures.) Rozin concludes that in disgust we are rejecting something about our own animality. Although he is not specific enough at this point, it is evident from his research that we do not reject all signs of our kinship with the other animals: not traits such as strength, speed, and beauty, for example. What we reject is all that is associated with decay and mortality: we're rejecting our own membership in animal weakness and vulnerability, decaying mortal animality.

All that might be harmless enough, although I would argue that it is always problematic to encourage this sort of self-loathing. In all known societies, however, people do not stop there, and we arrive at what I call "projective disgust." People seek to create a buffer zone between themselves and their own animality, by identifying a group (usually a powerless minority) who can be targeted as the quasi-animals and projecting onto that group various animal characteristics, which they have to no greater degree than the ones doing the projecting: bad smell, animal sexuality, and so on. The so-called thinking seems to be: if those quasi-animal humans stand between us and our own animal stench and decay, we are that much further from being animal and mortal ourselves. There is no society in which we do not find subgroups, to whom, irrationally, properties of smelliness, sliminess, hypersexuality, and in general hyperanimality are imputed.[3]

There are many varieties of disgust-stigma. In European anti-Semitism, Jews were depicted as hyperbodily, smelly, and hypersexual, but also as crafty and intelligent.[4] They were regarded with fear and envy, as well as disgust. African Americans, by contrast, were and unfortunately at times still are imagined as hypersexual and also smelly, bestial, and stupid. They were regarded with both disgust and bodily fear but not with envy. Again, African Americans have been imagined as physically powerful and aggressive. To upper Hindu castes who observed untouchability, untouchables were foul, weak, and not particularly aggressive.

In misogyny, women in so many cultures have been imagined as disgusting—and yet that disgust is frequently combined with sexual desire and arousal, in such a way that no less an authority than Sigmund Freud argued that disgust is an inevitable part of sexual arousal. Feminists are surely right to see in this disgust (so oddly linked with attraction) a linchpin of gender-based denials of moral and intellectual equality—and yet the disgust-reaction does not lead to avoidance of intimacy, but, rather, to an intimacy and domesticity characterized by anxious attempts to police female sexuality. It's not that women are never avoided as contaminating: taboos surrounding menstruation in many cultures testify to the power of misogynistic stigma. And that polite and sophisticated observer of morals, Adam Smith, observed that males like to avoid females after sexual desire is gratified: "When we have dined, we order the covers to be removed."[5] Contemporary US legal scholar William Ian Miller concurs, arguing that such male reactions are deep and tenacious and probably impede the achievement of gender equality.[6] But this type of avoidance, of course, is fully compatible with sharing a dwelling, food, and a bed.

To continue to another case: in contemporary homophobia, gay men are imagined as hypersexual and also as disgusting—and not as sexually desirable to the homophobic men who have these reactions.[7] The violent type of disgust-stigma associated with homosexuality is more or less entirely directed at gay men: lesbian acts were never illegal in Britain, and in the United States lesbian sex is rarely central to the political mobilization of hatred. In fact, lesbian sex is typically found appealing and arousing by straight men, not disgusting. The mobilization of disgust against gay men typically focuses on anal sex, imagining the mingling of bodily fluids, as, allegedly, semen, feces, and blood all stir around together.[8] These differences in forms of stigma are important, and yet a common set of threads runs through all.

An interesting puzzle is class. At times, class-related stigma appears to involve a form of bodily disgust. George Orwell argues that the upper classes will always feel disgust for the living conditions of the lower classes—citing, however, conditions that are ubiquitous in British house-keeping in all classes.[9] Miller reaches a similar conclusion, considering an instance of his own interaction with a manual laborer.[10] On the other hand, class relations involve many rational differences about policy, and are not solely mediated by disgust. Moreover, in nations with reasonable social mobility, class is a temporary status.

Now we begin to arrive at the heart of the matter, for our current purposes. Two instances of disgust-stigma are different from the others, and interestingly similar to one another. Disgust for people with physical and mental disabilities is directed at weakness and inability—seen, very likely, as a lot potentially open to us all. It is not linked to any type of envy, and not to any type of fear except the fear of becoming like that. Disgust for the bodies of aging people (who are often also members of the category of the disabled) has a similar flavor: no envy, no fear of superior power or intelligence, no fear, even, of ungovernable sexuality or a propensity to rape others: just a kind of horror at the prospect of being broken down and (allegedly) decaying, close to death. For "able-bodied" people, there's also comfort, albeit an uneasy comfort, in looking at the bodies of the people with disabilities: they are different, and I'm not like that. With aging bodies, no such comfort is available: however much a younger person tries to "other" the aging, at some level she knows that this is her in the future— unless she meets the yet worse fate of premature death.

Projective disgust always leads to some type of avoidance of bodily contact. Again, the type and extent vary. African Americans were forbidden to use white people's drinking fountains, swimming pools, lunch counters, hotel beds—and of course sexual contact was strictly forbidden and was considered to be a felony in many states (widely, though, white men had sexual relationships with, and sexually abused, black women). Yet, an African American might prepare and serve food for a white family. An Indian untouchable, by contrast, could never serve food in an upper-caste family, and, as noted, Dalits also could not share lodging or drinking taps. The crazy irrationalities of these ideas are manifold. As for gay men in America: given the reality of the closet, no ban on shared restaurants, lodgings, drinking fountains, or even swimming pools could realistically be imposed, but straight men still often find gay men creepy and seek to avoid any possible bodily contact with them. Women have often been segregated from male discussion and deliberation.

As for people with mental and physical disabilities, as children they have often been denied access to mainstream spaces, public and private. Many have been relegated to institutions; most, until recently, have been denied access to integrated education; most until recently have lacked full or meaningful access to public spaces, whether recreational or utilitarian (busses, trains, etc.). The testimony that led to the passage of the Americans with Disabilities Act shows that a common "justification" offered for such exclusions was that "normal" people said they found it upsetting to look at people with disabilities.

Disgust and the Aging Body

Projective disgust always targets imputed (and often fantasized) characteristics that are thought to be contaminating to the disgusted person, reminders of an animal nature that has not been embraced. What is special about the prejudice against aging bodies?

First, the shrinking from contact appears to be somewhat less mediated by culture than in most of our other cases. The stigma attached to wrinkles, drooping skin, and other signs of age seems to be culturally universal in some form, and preverbal children already show avoidance behavior when given a choice between an older and a younger person. It seems plausible that an aversion to aging bodies is based on an evolutionary tendency that is connected to reproductive fitness. Even if children's disgust is far from totally innate, getting many cues from surrounding culture, at least a part of it appears to be based on innate tendencies.[11]

Second, the stigma has at least some truth and is not a total fantasy. Aging people are indeed closer to death than younger people, and at least some of the stigmatized characteristics (drooping skin, age spots, wrinkles) are indeed signs of this nearness, although they are exacerbated by lack of exercise and self-care. Racial stigma and caste stigma, by contrast, rest entirely upon fantasy: the bodies of these groups smell no different from bodies in the dominant group, nor is the sexuality of the stigmatized group more "animal" than any other instance of human sexuality.

This is not to say that all aspects of the aging stigma are based on truth. The aging are widely believed to be less competent along all parameters, and to be incapable of understanding normal speech—explaining why medical personnel typically use a high-pitched hyperarticulate baby speech called "elderspeak" to address them.[12] Like people who use wheelchairs, who are often addressed in baby talk even though no mental impairment is present, aging people are assumed to be less competent as a class and across all life-functions, without assessing the abilities of the individual. And this is surely wrong. So there is a mixture of truth and fantasy, and the admixture of truth feeds the fantasy.

Third, the stigma is associated, from very early on, with the felt inevitability that one will enter the stigmatized group, if one lives long enough. It is the only out-group into which each and every member of the in-group of the young will inevitably move, if he or she lives long enough. This future, however distant, inflects the shrinking from the start. As time advances, it becomes not just a projection but a partial or total self-ascription. The self-ascription is characteristically mingled with uncertainty and vague dread. Unlike the progress of childhood, which, while hardly uniform in all, is uniform enough for age-related generalizations and bright-line rules to make at least some sense, the progress of aging is both hugely variable among individuals and different across the different aspects of human life. One may be mentally acute with one or more physical disabilities; one may be bad at sprinting while having undiminished ability to play the piano or (as Cicero's Cato notes) to give public orations. Even the mind is plural: one may have problems remembering names without any difficulty talking about politics or culture. So, the anxiety about whether the stigma applies to oneself ramifies to embrace the rich plurality of zones of life: as many activities as life contains, so many sources of anxiety about metaphorical or literal wrinkles and sag.

In short: disgust is always at some level self-disgust, as one perceives animality in others and shuns it in oneself. But with aging the truth is front and center: it really is for oneself that one fears. Stigma learned early and toward others gradually becomes self-stigma and self-exclusion, as one's own aging body is seen as a site of decay and future death—by oneself, as well as by others.

Now we can understand why having a colonoscopy is potentially such a significant experience. Its onset is usually around fifty, just when one is beginning the long self-ascriptive work of projective disgust. Its content is feces and decay, and thus it becomes a handy symbol for the entirety of the stigma: the aging body is smelly and decaying, just a pile of feces. It's just an animal, not a transcendent being. And what type of animal? A smelly ugly revolting sort.

Far better to get knocked out and avoid the whole confrontation with oneself.

Bias and Stigma: Contemporary Research

It is time to step back and take stock of what research has shown us up until now. One thing that is constantly said in the research is that more research is needed, so all these findings should be regarded as provisional.[13] Still, several findings seem reasonably solid.

First, stereotypes about aging people are in part explicit, in part implicit. As in other areas of bias research, it is now clear that the bias against aging operates powerfully at a nonconscious level, as prompts associated with aging (words like "old" and "aged") elicit negative reactions even when the subject is not aware of having any such bias.[14] Implicit bias toward the aging is likely to be based on childhood learning, deeply internalized; it will, therefore, be difficult to eradicate.[15]

The stereotype involves aversive reactions to aging bodies as such; but it also contains more specific beliefs. One is that the aging have declining cognitive capacity and memory. Thus, the very same mistakes and instances of forgetfulness are ascribed to normal human frailty when a younger person makes them, but to age when an aging person makes them.[16] Similarly, the same physical problems that are ascribed to treatable disease in younger people are ascribed to the inevitable effects of aging when the patient is older.[17] Since such stereotypes of inevitability have reigned for so long, we actually don't know very much about what the baseline of health is for people at various ages, in a variety of performance areas. Ignorance supports further stereotyping, both about others and, often, about oneself.

Even when the stereotype contains a positive element, the positive often contains hidden negativity. Thus the positive stereotype of an aging man emphasizes "wisdom"—not analytical ability or skill, or subversive challenges to existing norms. And women are denied even "wisdom"—the positive female stereotype is of the "perfect grandmother," which probably connotes nice subservient behavior and not anything associated with professional excellence or challenging ideas.

And as one might predict, the influence of both explicit and implicit bias has real effects on behavior. Where health is concerned, stereotypes prevent aging people from seeking treatment for treatable weaknesses and diseases; should they seek treatment, they may not get what they need, if medical personnel, influenced by stereotypes, believe the condition is just "normal aging." Mental performance has been experimentally shown to be directly affected by stereotypes: people do worse on tests of memory and other cognitive abilities when "primed" by references to stereotypes of aging.[18] Furthermore, the stress imposed by carrying around negative stereotypes about oneself has direct effects on health and well-being.[19]

The feeling that discrimination against older workers is just "natural" and is not discrimination at all is extremely widespread. A comprehensive study of discrimination against workers over the age of fifty-five in the United States shows that this problem is large, and it has been experimentally confirmed by tests in which fake résumés are submitted: some suggested age, others didn't.[20] The study concludes that people simply do not see this type of discrimination as unjust: it's just natural.

Sometimes aging people cordon themselves off from the ill effects of stereotyping by refusing to identify themselves with the denigrated group: retaining an idea of oneself as young and able has good effects.[21] On the other hand, this strategy forfeits the usual good effects of in-group solidarity.[22] In other cases of deprived groups suffering from stereotyping—racial, gender, and sexual orientation groups, and also disability groups—group solidarity has been important for revolutionary movements seeking better treatment from the world and seeking to enhance their own self-image. But it appears that aging may be different: because of the element of truth in the stereotype, accepting group membership can itself be stigmatizing.

Much depends on topic and context. If it is a question of political mobilization to seek better conditions—better nursing and other medical insurance, an end to compulsory retirement—group solidarity feels positive and forward-looking, not stigmatizing: it is about enabling activity and self-respect. The AARP has surely promoted a useful type of group solidarity and self-respect by making definite progress on many issues.

What about group segregation for a range of different activities? It seems that many seniors enjoy senior fitness classes, and in many sports a type of voluntary group segregation seems to improve enjoyment, presumably because it helps aging people avoid shame and stigma, although I enjoy the experience of finishing a half-marathon slowly in the company of twenty-somethings who have not trained carefully. Segregation may also be helpful in the way that AARP is helpful, because the aging body, to be productive, needs specialized attention. One of the nicest parts of the incipient prosenior revolution is that physical trainers do not tell aging people to do less. They typically tell them they need to do more. Thus, when I have some typical runner's injury, whether a hamstring strain or Achilles tendinitis, I am given specific therapy for that problem, but I am also told very firmly that I ought to be doing more core exercises and more exercises for foot tendons, which don't need so much specific attention earlier. So that's a way in which group segregation can promote achievement and useful activity.

But there are also many cases in which the segregation itself embodies a pernicious stereotype and seems likely to produce both lowered self-esteem and diminished performance. I was recently invited to join a new singing group "for older singers." It met at a senior living center, though many members would come in from outside, and it was said to focus on "lighter" repertory. This is surely a bad idea, though having a choral group for untrained singers or less serious singers is a better idea. Singing is a joyful activity that has no age limit, and the main ingredients are training, practice, and basic ability. Of course at the highest end of performance there is a likely terminus to professional performance. But choral singing at a high level does not have such built-in age limits, since a lot of it is about technical ability (sight reading, hearing pitch, musical learning, and taste), and if one can just make sure that one does not sing with too wide a vibrato, a seventy-year-old can happily join with the twenty-somethings.

There are many other contexts in which segregation by age would be stigmatizing. A work in progress workshop for "older law professors"? Opera and symphony performances for "older audiences"? (Well, all too many of those end up that way, because of lack of outreach to new and younger audiences, but that is a different problem.) Voting by age group, with different age groups having different political representatives? Surely modern democracies are wise to avoid that sort of group segregation.

One context that is especially vulnerable to stigmatizing segregation is that of friendship. Families have the advantage that they promote continued contact between the generations. This contact, however, is not always benign: it can reinforce the stereotype of the nonthreatening grandmother, the wise patriarch—rather than promoting attention to the capacities and preferred activities of the individual. Aging people whose only context for friendship is family are vulnerable to a narrowing of their perceived social role. Workplace friendships are more promising: another reason to oppose compulsory retirement is that it deprives active aging people of continued friendships with people of many different ages, shunting them off onto the stigmatized track of the "retired" or "emeritus/a." Choosing friends in a variety of different age groups works against complacency, keeps one open to challenges of many types, and prevents stigmatizing segregation and self-segregation.

The Care of the Self

One way aging people try to avoid stigma is through cosmetic surgery and nonsurgical cosmetic procedures, such as Botox, fillers, facial peels. Of course the obsession with such techniques, especially among women, is hardly confined to people who are aging: women of all ages, and a smaller number of men, seek liposuction, tummy tucks, nose jobs, and so forth. Some of these procedures are aimed at countering other stereotypes: the nose job for Jewish young women, in order to look like the WASP norm of beauty, and eye lifts in Korea, almost mandatory for high school girls, in order to create a Western eye slit. There are still other procedures popular in Korea that, similarly, embody a Western beauty ideal. In general, Korea seems to be the world's plastic surgery capital.[23] One in five women in Korea has had cosmetic surgery, as contrasted with one in twenty women in the United States. (This means a far higher ratio in affluent groups.) And the surgery begins very young: many women have had multiple procedures by the time they graduate from college.

Some cosmetic procedures that people elect are medically indicated: correcting a cleft palate would be at one end of this spectrum, and breast reduction surgery, or having a tummy tuck if one has had multiple large children, are somewhere in the middle; all these seem very different from pure beauty-oriented treatments. Many procedures, however, have no health or medical advantage; among these, many are aimed at conforming to a (mostly male) standard of female beauty. Since part of the norm of female beauty, and, to a lesser extent, of male beauty includes conforming to an ideal of youth, beauty procedures are all the more eagerly sought as age begins to advance. The pursuit of youthful beauty through surgery and other cosmetic procedures can become a virtual obsession.

What should we think about this? Becca Levy refers disparagingly to Botox as a futile and highly temporary attempt to avoid self-stigmatization. She doesn't seem to know its merits very well; one difficulty with third-person assessments is that one recognizes, typically, only those cases that are badly done: Botox injections that render the whole face immobile, facelifts that create a hideous mask-like tightness. So the first thing we should do before judging is to examine a range of real cases, prominently including those that would usually escape detection and leave the person looking like herself. These are, indeed, the cases that truly show the potential of cosmetic techniques: one should judge by best, not worst, cases.

Beyond this, we ought to avoid the tendency to romanticize the "natural." All of us alter our bodies in all sorts of ways, by exercise, by diet, by clothing, by hairstyling, by tooth care, by washing, by shaving legs and underarms, and much more. Human life is itself unnatural, a constant effort not to be what we would be if we did nothing to improve our bodies. So it's stupid to veto all cosmetic procedures simply by saying "unnatural." Indeed I believe that such a response itself embodies stigma: it's okay for women in their thirties to get their hair frosted or permed, but aging women should just yield to the inevitable. Nonsense. Most people accept hairstyling and hair dying at all ages, and they have no objection to tooth capping, even though such things can indeed make people look younger— sort of, since they look like themselves, and it is only to people who have internalized a stereotype that all aging people have yellow ugly teeth and gray hair that they look "young." Indeed, the suspect stereotype of the ugly smelly revolting aging person crops up prominently in the censorious condemnation of cosmetic procedures: why not just capitulate to the march of time and look terrible—as we know you really are, under the veneer of nice clothes, physical fitness, and facial care? We should not yield to such stigmatizing advice.

People must, then, steer their course between the Scylla of excessive deference to "nature" and the Charybdis of obsession with flight from age. We might begin by asking why the Korean obsession seems excessive. Two replies suggest themselves: first, a lot of the cosmetic procedures betray an unpleasant type of national self-hatred and an obsession with Western, and, specifically, American, standards: Western eyes, pointy chins, long oval rather than round faces. Second, as many of the people interviewed in the two excellent studies agree, women choose to have so many procedures because they believe with reason that they are going to be socially evaluated (and even evaluated in the workplace) only or primarily for their degree of conformity to a rigid norm of beauty, and not for other traits such as intelligence or character. Deferring to norms that efface so much of oneself and that express baneful stereotypes of women's abilities and capacities seems unhealthy.

After that extreme, where do we go? Such matters are profoundly personal, but a few useful guidelines might be these: (1) Don't use cosmetic procedures as substitutes for exercise and good diet; get what you can out of those strategies. (2) If you have a look that has become "you," don't efface that by attempts to conform to a stereotype—as with most breast implants, for example, or with the sort of overuse of Botox that removes the ability to smile. (3) Don't spend too much money, since there are lots of other more altruistic things to do with one's money. And (4) remember that surgery is always risky and has a long and difficult recovery period. For me, that puts it out of the question, since not exercising or singing for six weeks would be a torture. Others may judge differently. But (5) remember that the number of nonsurgical procedures (fillers, peels, Botox, "photofacials" for sun damage and age spots, and yet others more odd and exotic) are many and increasing all the time. These have no recovery time and don't cost much money. It seems to me that there is nothing wrong with wanting to look better, it's what we all do every day. And that looking better is what we are talking about, not looking younger. There is no such thing as a template in nature of the sixty-eight-year-old woman, or if there is (among our Neolithic ancestors) it is not anyone any of us would want to be. So one should remember that "younger" always invites the question, "Younger than what? Younger than I looked two weeks ago? Younger than you think a sixty-eight-year-old woman ought to look? Younger than you think I have a right to look?" The imputation of youth to healthy good looks is itself stigmatizing.

So my probody advice is not simple: it is not the advice to love how the body would be if you didn't take care of it. What would be reasons why an aging person would not take care of her body and try to make it more beautiful? Depression comes to mind, as does self-hatred—and, prominently, the stereotype that tells us that the aging body is ugly and discardable, like a piece of trash. Compared to that, I'll take cosmetic procedures any day.

Rebelling against Stigma

The stigma attached to the aging body is real and it has real, baneful effects, however much modern societies try to rationalize it as "nature." This sort of naturalizing of inequality is well known historically: it was the target of the movement against feudalism, the movement for racial justice, the movement for women's equality, the movement for lesbian, gay, and transgender equality, the movement for disability rights. Age is the new frontier, and we all must join to oppose this type of immoral—and in many nations illegal—discrimination.

In most movements for social justice, however, stigmatized people have also felt the need of a more informal antidisgust movement that creatively reshapes the stigma into something to be embraced. The formal civil rights movement was accompanied by the slogan "Black is beautiful," and a widespread social movement around that idea. The women's movement in my youth invented the slogan "Our Bodies, Ourselves," and set about reclaiming the female body as a site of curiosity and love, rather than stigma and disgust. There are many reasons to think that aging people need, in addition to the good political work of AARP, a movement akin to the feminist *Our Bodies* movement: a movement against self-disgust.

Following my argument, this movement would be best imagined as integrative rather than self-segregating—since, after all, the stigma against aging is lodged in all of us, regardless of age. There is little hope of limiting its harmful influence unless one begins with the young. The stigma is, at its core, a stigma about our embodiment and our mortality, so we ultimately will need to shift attitudes toward the body in order to counter stigma effectively. The *Our Bodies* movement was partly about autonomy. We said we won't let doctors take over our bodies and extract the babies, we will be awake and active, and give birth as ourselves. But it was also very much a rebellion against the idea that the female body is disgusting, a staple of misogyny the world over. Whether we read Walt Whitman or not, we were Whitmanians, saying, "I sing the body electric," that triumphant denunciation of all the shames and disgusts that Whitman saw behind the social phenomena of racial aversion, misogyny, and homophobia.

Whitman knew that we will not be able to love one another unless we first stop hiding from ourselves—meaning our bodies. For "if the body were not the soul, what is the soul?" If we can love our own bodies, we may possibly also love "the likes of [them] in other men and women." In a bold crescendo of antidisgust, Whitman then enumerates all the parts we might come to love—starting with the ones we already like pretty well, like "head, neck, ears," then continuing on to the trunk, but its rather pleasing outer parts such as "palm, knuckles, thumb, forefinger," and on down to the strong thighs supporting the trunk. But then, like my doctor's colonoscope, he delves within, caressing with his words "the lung-sponges, stomach-sac, the bowels sweet and clean . . . the thin red jellies within you or within me." These, he says, are actually poems, and they are his poems. "O I say these are not the parts and poems of the body only, but of the soul. / O I say now these are the soul."

Once we were Whitmanians. What has become of that youthful surge of profound self-love? As we age, we are yielding to all the forces we tried, back then, to combat: not only the forces of external medical control, but the more insidious force of self-loathing and self-disgust. Whitman knew that disgust was a social poison. Psychologists studying the emotion today confirm his intuitions about its link with prejudice and exclusion. Isn't it time, for all us aging boomers (using another of our old slogans), to "take back the night"—that is, time to lay claim to that uncharted territory within that we try so hard, and in so many ways, to avoid?

Notes

1. Portions of this essay appeared in a different form in the *New Republic*, October 13, 2014, 1011.

    Below, I draw on the following sources for research on the stigma associated with aging: Becca R. Levy, "Mind Matters: Cognitive and Physical Effects of Aging Self-Stereotypes," *Journal of Gerontology* 58B (2003), 203–11; Becca Levy and Mazarin Banaji, "Implicit Ageism," in *Ageism: Stereotyping and Prejudice against Older Persons*, ed. Todd R. Nelson (Cambridge, MA: MIT Press, 2002), 49–75; *When I'm 64*, Report of the National Academy of Sciences (Washington, DC: National Academies Press, 2006); Jennifer A. Richeson and J. Nicole Shelton, "A Social Psychological Perspective on the Stigmatization of Older Adults," in *When I'm 64*, 174–208.

2. See references to and discussion of the work of Paul Rozin and his colleagues in Martha C. Nussbaum, *Hiding from Humanity* (Princeton, NJ: Princeton University Press, 2004).

3. See the longer version of these arguments in *Hiding from Humanity*.

4. See references to the historical literature in *Hiding from Humanity*.

5. Smith, *The Theory of Moral Sentiments*, Book I.

6. William Ian Miller, *The Anatomy of Disgust* (Cambridge, MA: Harvard University Press, 1997).

7. See Nussbaum, *From Disgust to Humanity: Sexual Orientation and Constitutional Law* (New York: Oxford University Press, 2010).

8. See *From Disgust to Humanity* for illustrations from the pamphlet literature.

9. George Orwell, *The Road to Wigan Pier* (Harmondsworth: Penguin, in association with Secker & Warburg, 1962).

10. Miller, *The Anatomy of Disgust*.

11. Levy, "Mind Matters," 204.

12. Levy, "Mind Matters"; *When I'm 64*, summary.

13. *When I'm 64*, summary.

14. Levy, "Mind Matters"; Levy and Banaji, "Implicit Ageism."

15. Levy, "Mind Matters," 203.

16. *When I'm 64*, summary.

17. *When I'm 64*, summary.

18. *When I'm 64*, summary; Levy, "Mind Matters," 206.

19. Levy, "Mind Matters," 207.

20. See "As More Older People Look for Work," *New York Times*, August 18, 2016, 3.

21. *When I'm 64*, summary.

22. Levy, "Mind Matters," 204.

23. Two good articles on this topic are Patricia Marx, "About Face," *New Yorker* March 23, 2015, http://www.newyorker.com/magazine/2015/03/23/about-face, and Zara Stone, "The K-Pop Surgery Obsession," *Atlantic*, May 24, 2013, http://www.theatlantic.com/health/archive/2013/05/the-k-pop-plastic-surgery-obsession/276215/.

Chapter 5

Looking Back

WE WANT TO learn from experience, but what is gained from regret, and how serious is the danger of living in, or being captured by, the past? In contrast, what is wrong with living in the moment? How is disgust connected to age discrimination? How should we think about retirement communities that seem hedonistic to outsiders and are often segregated, and not just by age?

Living the Past Forward

THE PRESENT AND FUTURE VALUE
OF BACKWARD-LOOKING EMOTIONS

Martha

They live by memory rather than by hope; for what is left to them of life is but little as compared with the long past; and hope is of the future, memory of the past. This, again, is the cause of their loquacity; they are continually talking of the past, because they enjoy remembering it.

—ARISTOTLE, Rhetoric, *II.12, on the character of the elderly*

Oh, for God's sake, don't drag up that ancient history.

—JAMIE TYRONE, *in Eugene O'Neill,* Long Day's Journey into Night

AS PEOPLE AGE, they often spend more time thinking and talking about the past, usually their own past. That's hardly surprising: after all, they see less life ahead of them, and more life behind. Planning and hoping, even fearing, seem less productive than before—or, productive only in an altruistic mode, as aging people hope and fear for their children, grandchildren, and other younger loved ones. And to the extent that aging people spend time looking backward, they also tend to spend time with backward-looking emotions such as regret, guilt, retrospective contentment, and, of course, retrospective anger.

What's the point of these emotions? We can't change the past, so is there any value in these trips down memory lane? We clearly have a good deal of choice about this way of using our time, so what should we think and choose?

The ancient Greek and Roman Stoics made elaborate lists of the emotions, dividing them into four categories: emotions focused on a present good (for example, joy), emotions focused on a future good (for example, hope), emotions focused on a present bad (for example, grief), and emotions focused on a future bad (for example, fear). They recognized no category of past-directed emotions. Guilt and remorse did not enter their taxonomies. Such omissions do not show that Greeks and Romans failed to experience such emotions, since the lists are works of philosophical theory, not close reports of everyday experience. But it does mean that the Stoic thinkers believed that their compatriots would not view the omission of the past as a major gap, for that reason rejecting their theory. And, since their theory was extremely hostile to all emotions, it also means that they saw no major danger to human life in these past-directed attitudes, which might have provided further ammunition for their negative theory, and also no major benefit to human life that could provide potential disconfirmation of their theory. Since two of the most copious philosophical writers about emotions in Greco-Roman antiquity, Cicero and Seneca, were themselves aging (in their sixties) when they did much of their significant work on this topic,[1] we can also conclude that they saw no special relevance of these backward-looking emotions for aging people.

Leading Greco-Roman poets seem to agree with them. Tragic characters who are aging rarely look backward: or, if they do, it is either to point to a distinguished lineage (or, in Cicero's case, to boast of having risen from relatively humble origins), or in the mode of specific and immediate mourning. Thus Hecuba in Euripides's *Trojan Women*, kneeling over the corpse of her murdered grandson Astyanax, recalls the fond hopes he had confidently expressed, including his promise to perform the mourning rituals at her death and to lead a large contingent of young men in the funeral observance. That irony is clearly pertinent to her current terrible plight, since she, an aging woman, is the sole survivor of a royal line, with nobody left to mourn her.[2] Furthermore, as a slave she knows she is highly unlikely to receive a respectful burial. For these reasons, immediate grief is to be expected, and the backward-looking thoughts (not very far back) simply reinforce the magnitude of her present loss. It would have been very surprising, by contrast, for Hecuba to start thinking about how her own personality and emotions had been shaped by long-past events, or to find her expressing grief, regret, and remorse about events long past; we learn of no childhood memories of any aging tragic character. Grief is regarded as a painful emotion directed at a bad state of affairs in the present.

Even when we can access more personal and informal self-reports in ancient Greco-Roman society, we do not find people delving into their long-ago pasts in order to make sense of their present and future. Cicero talks to his Atticus about everything he considers important and much that he does not. He does not talk to Atticus about his own (or Atticus's) parents, even when commenting on the bad behavior of his brother Quintus, or Atticus's sister Pomponia. Nor, much though he adores his daughter Tullia, does it occur to him to wonder whether her remarkably bad judgment in (apparently) falling in love with her philandering third husband Dolabella can be traced to any childhood pattern. When she dies, he mourns with obsessive intensity, but he does not recall her childhood or their long-ago times together. Cicero is not a self-critical man, but he is introspective, and his failure to raise such questions can be understood to express a shared cultural view about what questions are worth asking and what emotions are worth investigating.

Aristotle does report that elderly people love talking about the past. But he does not suggest that they study it in search of self-understanding. Nor does he claim that they focus intense emotion on the events of their past. Indeed, the main emotion he reports is pleasure—the pleasure of diverting oneself from a possibly painful present to the memory of happier times. The philosopher Epicurus's famous deathbed letter makes a similar claim: the pleasant memory of conversations with friends, he says, has managed to overwhelm the pain of his fatal illnesses, dysentery and urinary obstruction.

Modern societies, by contrast, tend to see the past as a highly meaningful emotional category, and to see past-directed emotions as highly consequential for a person's present and future. Three factors contributing to this shift are Judeo-Christian belief, psychoanalysis, and the novel. Judaism and Christianity teach careful self-examination of past deeds and thoughts, attaching immense importance for a person's spiritual condition to backward-looking emotions of regret, remorse, and guilt. Christian beliefs about the afterlife make retrospective emotion a key to one's eternal life-condition: by confessing and bemoaning guilty deeds, one may be saved.

The relationship between psychoanalytic thought and Judeo-Christian belief is complicated and can hardly be discussed here, but psychoanalysis clearly reinforced the cultural idea that the past is highly salient for the present and future state of the self—while turning the focus away from sin and judgment and toward self-understanding. It is virtually a given that the patient has intense emotions directed backward toward early childhood, and a lot of the work of analysis is to make these emotions conscious and to understand how they affect present patterns. Psychoanalytic beliefs have had enormous influence in making modern societies interested in the backward-looking emotions. Whether or not people accept the details of any specific psychoanalytic theory, the idea that memory, and emotions focused on the past, are keys to present and future happiness has ubiquitously shaped people's ways of thinking and talking about themselves—and not just in Europe and North America.[3]

An even wider and longer influence is the novel. The heroes and heroines of novels live and move in time, and their emotions span the full range of temporal categories. Reading novels has taught us that we ought to ask about the past in order to understand the present and future of any character—and that people ought to ask about their own pasts in order to understand their own present and future. In the process, emotions of many kinds toward that past become extremely important. One way novels often dramatize that importance is through retrospective first-person narration, as an adult character both recalls the emotions he or she experienced long ago, and, at the same time, records intense present emotions toward those long-ago events and emotions. Novels, like and preceding the psychoanalysts, often show childhood as a particularly salient category. The genre of the Bildungsroman, which surely has a central place in the development of the novel in general, revolves around the development of a person's character, goals, and values as a result of childhood (and adolescent) experience—and the adult narrator typically interacts, emotionally, with his or her past. Few novelists are as pessimistic as Marcel Proust, who believes (or at least entrusts his story to a narrator who believes) that the past virtually dooms us to rigid repetition in the present, as we focus not on the people who are in front of us, but on people long gone, our parents and other intensely loved adults. But most novelists suggest, at least, that knowing a person's past is an important part of knowing them, and that a narrative study of personality, of the sort novels promote, in combination with past-directed emotions related to that study, is a valuable guide to self-understanding.

In short: when Aristotle's elderly people talked on and on about the past, they were understood, and probably understood themselves, as having a good time, not as accomplishing anything profoundly worthwhile. We, by contrast, tend to think that there is a project, or projects, to be undertaken, projects involving self-knowledge and intelligent self-narration, and that the backward-looking emotions are an important part of executing such projects.

But what, precisely, are these projects? What are better and worse ways of executing them? Are any of them really worthwhile, given that we can't change the past? Should we perhaps try to be more like the Greeks and Romans, remembering for pleasure and diversion from pain, but not looking to our past for profound meaning?

There are Greeks and Romans still living in our world. One of them was my grandmother. She lived to be 104, almost all of that time in good health, and I never heard her say one word about her past. She had had two husbands. One committed suicide in the Depression, and the other died of cancer when I was around eighteen. But she never looked back, except in the occasional humorous anecdote about other people, for example about funny things I did as a young child. I learned about her past from my mother, not her. Characteristic of her was the fact that right after the death of her second husband she asked me to sing a cheerful song for her. I remember the strangeness of doing just that, as she sat there impeccably, expensively dressed, in her elegant living room filled with fine furniture. (The painter John Koch,[4] who supported his important experimental work by painting society women, once did her portrait. It hangs in my living room. She looks very glamorous. "John Koch's best work is with naked subjects," a headline on the Internet reads. My grandmother was never naked.)

As she aged, she loved to talk with her older sisters[5] about their children and grandchildren. She gossiped about their marital problems, or their health issues, while knitting or crocheting an endless stream of afghans for any family member who didn't already have enough. She polished her precious antiques. With my sister and me, and later with my daughter, she loved talking about immediate things, such as what nice clothes of hers she might give us, what we wanted to eat for lunch, and how her precious pigs were doing. She collected and lavished amused attention on a range of ceramic, wood, and leather pigs whose stories she loved to tell to anyone young enough to listen. We gave her the nickname Piglet. We found her delightful.

Piglet had no interest in her past and no use for it. And since she had no pain until the last weeks of her life, she had no need even of Aristotelian memory in order to distract her from bitter reality. She was the most wholly present-oriented person I have ever seen. I often thought that this orientation helped explain her health and longevity.

But here is the thing about Piglet. Although her good spirits were admirable and her company delightful to those who did not spend a lot of time with her, there was a manipulativeness and a coldness in her that was painful to those (my mother and sister) who had to be at her beck and call. And this coldness went way back. She sent my mother to boarding school at the age of eight so that she could have fun traveling with her rich first husband. (Though a common practice in the British upper classes, this was highly unusual in the United States, and my mother felt abandoned.) When that husband seemed at risk of losing his money, she did not stand by him, but took my mother on a cruise to Europe. Photos show her laughing with men in SS uniform. On their return they found that, having exhausted all his financial options, he had killed himself by jumping from a hotel window, in order to give them the insurance money. I have his suicide letter. Undated (though I believe the date to be 1934), typed on stationary from the Hotel Fairfax on East Fifty-Fifth Street, where he jumped, it is addressed, "My dearest Gertrude." It speaks of not wanting to force Gertrude and Betty (my mother) to "drag along in poverty." It concludes: "I feel sure I am doing the wiser thing for the good of both of you. This has always been my controlling motive. . . . I love you both far better than life."

Although such attitudes of self-sacrifice were bred in many American men of his class, he also knew the wife he had. Gertrude would not have embraced poverty in exchange for his life. By her commitment to freedom from care, she virtually willed his demise. It was my mother, deeply loving, devastated, who saved the letter and passed it on to me.

This, then, was not exactly a life that ought to have fled from self-examination. There was a lot to know, a lot to rue. But why? What would self-examination have achieved? If I feel that she was a shallow person for not having undertaken a backward-looking project, am I just the dupe of deeply habitual ideas of confession, guilt, and the last judgment? Since she had done these bad things already, what sense, if any, is there in thinking that backward-looking emotion could have made her life better? Why should she have added self-inflicted pain to the pain she had already caused?

I'll use this case as a test for my idea that it is in some ways useful and valuable to examine one's past and to feel toward it a range of emotions.

The Backward-Looking Emotions

First, however, we need some definitions. What are these backward-looking emotions, and what thoughts do they typically include?

Let's begin with the happy ones. The main happy emotion looking backward is a type of *contented satisfaction* with what happened or what one has done. If intensely positive, it might even be described as *retrospective joy*. A close relative of these happy emotions is *retrospective pride*: one views oneself with pleasure or satisfaction, because one has been or done something good. And finally there is backward-looking *love*—which may be tinged with retrospective joy, or with grief, or with both of these.

The painful species seem more numerous and more complicated. *Grief* might be fixed on an immediate loss, but it may also look backward toward a loss a long time before. The Greek philosophers left out a part of grief when they thought of it as present-directed. *Regret* is a painful awareness that something bad happened, combined with the thought that it would have been better had that bad thing not happened. Closely related to regret is *remorse* or *guilt*. Whereas regret focuses on an event that happened, without characterizing it as wrongful or blameworthy, remorse or guilt (I see no important distinction) focuses on a deed that one has done. It involves the thought the deed was wrongful, and that one should not have done it. Not surprisingly, the Greeks don't recognize these retrospective categories.

And then there is anger. Anger is an unusually complex emotion, since it looks both backward and forward: backward toward a wrongful damage (sometimes close at hand, sometimes long past), forward toward some type of retribution.[6] Sometimes the retribution is imagined as still in the future (whether through one's own agency or through law or divine justice). But sometimes the imagined retribution may itself be located in the past: "X got what was coming to him, and a good thing too." In both cases, anger combines pain at the damage with pleasure at the imagined retribution. The ancient Greek and Roman philosophers focus on cases of anger in which the damage is present. Focusing on retribution, they categorized anger as a future-directed emotion. But of course there may be anger at events long ago.

There are obvious ways in which backward-looking emotions can go wrong. They can get the facts wrong, believing that events happened when they didn't, or failing to take note of salient events that happened, or getting crucial causal connections wrong (for example, thinking a damage wrongful when it was merely accidental). They can get the values wrong, thinking of events or people as more or less important than they were. For example, one might grieve for a trivial loss, like that of a paper clip, or one might be angry with another person for taking such a trivial item.

A further problem with backward-looking emotions as a group, particularly the painful ones, is that they often seem to involve an impossible wish to change the past. But is this really so? Sometimes this wish is clearly peripheral. Grief is sometimes accompanied by a wish that a dead person would return to life, but that wish is not essential to grief. One can have full grief while fully accepting the loss.

But still, one might say: why waste emotional energy on what is lost and gone? The answer seems to be: because grief expresses love's importance in one's life and is a testament to that attachment and to one's own nature as a person who cherishes such attachments. It is about the dead person, not about oneself, but it powerfully expresses the integrity of what one stands for.

Grief usually shifts as time goes on. At the moment of loss, one has the thought, "A person who is absolutely central to my life is gone." As time goes on and the person reweaves the fabric of her goals and concerns, such statements typically change tense: "A person who was absolutely central to my life is gone." This change of tense marks the fading of grief. And yet, grief of some sort may linger as one looks backward. Particularly if one is sizing up one's life as a whole, looking at the entire fabric in a way detached from present time, one may still see a large hole in that fabric. There's that loss there, and it is a fact about who I am and whom I've loved. In that way, even grief for a loss long ago may express something valuable about the person: she is such as to have loved in that way, and she acknowledges that love as a fact about her life.

Regret, like grief, can involve a wish that the bad event not have occurred, but as with grief: that wish seems peripheral, not part of the emotion itself. The main emphasis is, instead, on the idea that it *would have been better* had it not occurred. It would have been better if my children had not been exactly where they were on the highway, so that they were killed by a negligent driver. I feel that it would have been better had they stayed home or taken a different route, but my emotion does not centrally involve a wish to alter what cannot be altered. And it seems plausible that regret, like grief, can be a present acknowledgment of one's commitments and concerns: I am such that this type of event disrupts my life.

Guilt, similarly, may involve simply the thought that what I did was bad, and that it would have been better had I not done it, without the wish to undo what cannot be changed. And guilt, like grief, has a present expressive role that may also direct future choices. My thought that what I did was wrong is a thought that this act was unworthy of me and what I stand for. It is likely to be accompanied by determination that this bad act will not be repeated. Guilt of this sort is part of being a complete person, if one has moral commitments. However, we will shortly have reason to revisit this assessment.

So far, the retrospective emotions do not seem to be per se irrational. There is, however, a problem waiting in the wings: the problem of the retributive wish. Guilt is, basically, self-anger. And both guilt and anger at others, whether present or retrospective, typically involve a payback wish: the thought that someone should be made to suffer for the bad deed, and the belief that this suffering somehow counterbalances the bad deed. This idea is deeply human, and probably evolutionarily programmed. It is, nonetheless, irrational. The idea that inflicting retributive pain somehow counterbalances the pain or damage suffered and in general makes things better is an old but nonetheless incoherent form of human magical thinking. That is so whether the target of the retributive wish is another person or oneself. Punishment of the offender might achieve some useful goal in the future (deterrence, incapacitation, reform), or it might not: that is an empirical question. Similarly, inflicting torment upon oneself may lead to improvement or it may only lead to shutting down; by itself it achieves no valuable purpose.[7]

This objection does not pertain particularly to anger directed at (long) past misdeeds: it pertains equally to anger whose focus is present or recent. But since anger and self-anger (guilt) are prominent retrospective emotions, it is important to emphasize this difficulty.

What does seem valuable, in both the other-directed and the self-directed emotions, is a kind of quasi-anger that drops the payback wish in favor of future-oriented thoughts about the good. "That's outrageous: it must not happen again!" That emotion has much in common with ordinary anger, but it lacks the component of wishing that the doer suffer. It commits the person to a search for strategies to prevent the recurrence of the wrongful act, whatever the best strategies turn out to be (and of course those might include some type of punishment). Similarly, there's a self-oriented type of anger or quasi-anger that is outraged and determined to do better, but without a wish for self-punishment; it commits the self to a search for strategies of self-control or self-change. As with anger at others, self-punishment will be a valuable strategy only if it seems likely to make things better. Needless to say, it is often very difficult to distinguish the productive future-oriented versions of anger and self-anger from the empty versions focused on retrospective retribution.

We're beginning to get a sense of what might be good in having and thinking about retrospective emotions: they tell me who I am, what I have done, what I have been committed to, and they pose a question: do I stand by that, or not? That could be useful for self-change. But even when self-change is not at issue—one doesn't think ill of what one has loved or done—the retrospective emotion can play a valuable role in expressing and declaring who one is—if one avoids the danger of futile self-punishment. But we still need a deeper investigation of the errors and damages of living backward.

"The Past Is the Present, Isn't It?"

I now examine two cases in which living with a great proportion of one's emotional energy directed toward the past is destructive to both self and others—because it involves a failure to face the present and future.

Eugene O'Neill's *Long Day's Journey into* Night is one of the most lauded dramas in the history of the American theater.[8] It is also one of the most excruciating to watch. As you spend four hours with the four characters, the father, the mother, and the two sons, you feel increasingly stifled and trapped, and you want to go up on stage and shake them, to get them to stop their obsessive, futile, and destructive behavior, as they rehearse routines from the past and refuse to face up to the challenges of their present. The watcher of a Sophoclean tragedy wants to tell the characters what she knows, so that they will not behave in a way that, in the light of the truth, is horrible and doomed. Don't kill that old man at the crossroads, even in self-defense. Don't marry the attractive widowed queen. We know that the tragic hero would change his course of action immediately if he knew what we know. There's nothing deeply irrational about such heroes, they are just in the dark.

The tragedy in O'Neill is different. It could not be avoided by adding knowledge. The destructive pattern has become endemic to how these people live and who they are, in such a way that only a long struggle toward change could alter it. The journey mentioned in the title is a literal journey throughout the long day toward an ever-greater depth of misery and estrangement. But the title also alludes to the way in which the life-journey of the characters, instead of moving toward the light of the future, turns back to the fixity and darkness of the past. The play feels stifling because it is a world from which the breath of future possibility has long ago been drained. Emotionally, the journey into night is a gradual progression away from present or future-related emotions, such as hope, love, and even fear, toward a repetitive recitation of routines rooted in and focused on the past.

The basic story is this. (The characters obsessively tell this story during the one day of the play's action; we are invited to imagine that they rehearse it on other days as well.) Mary Tyrone, convent-educated, from an affluent middle-class family, surprises everyone by marrying an itinerant actor, the glamorous matinee idol James Tyrone. She tours with him and consequently has no fixed home. Her first child, Jamie, contracts measles and inadvertently communicates it to her second child, the infant Eugene, who dies. Despite being too weak to get pregnant again safely, she does, and has a difficult labor. In the aftermath of Edmund's birth, she becomes addicted to morphine. Perhaps this happened because her frugal husband chose inexpensive doctors. Mary has struggled with the addiction unsuccessfully ever since, thus for twenty-three years. (O'Neill gives Jamie's age as thirty-three, Edmund's as twenty-three.) She feels that this struggle is more difficult because her husband, during his vacations from acting, isolates her in a large but ill-repaired house in an environment where she lacks friends. Meanwhile, her older son Jamie has become a drifter and an alcoholic, in part bearing the guilt of imputed fratricide. Edmund, a talented writer, also has problems with alcohol, and, in addition, after several years at sea, has developed an infection that seems to be tuberculosis. The most functional member of the family is the father, who drinks a lot too, but never misses a performance, and appears to have some sense of order and agency, although the other family members are relentless in blaming most of their problems on him.[9]

The play begins on a note of hope and loving connection, as the mother's drug addiction seems to have been successfully treated. She is cheerful and has put on weight. People have begun to relax around her. Even the family's fear for Edmund's health seems hopeful, since they are actually facing the future and seem determined to do something about it. Love and connection are amply evident—at first. But we quickly learn that this day is not to be a day that moves into the future: instead, it is a day (and surely not the only one) when the past exercises its strangling grip on all the characters, as Mary starts her morphine injections again, unable to live with fear and hope, with the difficult present and future, where there are new choices to be made.[10]

O'Neill uses his own life as material, but he changes it in striking ways, omitting the happy future of the real-life characters: his own recovery from tuberculosis and later success, and, even more remarkably, his mother's successful drug treatment and eight years of sobriety, before her death from cancer, his father's continued success and relative longevity.

Of the four characters, only Jamie appears to have had the dead-end life assigned to him in the play. These changes, when so much else is veridical, give us a sense of O'Neill's project: to study the destructiveness of the backward-looking emotions, when permitted to dominate present-day human relationships.

The Tyrones talk constantly about the past, and most of the emotions they express are past-directed. Mary's reasonable fear for Edmund's health soon gets channeled into retrospective anger, as the need to choose a doctor and a sanitarium reminds her of many allegedly stingy choices made by James in the past, above all his choice of her doctor, on which she blames her addiction. By the end of the play, even Edmund's urgent declaration that he has tuberculosis cannot get through to her, since she is by then living entirely in the past.

Mary's dominant emotional mode is a passive-aggressive type of fatalism, which masks and ultimately expresses retrospective anger. Often she excuses her own relapse with fatalistic utterances—saying of Jamie, for example, "He can't help being what the past has made him. Any more than your father can. Or you. Or I" (66). Denying the possibility of choice in the present, she turns the present into a past, makes it as rigidly fixed as the past. And for her this means that James's alleged misdeeds, his stinginess, his constant touring, are to blame not only for what they caused in the past, but also for everything bad in the present. Retrospective blame is the mode of her entire life. Even her repeated statements of self-blame always turn out, as she elaborates, to be blame of James. And anger at James is the ultimate reason for her fatalism: rather than blaming him for one or more specific acts, she finds it convenient to lay her entire life at his door. Late in the play, when James tries to get through to her emotions, and cries out, "Mary! For God's sake, forget the past!" she replies, "Why? How can I? The past is the present, isn't it? It's the future too" (90).

For Jamie too, the long ago "misdeed" of becoming the inadvertent cause of his infant brother's death is treated as a fate robbing him of choice, so that all of his emotions, too, are past-directed. Near the play's end, he recites sardonically from Rossetti, "Look in my face. My name is Might-Have-Been; / I am also called No More, Too Late, Farewell" (171).

Edmund and his father are somewhat less immersed in the past. Both struggle toward real connection with others, both have a robust sense of the present and future—and yet both ultimately succumb to the forces of repetition and retrospection. Just as James found it easier to repeat again and again the role of Dumas's Count, rather than to take on any new artistic challenge, so too in his life he ultimately falls back on routine and repetition rather than seeking creative solutions for the family's problems. That is in essence what all the characters do: they choose the easy recycling of a repetitive role learned by memory and animated by retrospective emotions, over the challenge of a real present and future.

Anger often produces such repetitive and pointless routines of retrospective blaming, in which real problems and their scary difficulties are avoided and people act from a script learned long ago.[11] You started it. No, you did this bad thing first. And so it goes. Rigidity can be the stuff of comedy, but in O'Neill, where the stakes are so high, it is tragic instead. The tragedy consists, really, in the avoidability of tragedy and its willing embrace. The characters prefer to believe they are doomed, because that belief absolves them of responsibility for choice in the present. Being dead is easier than living. As the drama ends, Mary makes her final statement of retrospective anger: "Then in the spring something happened to me. I fell in love with James Tyrone and was so happy for a time." In other words, I was a happy girl, and then came that one disastrous fate. You made me who I am today, living in a night that has no exit.

Whatever retrospective emotions an aging life admits and even seeks, surely this way of avoiding present accountability is both futile, accomplishing nothing good, and ethically heinous. Life is not the afterlife, and the present is not the past. It is all too easy to live retrospectively, whether the people one blames are others or oneself, and whether the others are alive or dead. Accountability (of self and others) for past deeds is an important part of facing up to one's life, but accountability is distinct from a manufactured doom and from obsessive payback routines. Indeed, in its best form it brings the painful awareness that change is not impossible but all too possible.

The past sets more than one sort of trap for the unwary. A different problem involved in living backward is dramatized in a very strange novel, Michel Butor's *L'Emploi du Temps* (1957),[12] an experimental novel that is unjustly neglected. What is remarkable about it is the way it plays with time—and not only for literary effect: time plays havoc with the life of the central character, through an initially plausible commitment to clarity and self-knowledge.

Jacques Revel has come from France to midlands England, to take up a one-year post in a firm called Matthews & Sons in the fictional city of Bleston. The opening of the novel finds Revel in a train compartment with grimy windows, rain and brown fog outside, the scarce light refracted by the raindrops so that all he can see is glimmers of indistinct light. (The novel's first sentence is, "Les lueurs se sont multipliées," "Glimmers multiply" [9].) He experiences a desperate desire for clear vision. But before we have finished the first page, we find out that the train journey described is not in the character's present: it is a memory: "I see this again very clearly." And the top of the page tells us that the episode takes place in both May and October, the month of experiencing and the month of writing. This type of annotation occurs on every page of the novel, reminding readers that each episode takes place in at least two times, and frequently more than two (if Revel revisits and corrects an earlier narration of a past event).

Complaining of a "blurring of my self" (cet obscurcissement de moi-même [10]), Revel decides—or rather narrates his long-past decision—to keep a journal in order to keep his mind clear, undefiled by the grime and fog of Bleston. So the experiment begins: and at the time when it begins, Revel still has an external life. He meets his colleagues, he makes friends, he finds himself fascinated by two very different women, Rose and Ann. But each night as he sits down to write, he realizes that his description of past events has been incomplete—so, instead of writing only the day he just lived, he also dips back into the further past to render the journal more complete. This keeps happening, as his obsession with clarity turns him ever more to the past, as he feels the need to correct or flesh out earlier narrations. "This Saturday, this Sunday, how I would like to grasp them, how I would like to transcribe them completely, to lay them out on paper so that I could read them, so that they would become transparent to the light" (218). The ratio of text devoted to present or recent experience becomes ever smaller, the grip of the past ever more all-consuming. The people who used to be his friends, his potential lovers, appear at an increasing distance. Ann gets engaged to someone else, and this passes by with no emotion from Revel, since he is preoccupied with his retrospective project.

Revel is obviously an heir of Proust's Marcel, and the idea is similar: recapturing the past is very difficult; if one pursues it with commitment, as an end in itself, it will necessarily detach one from life and love. Proust suggests that the only fully lived life is the retrospective life: love and friendship are superficial, almost illusory, at least until their essence is recaptured in retrospective emotion. Butor's novel suggests a different moral: Revel's preoccupation with clarity about the past is destructive and unbalanced, a pathological response to his displaced circumstances and his hatred of England.

Revel is a young man, and we are allowed to think that once he is back in France he might recover his balance and enter life again. The animus against Bleston that increasingly propels the narrative—a lot of the last section is in the second person, addressed to the city itself—could be expected to fade amid the charms of Paris—which, of course (in Revel's mind at least) has no fog, no rain, and only clear light with no confusing glimmers!

Butor's title, however, has a special meaning for the aging. Time is getting shorter all the time, and the question of how to use it becomes ever more pressing. Time used in retrospective emotion and thought is time when one does not engage with one's friends, children, and grandchildren. This "use of time" is especially tempting when many friends and relations have died. One can easily think that all that matters is in the past. But there are always new and living people to attend to, and living backward can prevent many joyful connections. The moral is not to discard all backward-looking projects, but to budget the time spent on them and choose only those that seem likely to enrich the present and future, since that is all we really have.

Presentism: Perpetual Childhood?

So was my grandmother on the right track after all? Seeing the traps involved in retrospective emotion, one might easily conclude that her way of living is better, a kind of perpetual childhood in which the past simply ceases to exist. So what is missing in that pleasant life? Obviously her life involves a refusal to confront error and wrongdoing. And since there were misdeeds, indeed bad character traits as well, failing to face them means, too, a failure to be truthful about who one is: a veneer of niceness is put forward, while lurking in the background is something very different. There is a kind of bad faith in such a life, drawing people in by charm and giving an impersonation of life and love, but not really loving at all, and perhaps not even living at all, in the sense that change is ruled out. Her failure to experience grief or guilt is of a piece with an inability to love. When a husband dies, just cheerfully move on. And these emotional deficiencies yield a life in which one ceases to choose and move, just as much as Mary Tyrone: the perpetual present is as inflexible a trap as the perpetual past.

Introspection is generally valuable, and it is part of being a whole person. Trying to understand oneself by facing up to and trying to comprehend what one has done is part of being a full person in the present. That is why psychoanalysis, though it always looks backward, is not primarily a backward-looking process. It is urgently relevant to the task of living forward, for however long one has to live. But looking backward honestly will naturally entail many retrospective emotions, and not only the pleasant ones, since all lives contain losses and misdeeds.

If, then, there is error in turning the present and future into a past, there is an equal and opposite error in discarding the past in favor of a (therefore impoverished) present and future. It is possible for an entire community to live like my grandmother. In *Leisureville: Adventures in a World without Children*,[13] Andrew D. Blechman describes retirement communities in Florida and Arizona that focus on constructing a type of presentist hedonism that distracts aging people from introspection and painful emotion. The one, ubiquitous radio station keeps on repeating, "It's a beautiful day in The Villages!" Social problems are kept at bay. People don't search for meaning, they search for short-term pleasure in golf, food, and sex. Unlike Aristotle's aging people, they turn to the present rather than the past to distract themselves from the prospect of pain. I agree with Blechman in finding this lifestyle off-putting, even disgusting. I prefer my grandmother, since at least she was generous to her grandchildren and her great-grandchild, and support for our education occupied a good part of her planning.

But what's really wrong with the residents of Leisureville? Can I say more to defend my reaction, or is it an inexplicable judgment of personal taste? The residents seem superficial, but they are cheerful. And unlike many aging people, they are at least not isolated. So what's so bad about that? I believe, however, that these people have defects that are significant apart from the general distastefulness (to me) of their lifestyle. Part of the problem with these people is a complete absence of altruism, in people who have large resources. The avoidance of children is just a symptom of this lack of concern for a world outside the self, where resources might do good.

But there also seems to be something amiss with the presentism itself. Avoiding family and the past, these people avoid a lot of pain. Once again, however, I feel that there is a project of being a whole person that they are not executing, a project that requires facing difficulty, loss, and error. The presentist life is like the life we imagine many nonhuman animals leading, and that is fine for them; but human lives, and indeed the lives of some nonhuman animals, have richer possibilities: grief that acknowledges love, remorse that acknowledges ethical failure and the possibility of self-change.

Meaning and Self-Narration

There's a stronger thesis that we should at least consider: that finding or constructing a narrative out of the scattered materials of one's life is a way of making one's life more meaningful, more worth living. Retrospection, carried out in a certain way, is not just finding or affirming meaning, it is a way of constructing it. This thesis, associated with Nietzsche and some Romantics, involves an initially compelling picture of what it is for something to make sense. The general idea is that our lives can look like chance accretions of accidents, and there is something undignified about that, something not fully worthy of our humanity. Religious doctrines solve that problem by providing an external narrative of meaning against which life's shape, and its progress or regress, can be assessed. But if our sense or meaning is not given us by a religious narrative, then it is up to us to endow our lives with meaning. Making a narrative whole out of life's chance materials is a good way of doing that.

What retrospection does, on this account, is not just to face up to the past, it is to select and shape, to create a work of art where previously there was just chance. If we follow this path, we can see a double benefit in past-directed emotions: they are part of confronting who one is, but also, in the process, they play a role in narrating one's life story, as we strive, encountering our past, to shape it into a literary work of art.

There is much to admire in this ambition, but it also has its problematic aspects. First, it suffers acutely from the Butor problem: for the minute one undertakes retrospective narration, one is to that extent no longer living forward. Writing one's autobiography is thus highly likely to take one away from interactions in the present. Psychoanalysis does not appear to have this problem, since a good analyst keeps the analysand's mind on the present task of living, which retrospective understanding is supposed to aid. Nor does psychoanalysis generate the expectation that everything will fit together into a tidy and aesthetically pleasing whole, an expectation that clearly militates against ongoing living, which could all too easily disrupt the emerging pattern.

A further problem is that the narratorial idea of life's meaning seems hostile to life and its actual messiness. You take out what is "superfluous," "repetitious," "trivial," and so forth. But that's life too. You make sure that there is a clear, and possibly single or at least not too complicated, narrative arc. But lives are not like literary plots, they are typically much more multifaceted and multidirectional than that. Nor are real people like literary characters. They do not fit tidily into a plot, and relating to them well requires attending to what is messy, idiosyncratic, even boring from a literary viewpoint. Cicero and Atticus are excellent friends because they do not try to turn the daily into the plotted or formally neat. If they were tempted to showcase the heroic (a temptation that Cicero rarely avoids in other friendships!), they allowed the reality of the friend and the friend's daily experiences to displace this conventional desire. In relations between the sexes, there may be an even greater danger that the desire for tidy narrative will impose gender-based stereotypes on real people. Culture tells us what a "man's story" is supposed to be like, and what the shape of a "woman's story" involves. And all too often we feel satisfied with the shape of a life story only if it does take this conventional form.

The same problem obtains in one's relationship to oneself. One fails to listen to oneself in an intelligent way, if one is determined to slot one's own life into a familiar plot form. And often gender-based expectations will further skew that attention, demanding a heroic narrative for males, a narrative of love and connection for women.

We should not utterly reject the idea of self-narration, but we should warn ourselves of the dangers involved in embarking on that project without rethinking dominant social expectations that deform and simplify, without asking ourselves what rich reservoirs of meaning lie in daily conversations, in nonteleological interactions of many types. If we now consider the Whitmanian critique of bodily disgust that I have applauded in my essay on bodies, we can add that most narration omits ordinary bodily functions and thus exhibits a type of shame and self-shame that I have criticized elsewhere in this book. (Joyce's *Ulysses* lovingly subverts that type of narrative disgust.) So: narration only if you are prepared to tell, in all freedom, an unconventional and messy (in all senses) story.

LIVES NEED TO be lived backward, in some ways and with certain goals— self-understanding, self-change, the enrichment of ongoing life. These retrospective projects must avoid the twin dangers of pastism (Mary Tyrone) and presentism (my grandmother). And we now see that they must avoid, as well, the misanthropy of aestheticism, the hatred of life and self that consists in rejecting the untidy and the unshapely.

Notes

1. Cicero's *Tusculan Disputations*, his only work on the emotions, was written around 45 B.C.E., when he was sixty-one. Seneca's writings on the emotions span his career, but the *Letters to Lucilius*, one of the major such works, was written when he was in his midsixties. Both died by assassination within two years of the works in question (Seneca nominally by suicide but under orders from the emperor).

2. She does have two surviving daughters, Cassandra and Andromache (a daughter-in-law), but they are slaves too, and one of them has been driven insane by rape.

3. This is true not only in Euro-American cultures, but also in India, where psychoanalysis, though attacked by the Hindu Right, is very popular and influential.

4. 1909–1978. The portrait in question was probably painted in the mid-1950s.

5. One died at 102, one at 103, and one, the unhealthy one, at 95; all predeceased her.

6. See the analysis in my *Anger and Forgiveness: Resentment, Generosity, Justice* (New York: Oxford University Press, 2016).

7. See *Anger and Forgiveness*, chapter 4.

8. I use the edition by Yale University Press (2002), with preface by Harold Bloom. All page numbers refer to that edition.

9. These facts are also to some extent those of O'Neill's early life. O'Neill (1888–1953) spent two years in a tuberculosis sanitarium in 1912–1913, and was cured. His father James really was a remarkable actor, though many believed that he squandered his talent by playing the role of Dumas's Count of Monte Cristo more than six thousand times. He died in 1920 at the age of seventy-two, after a car accident. Despite the drug problems depicted in the play, which is set in 1911, Ella kicked the morphine habit for good in 1914, and went on to survive breast cancer as well, dying eventually of brain cancer at the age of sixty-four in 1922. Jamie died of alcoholism in the early 1920s; the story told in the play, that he inadvertently spread measles to the infant Eugene, who died of it, is true.

10. One unfortunate aspect of the play is that it portrays drug addiction as at least in part a character flaw.

11. See my *Anger and Forgiveness*, chapter 4, discussing Harriet Lerner's *The Dance of Anger* (New York: Harper and Row, 1985).

12. Paris: Les Editions de Minuit, 1957. There is an English translation under the title *Passing Time*; it's a bad translation of the title, since the idea of the "use" of time is central to the novel's tragedy. I have not used that translation, and all translations from the French are mine.

13. New York: Grove Press, 2009.

No Regrets, and a Cheer for Retirement Communities

Saul

AGING THOUGHTFULLY MUST involve some learning from the past. If what we learn can be generalized and conveyed to others, then we ought to have some good answers when younger people turn to us for wisdom or ask: "If you could do it all over again, what would you do differently? What do you regret?" It is not much of an answer to say one would have avoided a bad marriage, studied Mandarin, or bought Google stock, because these are things most of us know only with hindsight. They might represent misfortune, but not sincere regrets or sources of wisdom for young listeners. A better answer might be that one should have studied languages; we could and should have known that life would be richer, and our understanding of other people more complete, if we invested in language skills. When young people ask for advice, I think they are asking about just such regrets, in order to avoid serious errors by learning from ours. Such advice is more valuable when it is not self-justifying. "I found a good job, and stayed loyal to my employer for forty years, and this brought me great happiness" is unconvincing, both because the listener might think that times have changed and because it might seem that the speaker is justifying an unadventurous life story. In contrast, "I was disloyal three times, and each time my actions caused great pain to everyone, including me," has the ring of sagacity. The statement might be about work or about love, and it conveys information that seems hard or costly to acquire on one's own. Good advice can even come from unhappy or even dysfunctional people. They are marked by a tendency to dwell on past errors or bad luck, and their regrets are impediments to new adventures, experimentation, and satisfaction. But if one can generalize about errors, others might learn from them. Ideally we would learn from the regrets of others, and end up having none of our own.

Some advice of this kind is rather simple. "After age sixty, do not talk about your health problems unless you intend to bore people"; "Spend time with your parents and children because these opportunities are precious"; and "Travel and engage with diverse people" are good pieces of advice that come from years of experience and, in all likelihood, occasional regrets. But when it comes to larger questions about life, essays and novels do more than any one person's musings can possibly convey. Martha points to one such lesson: learn from the past but do not let it either suffocate you (*pastism*) or turn you into a shallow, self-absorbed person (*presentist*). I think Martha is much too tough on presentists, so I will say something in favor of happy people who know how to seize moments. There is room to admire people who completely change their lives as they age. But there is also the larger psychological question: Can an attitude or way of living life be learned?

Looking backward is a special problem for pessimists and people who carry negative thoughts wherever they go. Novelists, therapists, and kindergarten teachers recognize that we would lead happier lives if we spread good cheer rather than gloom, if only because other people would respond better to us. But telling people to "cheer up" is rarely successful. Besides, there are charming curmudgeons. How-to books about mourning try to find a middle road: recognize your grief, let it run its course, and then move on. It is not obvious that these instructions work for people who are prone to guilt or stress, not to mention depression. Many best-selling books succeed because people like reading about themselves—reinforcement is doled out with a little inspiration in the mix—not because they offer proven remedies. In principle, regret is valuable if one learns from it, or is forgiven because remorse has been demonstrated, but it probably works best for forward-looking, optimistic people—and they probably do not need advice in the first place. I fear that although Eugene O'Neill's *Long Day's Journey into Night* is a brilliant analysis of dysfunction, it is unlikely to do much for those hoping to learn from it. Some people are forward-looking happy types, with enough balance or retrospection to avoid sociopathic behavior, while others are just gloomy. If the gloom can be pierced with psycho-pharmacological tools, they are fortunate. If not, only a very few will work their way out of dark places.

Consider the difference between well-placed blame and misfortune. Gary drives too fast and under the influence of alcohol, and he tragically ends Amir's life. In a novel there would be some quirk that put Amir in the wrong place at the wrong time, but in real life people like Gary need to be deterred or educated in the first place. If you drive recklessly you have a much higher chance of killing someone; Gary may recover if his regret teaches him something, but the wakeup call comes at the expense of Amir's life. In contrast, Allie drives safely but because of some bad luck, such as invisible ice on the road, her automobile slides into Gregory and kills him. She may have trouble getting over this tragedy, and she may hold herself responsible, especially if Gregory is a child. She and Gary may both be regretful and unlucky, but only one is blameworthy. Again, I'm not sure that rational discussion will help Allie see that she should look forward and not be consumed by the regret. Famously, many people feel lifelong guilt for surviving a war or a traumatic event like the Holocaust, when many loved ones and neighbors perished. Some benefit from therapy and years of being reminded that they were victims and not at fault, but most of those who go forward cheerfully seem to be made of different stuff. So yes, (1) it is great when people can learn from the past without becoming lost in what might have been or in assigning blame, but it is also (2) good to deter blameworthy behavior. And, finally, (3) telling people to be optimally forward-looking may be as ineffective as telling sad sacks to cheer up.

AND THEN THERE are the presentists, as Martha calls them, including the inhabitants of The Villages in Florida, not to mention cruise ships, where many retired people enjoy self-absorbed lives. I may not yearn for these places, and I know Martha does not. But then she would like to keep working into her seventies and then eighties, while most people want to retire; she would like to be surrounded by graduate students and new ideas, while many people want to exclude young people and especially schoolchildren from their oases. Another colleague ridicules The Villages for its faux Western storefronts, mini-Disney affects, and (like other real-estate developments targeting retirees) advertisement of golf and other "white" activities.[1] But what is so awful about people wanting to enjoy the last third of life?

About 5 percent of American elderly now live in senior living communities. Florida's The Villages is the country's fastest growing and largest retirement destination. Marketed as a community for active seniors, most subcommunities in The Villages require at least one fifty-five-year-old in each residence; anyone under nineteen (of school age) must limit visits to thirty days per year. The housing stock and considerable leisure activities appeal to and reflect middle-American tastes. Residents organize and participate in hundreds of clubs and hobbies. They use numerous recreation centers, swimming pools, and golf courses, some of which are available to all residents with no additional charge. The infrastructure, landscaping, radio, newsletters, and advertising might best be described as upbeat or chirpy. There are plenty of classes and educational opportunities, though most focus on self-help and spirituality, with occasional historical re-enacters and other popular, rather than highbrow, programs. The same is true for music and other entertainment; there are heavy doses of dated pop music, and classical pieces are often abridged.

The development and popularity of places like The Villages is good, not bad, news. The wealthiest 1 percent, or even 10 percent, of retirees might prefer to live in Manhattan or Palm Springs, and to enjoy cultural amenities with people of all ages, but this is not within the reach of most Americans. Think of retirement from the perspective of the median retiree born between 1930 and 1960. These are people who grew up without air conditioning, without fancy schools and colleges, with Scout and church summer camps rather than music, drama, and computer camps. They observed an increasingly affluent society around them and, in some part, did not share in the affluence while they worked and raised families. The median income of The Villages suggests that residents have Social Security and then just a modest amount of other retirement income. They probably sold their homes in other parts of the United States and invested the proceeds in $200,000 to $500,000 homes in this central Florida development. Republicans outnumber Democrats here two to one. This is not Palm Beach or San Diego, where the average cost of housing is much higher. And it is much grayer than Clearwater, Florida, or Scottsdale, Arizona, which have the highest percentage of retirees among cities of one hundred thousand or more; in these two cities 20 percent of the population is over sixty-five, while in The Villages it is 57.5 percent. It is worth noting that most of the places that attract retirees, including Scottsdale, Palm Springs, and Chappaqua, New York (of Bill and Hillary Clinton fame), are just as white as The Villages, but have much higher median incomes and housing prices.

The Villages, and many places like it, may be growing rapidly, but most middle-income retirees prefer to stay in the homes and communities in which they worked and brought up families. Of course, some are not self-sufficient and must relocate to facilities in which care is provided. I like to think that the phenomenal growth of The Villages reflects the arrival of middle-income Americans who can finally enjoy some of the affluence of the nation they helped build. During most of their lives they observed people with higher incomes traveling abroad, buying second homes, sending children to private colleges, and subscribing to the *New Yorker*. In retirement, some might develop new preferences, but most just want to be left alone to enjoy the activities and television they already like. After forty years of work they have earned stress-free lives. Leisureville, as it is cleverly and fairly called, is their counterpart to the "safe spaces" that presentist college students demand. University professors typically object to both trends, and wish for young and old alike to be challenged with new ideas, drawn from the classics or from contemporary science. But the market is telling us that most senior citizens want challenges of a different kind, and do not want intellectual humiliation—as they often see it—or new stresses; they want physical and mental comfort food. The retirement community is a place where they can enjoy each other's company, experience more sex, and not feel stigmatized by their age. They had little control in their prior lives, as they were buffeted and occasionally rescued by economic cycles, erratic employers, government policies, health issues, and family problems or successes. Their retirement dream is to migrate to an environment they can control and in which they are valued.

It may be that they also want, or find themselves leading, segregated lives in this retirement period. The extra comfort apparently derived by many people from interacting with others of similar background or beliefs is somewhat generational. My parents' friends were all of their own religious sect and color. Mine are much more diverse in religious terms, and substantially more so when it comes to race and ethnicity. My children's friends are yet more diverse in terms of race, ethnicity, and sexuality, though perhaps less so with respect to politics. In large part the adult friendship patterns follow or reflect the demographic characteristics of the universities we attended. At present, Chinese American retirees, for example, can find retirement homes that cater to their language and food preferences. Lutheran retirees can find faith-based communities that appeal to them. Alpha Kappa Alpha is developing Ivy Acres, a retirement community in North Carolina aimed at African Americans over fifty-five. Even the Loyal Order of Moose has Moosehaven, Florida, a "City of Contentment" exclusively for its retired members. Real-estate developers often work with churches to develop communities aimed at particular audiences. They advertise cuisines, entertainment, and other amenities aimed at particular audiences—just as The Villages advertises golf. All these communities say that they welcome diverse residents, but the target audiences are unambiguous. Yet older people might find themselves in nursing homes that separate groups by floors, and provide food, music, and other services attractive to the particular, segregated ethnic group.

If this segregation seems like a step back in time, we ought not blame it on real-estate developers. Most people have preferences reflected in whom they marry and, later on, with whom they retire. My guess is that the next generation's retirement communities will be more diverse, in part because their schools, universities, and workplaces are far more diverse as a result of legal, social, and economic changes. I would be surprised if there were many Chinese American retirement communities in fifty years; middle-class and affluent Chinese Americans will often have married members of other groups and, besides, they will retire along with their neighbors and college classmates. Indeed, universities may be the sponsors and organizing principle of retirement communities.

It is true, as Martha characterizes it, that these retirees in Leisureville are presentist. But when they do look backward, the evidence is that most are content rather than regretful. If their children turned out well, they are especially satisfied and even boastful. If not, they focus on grandchildren or simply try to improve their golf games. They want safe spaces, and most citizens would think they have earned it. Their lives are not free of bad news. They have Fox and NPR for one thing, but they also have fellow residents' funerals to attend, and these remind the aging mourners that time is short. If they thought they had many years ahead, they might well learn languages, but inasmuch as they are realistic, they choose to enjoy one another's company, play golf, sing, knit, and do a hundred other things that time now allows. Surely we all sometimes envy their communities and wish that we too could live among so many people with preferences like our own.

Note

1. Lior Jacob Strahilevitz, "Historic Preservation and Its Even Less Authentic Alternative," in *Evidence and Innovation in Housing Law and Policy*, ed. Lee Fennell and Benjamin Keys (Cambridge: Cambridge University Press, 2017).

Chapter 6

Romance and Sex beyond Middle Age

HOW ARE MATURE women depicted in opera, theater, and film? What should a thoughtful person look for in love? Why does age matter in romance? How should we think about gap couples, where one partner is much older than the other?

Lies of Richard Strauss, Truths of Shakespeare

AGING WOMEN, SEX, AND LOVE

Martha

THERE ARE MANY ways to begin an essay on love and aging women. One is to begin with popular culture, and I shall indeed consider a group of movies in my concluding section. If I begin, instead, with a "highbrow" work, an opera in fact, this choice reveals not only my devotion to opera, but also my desire to confront myths about love and aging, at first at least, from a vantage point of some detachment. Richard Strauss's *Der Rosenkavalier* (1910), both highbrow and popular, at least in a bygone era, shows us certain baneful lies and prejudices. Its clarity derives in part from its cultural distance. But I shall return to our own world, where similar lies are to be found.

A Mendacious and Sentimental Opera

Der Rosenkavalier is one of a very small number of recognized major works of art[1] that deal extensively with the theme of love and sexuality in an aging woman. A leading critic, pointing out that it is probably the most popular opera written during the twentieth century, calls it "a sublime work whose charm and beauty never fails to seduce the affections of audiences."[2] (Well, not everyone!) And certainly many have agreed with this critic in admiring the opera's treatment of important themes. The daring erotic opening, which finds the Marschallin in bed with the teenage boy Octavian, right after an episode of sexual pleasure boldly depicted by the orchestra during the overture, makes many people think that we will now have a serious exploration of the theme of female aging, and perhaps of age difference as well. As the drama unfolds, and the Marschallin accepts the need for her to give up Octavian so that a woman his own age can have him, she ruminates in a bittersweet way on the need to yield to the inevitable march of time, thus forgoing passionate intimacy and, in effect, returning to the convent from which her (totally absent) husband took her many years before. These ruminations, and the entire configuration of the plot, have been taken to be profound, and it was surely Strauss's intention to depict the Marschallin as a good and wise woman, normative for what women should be and do as they age. "Her wisdom and omniscience are overpowering," gushes the credulous critic Burton Fischer. And he summarizes:

> The Marschallin possesses an enlightened gift of consciousness and awareness which provides her with a profound understanding of the present, past, and future: Time. Her acute sensibilities enable her to come to terms with herself and direct the story . . . to its rightful conclusion.[3]

Fischer's hyperbolic rhetoric is a bit irritating, but there is no doubt that many interpreters and audience members have responded in exactly this way. And there is no doubt that Strauss wanted them so to respond: his Marschallin is one of a series of wise and serene women who, in his mature years, take over from the demented and yet far more psychologically interesting heroines (Elektra, Salome) of his earlier years.

Let me anticipate your response by giving the Marschallin some credit. She is a kind person, who wants others to be happy. She is not possessive or tyrannical. She has good manners. And she does have at least one good line about aging, at the end of her famous act 1 aria: "And in the 'how'—there lies the whole difference" ("und in dem Wie—da liegt der ganze Unterschied")—expressing the important idea that aging itself happens inevitably, but people have many choices about how to inhabit it. There's something nice about the musical setting of that line too—it ends not ponderously but lightly, suspended in the air, and one may even sing it with a trill of laughter.

And yet. The first lie of Strauss and his librettist Hugo von Hoffmanstahl, the one I shall call "the obvious lie," is the lie about inevitability. For a woman, according to the "wisdom" of this opera, getting old means surrender and renunciation. A woman's life, as she ages, must of necessity end up as sexless as the convent girl's life from which it emerged. That's its "rightful ending." Audiences typically swallow the lie and applaud her sage retreat. And they swallow it even though the actual age of the Marschallin is unspecified in the libretto, and was later specified by Strauss as thirty-two. I suspect that women in the audience, and some men too, imagine the age as considerably older, but even so: they accept a cultural myth that it would have been interesting to have challenged. Strauss plays a double game: he gains a reputation for daring by broaching this theme, and yet he satisfies his audience by saying something utterly conventional about it. Far from challenging his audience (as he appears to do and gets credit for doing), he comforts them and insulates them from real doubt and imagination.

Well, that's what readers could have guessed I would say, even without knowing anything about the opera. So not just the lie, but my critique, so far, is obvious.

Now, however, we come to the more subtle lie. Why do not just audiences in Strauss's time, but even contemporary audiences, accept the inevitability of the Marschallin's resignation? Let us consider her erotic choice. This is a woman who, by her own account, was taken from the convent, without much in the way of consent, into a loveless marriage, and with a husband who is off hunting throughout the entire opera and doesn't even bother to put in an appearance.[4] So, if she were really the intelligent and wise woman she is supposed to be, what do we think she would look for in a lover? Sex certainly, but that is not the exclusive offering of teenage boys. She would very likely also be looking for conversation, for humor, and for real personal love. Instead, she turns to a boy who is no more than seventeen (the age specified by Strauss), and possibly somewhat younger, since it is supposed to be plausible that the role is sung by a female mezzo-soprano. She seeks out a relationship that is based entirely on his infatuated sexual eagerness, and one that offers absolutely no possibilities of conversation or genuine personal intimacy, since Octavian, so far as we are allowed to know him, is also a very stupid teenager, albeit with pretty manners. Among teenage boys in opera, Mozart's Cherubino (the acknowledged prototype for Octavian) has much more depth. He prefers love to mere infatuated sexuality, and he has the ability to compose a very beautiful song to express his emotions. (The great aria "Voi che sapete" is represented as his own poetic and musical creation, thus giving his character a texture and interest that Octavian utterly lacks. Of course Octavian too sings lovely phrases, but not about love, and with no suggestion that he has composed them.) Cherubino also has a wonderful sense of humor, whereas Octavian is pretty deficient in that department (probably because Strauss and Hoffmanstahl are not Mozart and Da Ponte).

The world of eighteenth-century Vienna surely contained many men of far greater interest, many of them interested in love affairs with married women, since the world the opera depicts is a permissive one. So what has this wise woman with "acute sensibilities" and "profound understanding" done? Out of all the men around, she has chosen one who is interested in sex alone, who has no capacity for intelligent conversation, and who has no interest at all in her as a person, except as a beautiful and mature sex teacher, and a safe available object, since in his world unmarried women of good family would have been off limits. Why did she make this choice? Insecurity? A desire for control and hierarchy? No plausible motive is ever suggested. And this absence of motive, particularly in one so wise, confirms the lie: the only explanation offered (implicitly) is that this is the only option she has.

This "choice" of hers, of course, explains why the demise of the relationship is felt as inevitable. There's nothing to sustain it, and so Octavian may as well go on and marry a rich heiress to whom he has nothing interesting to say either, doing as society expects him to do. Soon he will be off hunting in the countryside, and Sophie will be alone (living out the "inevitable" in her own generation). We may even feel relief about the demise, in the twenty-first century, since there is a suggestion of pedophilia in the Marschallin/Octavian relationship, and more than a suggestion of inappropriate asymmetry and control.

This inappropriateness, of course, has nothing at all to do with age difference per se (as most commentators oddly suggest that it does). Age difference in itself means little or nothing if both parties are mature adults with intelligence, character, wit, and conversation. The inappropriateness is all about the fact that Octavian (besides being stupid) is much too young for a mature relationship.

One qualification must now be made, in response to some (male) readers, who feel that I have slighted the charms of the seventeen-year-old boy. Many mature men, perhaps all, have a boyish self, a capacity for sexual curiosity and delighted receptivity, that is one important aspect of their allure. I happily grant that this boyish aspect, and the corresponding idea of the wise female teacher, can be delightful. And just maybe an aging woman, who may possibly have more developed maternal capacities than a younger woman, can deal especially well with this aspect.

As Donald Winnicott beautifully puts it, the job of a good mother is "to continue to be herself, to be empathetic towards her infant, to be there to receive the spontaneous gesture, and to be pleased."[5] That indeed is also a fine description of a good sexual partner—since all adults are also infants, and good sex deals lovingly with infantile themes. And although Winnicott emphasized that "mother" is a role that could be played by an adult of either sex, it's certainly true that culturally, the role of mothering infants is likely to be more strongly developed in females, in a way that may make them especially ready to be pleased by the baby in the male, and good at welcoming it (him). All right, I grant all that, gladly. I do not grant, however, that this nice reality lends any attractiveness to the exploit of seducing an actual teenage boy, or makes the choice to do so any less sad, even pathetic.

So here's the subtle lie: a lonely aging woman, in an unhappy marriage, described as beautiful, cannot find any type of real love, or any type of genuinely interesting and complicated lover. All she can find is a hormonal kid who would sleep with anyone, and she takes what she can get. So she fools herself, and even (by act 3) calls it "complete love." Of course there are many such women in recent life and literature, Mrs. Robinson being perhaps the most famous example. But we rightly think of them as unwise, sad, and predatory, like those high school teachers who occasionally turn up in our criminal courts, not as wise, profound, and normative for how an aging woman ought to behave or genuinely indicative of what her choices are. The subtle lie is that a wise woman, seeing that she is aging, will naturally make a staggeringly inappropriate erotic choice, jettisoning the search for love (or not embarking on it, since she apparently has never searched for it) in a desperate burst of sexual eagerness. And then, being wise, she will give that up and become resigned to a sexless life—why? Apparently because she is aging and no intelligent man, no male not totally preoccupied with teenage hormonal excess, will look in her direction. That's not just a lie, it's a generative lie, since when people come to believe it, that belief informs choice. (*The Graduate* [1967] lies in similar fashion, and with similar misogyny, influencing a new public.)

And now we arrive at a further dimension of Strauss's mendacity. Why on earth did he choose this plot, and why, in particular, did he represent Octavian as so extremely young? Maybe he believed his own subtle lie about the choices open to an aging woman. But maybe not. He has a further motive, on the level of performance. He wants the role of Octavian to be sung by a female mezzo-soprano, and, given operatic conventions at least at the start of the twentieth century,[6] he can only set the role for a female mezzo if he makes Octavian a young teenager. The choice of a mezzo has clear musical advantages, and it does enable him to write some very beautiful music with close harmonies. But let's face it: he is also creating a form of pornography that has long been familiar, in which straight men are aroused by watching the sexual embraces of two women. Males in the audience can watch the daringly erotic opening scene without making this connection consciously, because Octavian is supposed to be a male. But let's face it again: given the bodies of mezzos, the charade is likely to be unpersuasive, and so they are at the same time enjoying a pornographic pleasure that they probably would feel somewhat ambivalent about enjoying, particularly in the presence of their wives or female partners, if Strauss didn't help them by playing his mendacious double game. (To explain my focus on straight men: the opera is not an especial favorite among gay men, except insofar as all opera is favored; works such as Britten's *Billy Budd*, which show the male body to advantage, are far more favored in that market.) And women? Well, the evidence of the work's popularity suggests that many fall victim to its lies and embrace the romance in its represented form. Others dissent. I dissent.

Now we arrive at a third lie, the subtlest of all. The lie is that it is only in this form—where the aging woman is stupid and makes a staggeringly bad choice, and where she then comes to her senses and renounces that choice—that an audience will accept the representation of the sex life and emotions of an aging woman. In other words, the aging woman has to be punished—and doubly punished, first by being thrust into a stupid and shallow relationship, and then by being made to give it up with high-minded talk about time and inevitability. It is very like the old days in which gay male relationships in fiction had to end with a death. As E. M. Forster remarked in his "Terminal Note" to *Maurice*, explaining why he postponed its publication (it was written in 1913, and finally published only posthumously in 1971), the problem was not that the novel dealt with gay male love, it was that it has a happy ending:

A happy ending was imperative. I shouldn't have bothered to write otherwise. I was determined that in fiction anyway two men should fall in love and remain in it for the ever and ever that fiction allows. . . . If it ended unhappily, with a lad dangling from a noose or with a suicide pact, all would be well for there is no pornography or seduction of minors. But the lovers get away unpunished and consequently recommend crime.[7]

Forster was of course speaking literally, since homosexual sodomy was not decriminalized in Britain until 1967. Sex between an aging woman and a consenting male partner has never been illegal! (This omission of legislators has long been the Achilles heel of Catholic natural-law arguments against the decriminalization of sodomy: for on this view all sex not open to reproduction could, and some say should, be repressed by law.)[8] But the issue, culturally and socially, is much the same. Audiences then wanted to punish gay men for their sex lives, since they disapproved, and wanted the novelist to register that disapproval. Audiences then and now want to punish the aging woman, and thus, aided by Strauss, they construct an aesthetic fiction of the "inevitability" of her renunciation and the "profound wisdom" of her acceptance.

More generally, a main activity of fiction, especially in the nineteenth and early twentieth centuries, but still all too often today, has been to assign a "comeuppance" to people who are regarded as sexual "deviants," including the unwed mother, the ambitious career woman, the adulteress, the woman who would simply like an intelligent partner.[9] To this catalog we may easily answer the aging woman who does not display the "wisdom" of resignation.

Is this third lie, however, a lie? Is it really possible, audiences being what they are, to represent the sexual choices of an aging woman attractively, showing her as genuinely wise, making a good and interesting choice, and then being happy in that choice, at least as long as fiction or history allows? To see that the answer to this question is "yes," we need only turn to a playwright far deeper and far more admired than Hugo Hoffmanstahl: to Shakespeare, and *Antony and Cleopatra*. Of course Shakespeare had history at his back, and Cleopatra is one of history's most fascinating female protagonists. Her love affair with Marc Antony was also amply attested, and was known to have lasted, not "ever after," since Augustus put a stop to that, but until the death of both. Still, Shakespeare chose that tale out of countless tales he might have dramatized. And having lived by then through the remarkable reign of a female monarch, aging throughout his career (until she died in 1601 at the age of sixty-eight), and who famously had (or didn't) a longtime lover, he knew that he could carry his audience along.

Let us then turn to *Antony and Cleopatra*.

Love in and through Time

Before we can approach that play, however, we need to see it in context, as one of a pair of bookends. Shakespeare of course approached the topic of erotic love in more or less every play he wrote,[10] but there are two plays that seem almost designed to be read together, as studies of love at two particular stages of life. They are also bookends in Shakespeare's short life (1564–1616). *Romeo and Juliet* dates from 1595, only about six years after his dramatic debut. *Antony and Cleopatra* was produced in 1606, and is thus one of his last sole-authored plays. Although a mere eleven years divides the two, those are years of astonishing productivity, marked by deepening insight and maturity. When he wrote *Romeo*, he was not in his first youth, being thirty-one, but the experiences of youth were clearly a theme available to him throughout the early part of his career. When he wrote *Antony*, he was already forty-two, and in Elizabethan terms could certainly be said to be aging. To write convincingly about aging, it helps to get close to it, at least.

As Tzachi Zamir points out, *Romeo and Juliet* conveys the hyperbolic, extravagant, rather abstract character of young love, its focus on a generalized and aestheticized image of the body ("I ne'er saw true beauty till this night"), its humorless mutual absorption, and its search for transcendence of mere earthy and bodily humanity. Juliet is the sun, her eyes "two of the fairest stars in all the heaven." She is a "bright angel," soaring above the heads of mere mortals.[11] This sort of love works by bracketing reality; it is actively hostile to fact and evidence. Because it is determined to rise above the earth, it is also lacking in particularity: Juliet is an abstract image, an angel, and neither Romeo nor the audience knows a great deal about the earthy attributes that distinguish her from others. It isn't really about the body, and indeed seems almost to spurn the real quirky lumpy body, with all of its fluids, tastes, and smells. Indeed those senses are virtually absent from the lovers' vocabulary, which is all drawn from the realm of sight, and idealized sight at that.

One sign of the lovers' preoccupation with the ideal is the play's constant fascination with images of sleep and dreaming; and Zamir, like many critics before him, notes that the play itself draws readers into a lulled and dreamy state. Such a state might be seen as mere forgetfulness; it might also be seen as infantile narcissism. Zamir ultimately rejects both of these interpretations, in favor of one that focuses on the transfiguring experience of the perception of beauty. By allowing ourselves to be drawn into this complex state, he thinks, we learn more fully to understand our relationship to aesthetic beauty and the blindness to daily life that its perception frequently involves.

The dreamy state Zamir describes may not, however, be so favorable to the appreciation of human interactions or deep human meaning. Certainly the play *Romeo and Juliet* could not be understood at all from the detached transcendent point of view.

I prefer one of Zamir's rejected interpretations: the play as a whole, including those dreamy stretches, shows the infantile narcissism of very young love. This love is in a sense beautiful. But it has nothing to do with true concern for another human being, or even with delighted sexual reciprocity: idealizing someone is far removed from responsiveness to that person's needs. Indeed, it is so contemptuous of the body that it's hard to see it yielding any satisfactory type of sexual interaction. These very young people more or less forget that they have bodies—perhaps because their bodies are so fit and healthy that they do not call attention to themselves.[12] The body is just an attractive form, not a real pulsing entity with hungers and limits. That's a very immature attitude to bodies, unlikely to withstand the reality of life with another person. Indeed, the persistence of this immature attitude is the cause of many breakups later in life.

So: teenagers, whether male or female (and whether older or younger!) are just not good at erotic love with a real person.[13]

Now we turn to *Antony and Cleopatra*.[14] That play depicts what we might call mature love, love between people who enjoy being grown-ups together and who have no project of transcending human life, because they are having too much fun in life as it is. Romeo and Juliet don't eat; Antony and Cleopatra eat all the time. Romeo and Juliet have no occupation; Antony and Cleopatra are friends and supportive colleagues with a great deal of work to do running their respective and interlocking empires. Romeo and Juliet have no sense of humor; Antony and Cleopatra live by elaborate jokes and highly personal forms of teasing (what Zamir calls "idiosyncratic practices") ("That time,—Oh times!—I laugh'd him out of patience"). Romeo and Juliet, utterly absorbed, pay no attention to others around them; Antony and Cleopatra love to gossip about the odd people in their world, spend evenings wandering through the streets watching the funny things people do. Romeo and Juliet speak to one another only in terms of worshipful hyperbole. Antony knows how to make contact with Cleopatra through insults, even about her age (he calls her his "serpent of old Nile"); she knows how to turn a story about a fishhook into a running joke that renews laughter each time it is mentioned. All this suggests a romance that, unlike that of the younger couple (as Zamir says), "does not work through transcending life, through perpetually setting its intensities at odds with what life is, but rather structures itself through life and the daily pleasures it affords."[15]

One sign of the difference is the role played by time. Romeo and Juliet are aware of the hours of the day and night, but not, or barely, of the seasons of the year and the years of a life. The love of Antony and Cleopatra is itself a piece of time. As in history, so here: they are together for at least a decade, and the texture of time past, present, and future constantly seasons their love.

The human body is a river of time, not an ideal aesthetic form. And Antony and Cleopatra pay attention to one another's real bodies, not to an idealized image of the body. And (by contrast to the teenage lovers) the body is always seen as animated by a lively searching and idiosyncratic mind that makes contact with another particular mind through intimate conversation. Cleopatra is clearly supposed to be attractive, but, as Zamir notes, the play, by contrast to Shakespeare's sources, downplays this aspect. It is her complicated personality, full of surprises, to which Shakespeare most draws our attention. ("Age cannot wither her, nor custom stale her infinite variety.") Her mode of seduction is above all mental. "Cunning past men's thought," as Antony describes her, she ingeniously elaborates a whole battery of stratagems to keep herself in the forefront of his attention: flirtation, capricious annoyance, the constant private teasing, frustrating allusions to significant undelivered information; but also, shared ambition, trusting collaboration, sincere deeply felt admiration for his achievements, insistence on her own equality. (Charmian advises deference and flattery; she, appropriately contemptuous: "Thou teachest like a fool; the way to lose him.")

Our teenage lovers seem totally unaware that every human being has flaws and personal vulnerabilities that real love needs to handle gently and respectfully. Not so these aging lovers. In the scene after the battle of Actium, Cleopatra expresses her love for Antony in her delicate attunement to the phases of Antony's career, her subtle sense of when to approach him and of what should and should not be said. Critics rarely give Cleopatra the credit for empathy that she clearly deserves.

But does she really love Antony? In part because many critics don't like Cleopatra, feeling that any such complicated, capricious, and powerful woman must be incapable of love, we have to raise this question.

Perhaps it is prompted, too, by the fact that this aging love lacks so much of what we culturally associate with ideal love: it has no outsize rapture, it is so immersed in the daily movement of work and conversation. Zamir, who is unduly obsessed with this question, eventually finds an affirmative answer in the scene in which news of Antony's marriage to Octavia is delivered to Cleopatra by a messenger—whom she first upbraids and then, in a childish tantrum, drags physically around the room by his hair. (Stage direction: "She hales him up and down.") Her angry reaction, says Zamir, must convince "even the most cynical of audiences that this woman's love . . . is genuine."

But this is far too simple. First of all, jealousy is no proof of love. It can as easily or more easily, be a proof of a longing for control that is poisonous to love. But in any case, Cleopatra's reaction is not a pure case of erotic jealousy. It cannot be, since Cleopatra knows the marriage, politically motivated, isn't based on overwhelming passion. And she intuits quickly that Octavia is no rival in brains or fascination. It is important that Octavia is described as "of a holy, cold, and still conversation." With her "modest eyes and still conclusion," she "shows a body rather than a life." (In fairness to Octavia, we should observe that, though the first of these judgments comes from the relatively impartial Enobarbus, the second remarkable insult is uttered by Cleopatra herself, the third by that same messenger, no doubt averse to a second "haling," and seeing exactly what Cleopatra wants to think about Antony's marital relationship.) So jealousy, focused on the sexuality and spirit of the rival, is not what her emotion is. She does eventually get round to asking what Octavia looks like, but that's an afterthought, well after that unfortunate messenger has been dragged about, *and* after she has asked him, three times, "He is married?"

It's not erotic jealousy, then, it is frustration at the circumstances of her life. This woman, who is at the top of her game, who is unique, who has wit, achievement, success, glamour, who rules a kingdom—sees suddenly that she is circumscribed in love by a contractual relationship. This fact seems to her so completely outrageous and absurd that she can only react by behaving, herself, in an absurd, even infantile, way.

She does love him, but it is not jealousy that is the proof, it is her regal protest against mere social impediments—and, far more, her utterly submissive tolerance of them, as she accepts and lives with—manhandled messenger notwithstanding—the limitations entailed by his news. (But does she really accept limitation, or is all that dragging by the hair, that funny threat to put the messenger in brine and turn him into a pickle, itself one more outsized joke, a theatrical display of determination and indomitability? She's certainly capable of games more elaborate by far. An actress might play the scene in many ways.) In short: there's a proof of love in that very acceptance of limit. Octavia doesn't have to love passionately, because her contract has a different basis, and it is what it is whether she loves him or not. Time itself is the evidence of Cleopatra's love.

More generally, aging love always has baggage. Everyone has a past and a present, and all of that challenges the relationship. Time can be a source of richness; it can be a source of pain. It can be both at the same time. What is certain is that living with a partner's whole past and present life is a huge challenge that young lovers do not have to face, and facing it well requires many qualities—a sense of one's own limits, humor, altruism, endurance, humility, self-knowledge—that young lovers are not called upon to develop.

Romeo and Juliet's love transfigured the world by raising love into the heavens: Juliet is the sun, and, as with the sun, we have no idea what, if anything, makes her laugh. Antony and Cleopatra transfigure the world from within, making each daily experience more vivid, funny, and surprising. Without each other, they both feel, the world is sadly boring. "Shall I abide in this dull world," she asks him as he dies, "which in thy absence is no better than a sty?" What's piggish, in her book, is not the body, it's the absence of interesting conversation. So the world needs to be transfigured here too, but the transfiguration is human and particular, rather than celestial and abstract.

Philosophy is almost entirely silent on the topic of erotic love in an aging woman. (Even Beauvoir ignores the topic.) More generally, no philosopher I know of has ever given a decent account of the complexities of "mature love" in any sort of couple. Nor is this failure just an accident, or a social fact about cultural reticence. Philosophy needs literature at this point. Abstract prose by itself could not convey the quirky uneven particularistic nature of this type of love, the way genuine feeling is embodied in a fish story. The experience of the spectator or reader, as she goes through the variegated moods of this relationship, is epistemically significant, putting her in a position to make and assess claims about "mature" love as no abstract account could.

So what do we learn from this woman, who, unlike the Marschallin, makes a deep, satisfying, and mature choice? We see that mature love is both sexual and personal and that its sexuality is itself personal, based upon memory, humor, shared history. For that reason it has a depth that youthful love can't have, and that the Marschallin's vain attempt to find love with a seventeen-year-old could never deliver. Love in an aging woman brings with it, or can, a sense of time that makes the bodies of both lovers concrete particulars, rather than fantasized ideals, and this is in many ways deeply satisfying, involving acceptance of oneself and one's finitude, and that of one's lover (of whatever age, but much older than seventeen!). Love in an aging woman also has a social context and a politics that may enrich the love, but may also limit it and hem it in. For Antony and Cleopatra, love is comic because of its bodily and daily texture, and for that reason it is also tragic, open to huge and irreparable loss.

Aging Women as Movie Stars

Aging women used to be totally neglected in the movies—or, if they appeared at all, they would be displayed as mothers and grandmothers, never as romantic and sexual partners. The demographics of the baby boomer generation, together with the fact that aging people appear to be more likely to go out to the movies, rather than sticking to TV or video, has given rise to a niche market, and we are seeing a steady stream of movies about aging women having sexual relationships and falling in love. We can get some insight into contemporary views, meanwhile following the thread of our discussion of mature love and time, by thinking about four recent films: *Something's Gotta Give* (2003), starring Diane Keaton and Jack Nicholson; *It's Complicated* (2009), starring Meryl Streep, Alec Baldwin, and Steve Martin; *I'll See You in My Dreams* (2015), starring Blythe Danner and Sam Elliott; and, saving the best for last, *The Hundred-Foot Journey* (2014), starring Helen Mirren and Om Puri.

Some general observations first. The women in these movies range in actual actor age at time of release from fifty-seven (Keaton) to seventy-two (Danner). (I could also have included the marvelous pair of eighty-year-olds Judi Dench and Maggie Smith, in *The Best Exotic Marigold Hotel* [2011] and its 2015 sequel—but for the fact that these frothy movies are much less interesting.) The women are depicted as, and are, extremely attractive, both to men of roughly their own age and to much younger men (the depressed young pool cleaner in *I'll See You*, who has a crush on Danner but never expresses it physically, and above all the attractive doctor played by Keanu Reeves in *Something*, who seriously and for a considerable time dates Keaton, twenty years his senior). They are most definitely interested in sex, not just in companionship, or sentiment, although they ultimately prefer love to sex without love. And the men respond to their aliveness.

One must immediately introduce a qualification. These movies all suggest that aging women, if they are to remain sexually attractive, have to take care of themselves much more carefully than men of the same age. There is no female Alec Baldwin or Jack Nicholson, paunchy and overindulged; no female Om Puri, face scarred and pitted. They do have wrinkles, and Mirren in particular has made much of not having cosmetic surgery and not even doing much about exercise; but she looks better than she did at forty. They must, accordingly, have a degree of affluence that permits self-care. They do not have to be queens, but they all have money—and the fine portrayal of aging by Patricia Arquette in *Boyhood* (2014) shows that age takes its toll more rapidly in a different social class. Although these films do not endorse the lies of Richard Strauss, then, they do narrow the criteria for continuing sexual attractiveness, in a gender-unequal and class-unequal way.

Another interesting thread linking these films is that, with the exception of Danner's character, who lives on inherited money, these women are successful working women, and they are happily involved in and at the top of their professions. One bakery owner (Streep), one famous chef (Mirren), one playwright (Keaton). In all three cases, which are also the most convincing and appealing cases of aging sexuality, the women's Cleopatra-esque intelligence and mastery (not exclusive of earthiness, humor, and vulnerability) is a large part of their romantic appeal.

But before we can discuss the types of love and sexuality displayed in these movies, we need to describe the movies themselves briefly, focusing on the central relationships:

Something's Gotta Give (2003). Keaton and Nicholson act their real-life ages, at time of filming fifty-six and sixty-three. Keaton plays a successful playwright with a temporary writer's block. Nicholson is a playboy who dates younger women; he strikes up a relationship with Keaton's daughter. When they go to the beach house for a tryst, they are surprised to discover Keaton there, and sparks of wit and hostility fly between Keaton and Nicholson. Nicholson has a sudden heart attack, and is cared for in the hospital by an attractive doctor age thirty-six, played by Keanu Reeves, who develops a crush on Keaton. Convalescing at Keaton's house (and having broken up with her daughter), Nicholson becomes fascinated by Keaton, and they have a brief affair, but, as is his pattern, he simply walks away, leaving her angry enough to write him into her highly successful play. The two meet up again at the play's opening—Keaton is now dating Reeves—and this time Nicholson, chastened and lonely, decides that he wants a real relationship. They get married.

It's Complicated (2009). The three stars have the following real ages at the time of the film's release: Meryl Streep, sixty; Alec Baldwin, fifty-one; Steve Martin, sixty-four. Streep plays a successful bakery owner who is divorced from Alec Baldwin, who has remarried. Meeting up in connection with their children, they start having a secret affair. Meanwhile, Streep begins to fall for the architect who is working on her house (Martin). Eventually the Streep-Baldwin affair ends, and Streep and Martin end up together.

I'll See You in My Dreams (2015). At the time of release, Blythe Danner was seventy-two, Sam Elliott seventy. Danner plays a rich widow who lives in a nice house with a pool, tended by a depressed young man who develops a crush on her. She hangs out with a group of women who live in an elite seniors community; with them, she starts trying to meet men—after not dating for many years, and after her beloved dog dies. Sam Elliott spots her while they are shopping and begins to pursue her. A rich retiree with a yacht, he convinces her to date him and they begin a sexual relationship, her first in many years. Meanwhile, with the support of Lloyd the pool boy, she rediscovers her love of singing. Elliott suddenly dies of a heart attack.

The Hundred-Foot Journey (2014). Madame Mallory (Mirren, age sixty-eight at the time of release) runs a famous French restaurant in a rural French town. A family of Indians arrives in the town more or less by accident; under the aegis of the family's father (Puri, age sixty-three at the time of release), they open an Indian restaurant across the street from the great chef's establishment. Much of the plot concerns the efforts of the Indian son to become a top-of-the-line French chef, his on-and-off romance with a young French woman, and his rise to culinary stardom—eventually with the aid of Mme. Mallory herself. Along the way, however, a bitter and hilarious rivalry between the two restaurants makes comic enemies of Mirren and Puri, who scheme against one another and show contempt for one another's rival styles—pure high-end cuisine on the one hand, earthy delicious Indian food on the other. These same contrasting styles embodied in the two people lead, gradually, to romance, as Mirren's aloofness gives way before Puri's earthy physicality, and as she elicits his hidden grace and graciousness. (The scene in which the two dance together silently, alone in the restaurant, is a triumph worthy of Shakespeare.)

All right, what do we observe? First, we learn that both women and men cease being either sexy or romantic when they have no work to do. The warm reviews that greeted *I'll See You* are utterly incomprehensible to me, almost as incomprehensible as the overpraise of *Rosenkavalier*. The whole world depicted in the movie is boring, and even repugnant, and so are the people in it—because they are parasites. That is the word that kept coming into my head as I watched. The single women depicted, Danner and her female friends Rhea Perlman and June Squibb, have no interests and no conversation. All they do is play bridge and go speed dating. None has even a serious hobby. None cares about politics or culture, or what is happening in the larger world. None has any altruism or any aspiration. Exactly the same is true of Elliott, who smokes revolting cigars and boasts about his yacht. Danner and he deserve each other, since neither has deep emotions, or any discernible inner life. Since Danner is a fine actress, she does gesture at a real vulnerable person, and the scene in which she redis-covers sexual desire would be appealing, were it not for the total blank with whom she is playing it. But it is only the hapless pool boy and failed poet (Martin Starr) who inspires real sympathy, since only he has a dream and a commitment. The lesson of this disastrous and unpleasant film is that human complexity itself is vulnerable: use it or lose it.

A corollary of this observation is that money cannot buy love, and when one has no work to do it is a great hindrance to real love, encour-aging lassitude and detachment from life. Money up to a point is a good thing; the lovers in the other two movies are clearly advantaged in life and love by being reasonably comfortable and being able to do work that they care about rather than just getting by. Of the whole group only Puri's character has a history of real poverty, and his indomitable face evinces a special sort of dedication to work that comes from the determination to survive. (Puri, a lead actor for decades in Bollywood films, where he has often played heavies, has a Shakespearean weight that comes in part from the suffering expressed by the pits and lines in his face and the folds in his body. He died in January 2017.)

Like Puri and unlike Danner and Elliott, all of the other lovers are very much alive—and that is in large part because, with or without love, they have a lot of work to do. They are not waiting around for love to strike out of the blue, and none is depressed. They are excellent profes-sionals pursuing excellence, and that makes it possible for them to find love, since they are immersed in life. In other words, professional com-mitment, far from being a distraction from personal life, is a great help to it in later years, keeping the whole personality vivid and vigorous. The two women love their work and are widely admired for it. Puri identifies deeply with the family enterprise; although he is not a creative talent, he is a clever businessman. Baldwin is a successful lawyer; although we hear little about love of work, he is clearly intellectually vibrant. The odd one in this group is Martin, whose character, a fine architect, is supposed to be a visionary romantic creative personality. But Martin is just miscast in that sort of role, and he only ends up looking awkward and unconvincing. The movie is therefore unbalanced: we want Streep to end up with Baldwin.

Is Keanu Reeves unconvincing as a lover of Keaton's for similar reasons (bad casting, bad acting)? I don't think so. He is a good actor, and he plays well the role that has been written for him. The script does make us think that his youth is a big disadvantage, in terms of understanding his complicated lover and matching her in wit and self-knowledge; but his age (thirty-six) is not the real problem. The real problem is his flat do-gooder seriousness; he's a committed doctor with little humor or challenge. He is just too sweetly bland. In short, it is not that he is a younger man, it is that he is a boring younger man, and he would have become a boring older man—whereas Nicholson was intensely interesting even when young (as in *Five Easy Pieces*). Mature love wants something different.

Shakespeare's insights hold up remarkably well in a new era. Mature love is compelling to the extent that people bring to it their past, the vicissitudes of their lengthy lives, and a sense of both comedy and tragedy that comes from constant awareness of the past. They are ready to be human, we might say, because they no longer expect everything to be perfect, and they have all suffered loss. They are comfortable in their bodies, because they understand that the body is funny as well as potentially tragic. The wonderful zest of the sex between Streep and Baldwin comes in large part from this sense of inhabited time, as the two actors very convincingly create a whole history and inhabit it with comic acceptance. (This is yet one further reason why the new relationship with Martin is unconvincing.) In fact (to continue a motif of my *Rosenkavalier* discussion), their sexual relationship is convincing in part because they know one another's different phases or strata, as Baldwin reveals a childlike self that Streep has obviously uncovered and gratified before.

The other two women are initially a provocative counterpoint—both to their men and to Streep—since both Keaton and Mirren are initially self-protective and aloof. Keaton has to some extent retreated from emotional life, living in her solitary beach house and experiencing life through her writing. Mirren is so successful that everyone is afraid of her, and she has become unaccustomed to being human. In both cases, roguish and unchivalrous men bring them back to vulnerable humanity through a combination of humor and, in Puri's case, initial hostility, and the two women enjoy the rediscovery of their own vulnerability. (I note that this theme is an old one in Hollywood romantic comedy, and has been shrewdly studied by Stanley Cavell, especially apropos of Katherine Hepburn, in his wonderful *Pursuits of Happiness*.)[16] But it's not that the men are creeps: the women elicit their capacity for respect, decency, and even grace.

Movies tell many lies about aging, and, especially, about aging women. They used to be far more in hock to stigmatizing mendacity, even, than Richard Strauss, who at least gives the Marschallin some extremely beautiful music to sing. The longevity and determination of a set of impressive actresses, together with directors and screenwriters willing to take a risk to tell their story, has made the world of our popular culture a more truthful and also a more Shakespearean place.

But wait a moment. Hasn't this entire essay been built upon a lie—and the most common, and perhaps most baneful, lie of all? That is, the staggering lie that love arrives only in neat couples, and that a person can love only one person at a time. Choosing a new lover means rejecting the old, and the destiny of woman is to be with one man ever after—or at least with a succession of ones. These movies all end with the "true love" being discovered and embraced (or in the case of Blythe Danner, mourned). And any other love has to be banished, especially in America. Life, however, is so much more untidy and so much richer in possibilities for happiness. Aging women should have learned a thing or two about the limitations of emotional exclusivity. Why, for example, should Diane Keaton not date both Keanu Reeves and Jack Nicholson, but for the fact that audiences demand a tidy resolution, and thus the filmmakers feel constrained to make Reeves boring and Nicholson overwhelmingly more interesting. Why, too, should Streep not continue her affair with her ex-husband while trying to find out whether Steve Martin has any capacity for humor or playfulness? But again, audiences would never permit that. These women still basically believe the old Cinderella story—because audiences believe it.

Real life is better, or can be. So in addition to the sexiness of older women, Hollywood now should take on a new challenge: the real complexities of human affections, and the joy that can be derived from openness to surprise, when cultural shibboleths about "the only one" are banished.

Notes

1. I say "major," not "great," because many are rightly skeptical of its faux senti-mentality. Strauss did write one great and utterly nonmendacious opera, *Elektra* (1909). But, perhaps jolted by the irate reaction to this experimental and pro-found work, he turned thereafter primarily to kitsch.

2. Burton D. Fischer, *Richard Strauss's "Der Rosenkavalier"* (New York: Opera Journeys, 2011), 30.

3. Fischer, *Richard Strauss's "Der Rosenkavalier,"* 31.

4. Here lies a major difference from *The Marriage of Figaro*, this opera's admitted prototype: for Rosina (the Countess) passionately loves her husband, and has been loved by him. What she wants is the return of that love, and maybe she gets it and maybe she doesn't. In any case, she meanwhile has a sane and appropri-ately cautious view of the ardor of Cherubino.

5. Donald Winnicott, "The Capacity for Concern" (1963), in *The Maturational Processes and the Facilitating Environment* (Madison, CT: International Universities Press, 1965), 76.

6. In earlier eras there is more flexibility—largely because many such transgender roles were sung by castrati, who could credibly impersonate mature and power-ful men while singing in a soprano or mezzo register.

7. E. M. Forster, *Maurice* (New York: Norton, 1971), 250. I apologize for focusing henceforth in this essay on straight couples, but I think the issues are compara-ble for gay and trans couples. Cleopatra, after all, was played by a male actor.

8. The standard solution, in the writings of Grisez, Finnis, and George, is to assert that heterosexual relations with a woman past menopause are "the right sort of thing" to engender a child, if there were no bodily impediment. Who knows? There might be a miracle. This view gives God insufficient credit for inven-tion: for if a miracle can cause a woman in her sixties to become pregnant, why could God not arrange a pregnancy for two men: new organs miraculously appear!

9. See Blakey Vermeule, *Why Do We Care about Literary Characters* (Baltimore, MD: Johns Hopkins University Press, 2011).

10. *Julius Caesar* and *Coriolanus* seem to be exceptions, but it is difficult to name any other.

11. See Zamir, *Double Vision: Moral Philosophy and Shakespearean Drama* (Princeton, NJ: Princeton University Press, 2007).

12. Compare Plato's account of why gymnastics is important for the young: if your body is fit and well trained, you can more easily ignore its demands (*Republic* II).

13. Juliet's age is specified as almost fourteen; Romeo is somewhat older, but prob-ably not as old as eighteen, which would have involved him in adult military responsibilities.

14. To dispose of the age question: historically speaking, Cleopatra (69–30 B.C.E.) is almost forty, and Antony (83–30 B.C.E.) fourteen years older. In terms of dramatic depiction, however, they appear to be coeval, and Antony certainly has the infantile side as already mentioned, so he appears at times younger. History typically contrasts Cleopatra's romance with the much older Julius Caesar (100–44 B.C.E.) with her romance with Antony, who is typically depicted as childlike and somewhat passive. But she did bear children to both (Caesarion was born in 47 B.C.E., when she was twenty-two; Cleopatra Selene was born to Cleopatra and Antony in around 40 B.C.E., and lived to 6 B.C.E.; her twin brother, Alexander Helios, died shortly after his parents, as did a younger brother, Ptolemy Philadelphus); so her real-life age is significant to at least that extent.

15. Zamir, *Double Vision*.

16. Cambridge, MA: Harvard University Press, 1981.

The Adventures of Ben Franklin, Ivana Trump, and Rejected Lovers of All Ages

Saul

"NOTHING VENTURED, NOTHING GAINED" is a confusing aphorism attributed to Benjamin Franklin. Franklin himself ventured at all ages. He was a significant publisher at age twenty-three and, eventually, governor of Pennsylvania until age eighty-two. He also ventured in his personal relationships. He advised men to prefer older women, and we can surmise that during the first half of his adult life he had experiences upon which he based this advice. But as he aged, he apparently enjoyed relations with a series of much younger women. Operas may lead us to think about younger men with much older women, recent movies encourage us to see that spontaneous romance is available to mature couples, and we have plenty of experience in both fiction and everyday life with gap couples, as I will call them, where the man is significantly older than the woman. (I do not mean to limit my observations here to straight couples, as will become apparent.) It is interesting that Ben Franklin says nothing about relationships between people of similar age, who are most likely to have things in common, and yet these appeal most to Martha Nussbaum. If I picture Martha herself enjoying Ben's wit and attention, it is either when they are of similar ages or when Ben is much younger than she. In this essay, I explore the question of whether aging ought to bring adventure, or should instead encourage people to double down on their relationships. I work toward the idea that in the near future we might see many more relationships between older women and younger men.

Let me begin with two observations about gap couples. The first is about finances and the second concerns parental influence. It is hard to find examples of significant age gaps (where the older person is more than one and a half times the younger person's age, let us say, and) where the older partner does not offer significant financial security to the younger one. Some younger women may prefer older men because they are more interesting or have more life experience, but it is telling that affluent women rarely find much-older, working-class or impoverished men so interesting. If there is a cultural distaste for these double-gap couples, of significantly different ages *and* economic circumstances, it is because the parties are not trusted, and the relationships cause us to fear that love is overly commodified. The relationship can seem like the modern version of an arranged marriage or even a business arrangement that is primarily in the older person's interest; romantics rarely find these attractive. As an illustrative example, when Donald Trump was thirty-one, he married Ivana, who was close in age; long after their divorce, which left her wealthy, Ivana married someone twenty-three years younger than herself. At age forty-seven, Donald Trump's second marriage was to a thirty-year-old. And his third marriage, at age fifty-nine, was to a woman who was thirty-five, though their relationship began when she was thirty-three. The pattern is not terribly unusual for a very wealthy man, and perhaps especially so for one involved in the real-estate and entertainment industries. It is, however, remarkable for a woman. Susan Sarandon is an exception, having twice married and remained for some time with a much younger man. She has described "soul" as more important than age in her choice of partners. That would have been a nice or even strategic thing for Trump to have said when running for president, but his comments about love interests seemed directed at male rather than female voters. In any event, the point is not the familiar one about men enjoying greater age range than women in their searches, but rather that it is wealthy people who attract much younger partners. It is no accident that the young Ben Franklin took up with older women of means, who introduced him to luxuries.

When a woman in her twenties is attracted to an older man, onlookers often say that she is looking for a father figure. If the woman is twice that age, and the man again twice her age, observations are more likely to concern wealth and life expectancy. Somewhat similarly and equally annoying, a younger man who finds a mature female partner might be accused of looking for someone to mother him. Such claims are common if the younger person were orphaned or abandoned at a young age, but I can find no statistical evidence that there is any connection between one's relationship with a parent and the age of one's spouse. Moreover, my observation of more than thirty years of students' personal choices is that there has been a profound shift in the connection between upbringing and marriage. In the 1970s and 1980s many young Americans had difficult relationships with their parents, and went through periods of rebellion and estrangement. The era was one on which parents were encouraged to set firm rules because children were said to need and want boundaries. It was also a period of political and social upheaval. It was an insult to tell a romantic partner: "You remind me of my (or your) mother." My generation was escaping from the influence of the previous generation, or at least it thought it was. Movies like *The Graduate* (1967) reflect this style of coming of age. But all this seems bewildering to today's university students. Their parents have been encouraged to be supportive rather than authoritarian, and it is much easier to have affection for those who support us through thick and thin. Parents can now be one's best friends, and they provide support rather than fear or constant judgment. Consequently, it is now completely natural to hear a twenty-something say that he or she is looking for a partner who is like his or her father or mother. Today's twenty-somethings want their parents to approve of their romantic choices. Martha notices Diane Keaton and Jack Nicholson coming together in *Something's Gotta Give* (2003), but when I saw that film my focus was on Diane Keaton's obsession with her daughters' approval, and they with hers. If rebellion is partly responsible for gap couples, then we might see fewer of these when our most-supported generation matures.

Supportive parenting may also have something to do with the trend toward later marriages and toward unmarried children returning to their parents' homes, and living under one roof. These developments are usually associated with education and a tough employment market, respectively, but it is easy to confuse cause and effect, and there are probably multiple causes for each of these phenomena. Still, positive parenting seems likely to bring about more caregiving by children, as their parents age. If so, we might see yet further change in the residential patterns of our elderly citizens, as multigeneration living may come back into vogue.

In drawing attention to the pattern of increasing age gaps in President Trump's marriages, I intended to highlight not just the hidden variable of economic dependence but also the fact that age gaps are often found in second or third marriages. When men separate from partners of their own age and reignite with much younger women, they are often maligned by (older) women—even if they are (or think they are) envied by other aging men. Critical observers sometimes think of the males in these couples as immature, as having trouble coming to grips with middle age, and as embarking on a hopeless or even pathetic venture. A younger woman at one's side will not, after all, reverse the aging process. But the same criticism could be directed back at many aging women. If men are doomed to disappointment because they will age regardless of their trophy companions, then women will also age regardless of their plastic surgeries—a topic taken up at some length in chapter 4. The differences between these strategies are interesting. First, plastic surgery is victimless, but gap-coupling leaves a wounded party if it is preceded by the breakup of a long-term relationship. The second difference incorporates the asymmetry developed in chapter 4; many women fear that a younger partner highlights their more advanced age, while men somehow feel younger, or are more boastful or vigorous, when paired with a much younger partner. Generalities have so many exceptions that they are painful to advance, but there may be something to the idea that many women care more about how they appear while more men care about what they have acquired or attracted.

Gap couples fit awkwardly in social settings, even when no earlier partner was rejected in favor of a younger one. Public displays of affection by gap couples often make onlookers uncomfortable. The older partner is not easily included in social events arranged by the younger partner's friends. Each partner is likely to maintain friends of his and her own age, and there is less integration of the friendship groups than with most similarly aged partners. We do not expect Melania Trump's friends to know her husband, Donald, well. It saddens me to think that she probably had difficulty making new friends, and the problem is yet worse for a First Lady. It is difficult to imagine other mothers in her kid's (Barron's) school befriending her. And inasmuch as she immigrated as an adult, she is unlikely to have many long-term friends nearby. Nor does she have peers in a workplace or another source of new friends.

Ivana Trump, Donald's first spouse, also found a newer model after she and Donald Trump split, and she emerged from the divorce with substantial wealth. But Donald's second wife, the American actress Marla Maples, has not gap-coupled; she probably had few opportunities to do so because her divorce from Trump was, apparently, governed rather strictly by a prenuptial agreement. Marla does not seem to attract sympathy, perhaps because she was ousted in the very manner in which she had previously displaced another. The lack of sympathy for this rejected woman may also reflect acceptance of freely negotiated bargains. Marla knew what she was getting into, had agreed to a prenup, did not (unlike Ivana) add great value by running a Trump business, and was probably not surprised when her run on the Trump stage came to an end. Ivana's situation lets us separate romantic rejection from economic dependence. The split might be seen as a kind of breach of contract, as discussed presently, but the financial outcome dramatically mitigates any claim of wrongdoing.

LET ME SHIFT gears and consider two young people who begin dating one another at a time of life when a permanent and long-term partnership is on their minds. Imagine that Deborah is smitten with Ben, and when Ben ends the relationship after a few months, Deborah is crushed. Heartless as it sounds, Deborah should be grateful. She is, by hypothesis, looking for a long-term partner, and Ben has helped Deborah by encouraging her to move on and look elsewhere. Most of us do not want to love people who do not love us in return, and so we can imagine that Deborah is unlikely to want a relationship with Ben if the latter no longer reciprocates. She might be disappointed, but it can hardly be a tragedy to search for a partner, develop a relationship, enjoy time together, and then learn that at least one person in the pair thinks the relationship ought to end. None of us really expects or wants everyone in the world to find us desirable and suitable. We may want a chance for the other person to get to know us but, after a few months of dating, Ben is probably in a good position to assess whether his relationship with Deborah is enduring. Deborah is lucky that Ben is decisive and honest; the rejection is good news, or at least that is my claim. (History-minded readers will notice that Deborah was the given name of Ben Franklin's common-law wife. The similarity ends there, however, as Deborah Franklin remained a kind of part-time spouse because of her Ben's foreign trips and dalliances.)

When I advance this optimistic view of rejection, young people like the present-day Deborah often say something like, "I am upset because if Ben had invested a little more, he would have come to see that we are perfect for one another." Perhaps. On the other hand, Ben has similar goals, and there is every reason to think that he has thought about the benefits of trying harder. For every happy ending where one party talked the other into rethinking a rejection and trying harder, there are probably three or four where, after the fact, at least one of the parties thinks that the relationship should have ended earlier, so that both could have moved on with their lives. As is often the case, my inner economist tells me that the right way to think about things is to be forward-looking. The months or years sunk into a relationship are gone, and hopefully they were intrinsically reward-ing. Life is a journey, not a destination, as the saying goes. I think of this as the optimist-economist's view of rejection.

This rosy and counterintuitive view of rejection extends to other endeavors where there is a kind of sorting going on. It can, for example, be good to be fired from a job, because it is an opportunity to look else-where and find a job where one will flourish. In turn, many employers come to learn that firing an employee is not as horrible as it seems; often the employee will benefit when forced to move on to something else.

It goes without saying that it would be more convenient to be rejected early on by a potential employer, and perhaps even by a potential roman-tic partner. The longer one stays in a position, the harder the forced departure. Losing a job is painful in part because one has invested a good deal in coworkers and in the skills required for the job. The sort of cold, search-theory view of rejection that I advance here suggests that the benefit of a romantic rebuff or re-entry into the marketplace declines with age. If I have forty years of work ahead of me, then rejection by an employer is valuable now because I can get back to the task of looking for more fulfilling work, where appreciation runs in both directions. But if I expect to retire in three years, further search is less valuable, and rejection by an employer will be crushing and disheartening. Is the same true for love?

The forward-looking, optimistic claim about the end of a relationship is harder to swallow the longer the relationship. If my spouse announced tomorrow that she would like to move on and end our relationship after three decades of marriage, I am sure I would not be cheerful about it, despite my inner economist. In principle I should be grateful for the rejec-tion; I want what is good for her, and if she is sure that I am no longer an asset in her calculation, then perhaps I should trust her judgment. Besides, what fun would it be to find that someone stayed with you just to avoid hurting your feelings? I would surely feel sadness, and perhaps I would sink into bitterness, though I cannot imagine that, inasmuch as I am forward-looking. The question is whether the inevitable sadness is the product of a kind of irrational, backward-looking calculation. The many years of marriage might seem false or wasted; the rejected party might feel abandoned and yet wronged for not having been told sooner to go invest in another. But we know not to say that it would have been better never to have loved at all. Nothing ventured, nothing gained, and all that. Perhaps the spouse who leaves is just as surprised and disappointed as the one who is rejected. There must be something more to the sadness of rejection after many years.

CONSIDER, AS SOMETHING OF AN ANALOGY, the phenomenon of mourning. Here the forward-looking economist claims to be a realist rather than an optimist. If a friend or family member dies, the forward-looking person might like to say: "I loved this person, but he is now dead. There is no point in feeling bad about that because grieving, like anger, is a waste of energy. I can switch instantly from news of the death to a forward-looking posture. It turns out I overinvested in this person, though the time spent together was good."

But this hypothetical economist is superhuman. Grieving rituals are so old and embedded in every culture that there must be something to them. One possibility is that mourning, and even wailing—as occurs in many societies, and seems triggered and authentic rather than staged—helps us think that when we die, others will care about us. The expectation that they will be grief-stricken when we pass on makes us feel better about our lives and our relationships with others. In turn, we invest in these relationships, and the entire community is strengthened. We learn or even evolve to dwell for a time on the death of another, as it contributes to our self-worth and effort far more than it wastes time and prevents us from being forward-looking. A second, better explanation that also fits the economist's forward-looking style is that mourning helps us appreciate our own mortality. Just as attending a wedding can lead to a resolve about one's own marriage, going forward, grieving at a funeral offers an opportunity to think about mortality, and to focus on leading a meaningful life in the time ahead.

One or both of these explanations about postdeath behavior illuminate the fragility that often follows the end of a romance. On the one hand, a forward-looking lover should accept rejection as useful news that it is time to move on and perhaps to invest in a new partner. But the pain of rejection, or simply of a failed relationship, might also be useful to a forward-looking person. It highlights the value of a relationship and encourages the person to appreciate the next one more, and also to work harder on it. Deborah's pain probably makes her—and Ben—take the next relationship more seriously.

As we age, these observations about romance and rejection take on slightly different forms. When rejection comes after many years, it is natural, though not forward-looking, for the rejected partner to feel betrayed and seriously wronged. If Ben leaves Deborah after twenty years together, she will feel cheated. She might say that she and Ben had a kind of mutual insurance policy. She would not have left him if he took ill, and she never sought out other partners in order to see whether she could do a bit better. She was committed for life to her relationship with Ben. When Ben says, "I just don't love you anymore, so what's the point," his friends might tell him what he wants to hear, that we only live once and should pursue the adventures that seem exciting. If Ben leaves because he has become attracted to a younger woman, Deborah is likely to feel especially wronged. This may be because she will feel that she gave up opportunities and her youthful attraction to Ben; in return, his inner compass should have prevented him from breaking the implicit or explicit contract.

But what if the aging Ben has really tried? Once we appreciate the value of rejection, but also perceive the decline in its value over time, there is also the question of when to try harder in a relationship or life endeavor, and when to avoid further disappointment. We can identify with both Ben and Deborah. Ben knows that Deborah has good qualities and has been a loyal partner; her commitment to Ben is valuable and may be the sort of thing that can make Ben very happy. But Ben needs to decide whether to stick with Deborah in order to allow the relationship to recover or to search for another partner. Does this depend on Ben's age? There are conflicting intuitions here. On the one hand, the older the couple, the more Ben should invest in rescuing the relationship both because he will cause more pain if he ends it and because he has fewer years remaining in which some hypothetical other relationship will really prove superior to the one he has already found. The contrary intuition is that Ben only lives once, and the longer he waits to make the break, the harder it will be for him and Deborah to recover. There may not be a single answer to this question, but the decision seems very different for the aging couple than for the young one.

A modern and revealing twist on this question involves the breakup of long-term couples because of sexual orientation. *Grace and Frankie* (2015), a popular Netflix series, gets to the point by beginning with the breakup of two forty-year marriages, with the men announcing they are leaving their spouses, played by Jane Fonda and Lily Tomlin, in order to be with each other. The men have been lovers, and not simply business partners, for the last twenty years, and they are now ready to be liberated and to wed one another. The plot thus taps into a reason for breakup that is hard to dispute in the modern era, and one that is not anyone's fault. The series has a grand old time exploring the lives of the aging, newly single women, brought together by their divorces. The modern, out-of-the-closet twist is a bit unfair. It prevents the audience from thinking that the men should work harder on their long-term marriages; the women should be understanding and even grateful that the competition was not younger women. And in case we need more help in seeing that it was time for these long-term marriages to end, the men, played by Martin Sheen and Sam Waterston, are just as quirky as the women, but they are written to be less controlling and self-absorbed. Finally, the lovers are of similar age, so we are not distracted by gap-coupling. The men's relationship is attractive, and we want their ex-wives to come to see that it is all for the best, despite their initial shock and claim of humiliation. If they are angry, it should be because the men were not honest much earlier. *Grace and Frankie* may not have the gravitas of a Strauss opera, but the central conceit rings true and supports the forward-looking view of relationships. The end of a long-term relationship is an opportunity rather than a tragedy. I'm inclined to think that Ben and Deborah, like the actual Franklins, should move on, just as Grace and Frankie's husbands do.

But why should anything be different if a long-term marriage ends not because it is finally safe to emerge from the closet, but because one of the parties has changed and recognized failings in the current relationship or anticipates adventure in a new relationship? A conventional view is that long-term partners have a contract (through marriage or otherwise) of mutual support through thick and thin. Lawyers might say that breach of this contract would be regarded as excused by impossibility, as contract law calls it, if one of the parties discovered or came to terms with a sexual identity that was inconsistent with the earlier contract. Impossibility follows because an underlying assumption of the contract is false. But law does not insist on adherence to conventional contracts that are not impossible to complete. It provides remedies for breach. Trump would say that when his marriage to Marla Maples ended, he paid exactly as their (prenuptial) contract demanded. In the absence of such an arrangement, a court can determine damages for breach, but it would be unusual to insist that a party must remain in a personal relationship. Promises can be broken, albeit with remedial consequences.

THIS, THEN, IS THE "LIE," if not one of many, that operas and films tell about aging men and women. It is not that aging people are sexless or unattractive. The lie is that there is a way of knowing whether a couple will continue to find both comfort and novelty together, or whether one or both will change and require a completely new adventure. It is easy to celebrate couples who stay together for fifty years, though the toastmaster always points out that there were some tough times the two must have worked through. It is more difficult to rejoice when a couple grows apart and the two proceed on separate journeys. But perhaps we ought to try to celebrate the energy and optimism that launch this next adventure.

I suspect that one reason we find breakups unnerving, and especially so when they are followed by gap-coupling, is that we have developed a strong preference for gender equality, and our experience is that when a couple divides, the aging man has more romantic opportunities ahead of him than does the aging woman. If he has such a relationship in progress, and it is with a much younger partner, the breakup seems worse. We regard this as unfair, and the only way we can protect the abandoned loser is to discourage breakups by applauding long-term couples and even regarding gap couples with disfavor. But if gap-coupling is largely limited to cases of economic inequality, then perhaps as more women join the 1 percent we will observe more older women with younger partners—and we will grow more comfortable with rejection followed by adventure. On the other hand, we may not see many gap couples with older women, if women (more than men) feel that they look older when standing next to a younger partner. This obsessive quest for youth in oneself rather than in one's partners might continue to make "reverse" gap-coupling unusual. Finally, the current pattern is self-sustaining. We have many Trumps, but few Sarandons and Marschallins. The French political sensation, Emmanuel Macron, was seventeen when he first proposed marriage to his wife (twenty-four years his senior), Brigitte Trogneux. She is sometimes described as Macron's coach, but not a mother figure or benefactor. In any event, romantic patterns in France are noted but rarely copied in the United States. In the absence of other role models, aging women may only rarely initiate romance with younger partners, or the other way around. But if this changes because of the rising number of self-made affluent women, then I suspect we will develop a new attitude toward gap couples and toward breakups as well. If aging is in part about becoming more comfortable in one's own skin, then we should hope for more adventures of this kind.

Chapter 7

Inequality and an Aging Population

THE PROBLEM OF growing inequality is all around us, and has permeated the political arena. Are the elderly poor a special problem? How might Social Security reform change things for the better, especially for people who have not saved for retirement? To what are the elderly entitled in an affluent and just society, and how can we deliver these things?

Inequality and the Elderly Poor

Saul

HOW CAN WE help the elderly poor? Most older Americans have ridden several waves of prosperity, so that the generation now retiring is the wealthiest the country has ever seen. But the most successful generation has its share of vulnerable members; there is a subset of elderly poor, and then millions of struggling retirees only slightly better off. This chapter offers a picture of wealth and poverty among aging Americans, and suggests a bold expansion of Social Security. It is a suggestion that many of us who are skeptical of big government will at first find implausible or unwise. The idea is to produce a "livable benefit" and to avoid costly political battles and class warfare.

Identifying the Elderly Poor

Let us begin with a snapshot of the problem, and some facts about wealth and poverty in the United States.[1] More than one-third of private wealth is held by 1 percent of the population, and the elderly are overrepresented in this group. At the same time, a majority of adults have insufficient savings to meet a modest emergency, and must anticipate assistance from the government, friends, or family. A bare majority has no retirement savings, though this category—like the inability to meet financial emergencies— excludes the equity value in homes. In the event of such crises, some of these people are able to sell assets or borrow, but many cannot, or do not know how to do so. Nearly all older Americans can rely on Social Security benefits, as only 3 or 4 percent of those beyond normal retirement age receive no Social Security benefits at all. This small group is comprised mostly of infrequent workers who never qualified for benefits and late-arriving immigrants. The group is disproportionately poor, but not dramatically unrepresentative of the population of that age in terms of gender and race.

It is apparent that most of the people normally labeled as the elderly poor are not penniless, but are instead without substantial savings and able to live only as well as various governmental programs, including Medicaid and Social Security, allow. The maximum annual Social Security benefit for a single person who retires at age sixty-six is, as of this writing, $31,668, but most recipients do not qualify for the maximum benefit. The average benefit is only about half that, while the minimum cost of living for a single person of that age who rents his or her residence, is calculated to be about $24,000. The poverty level is much lower than that, while the cost of living in expensive cities much higher. Social Security comprises at least 90 percent of income for 22 percent of older couples and for 45 percent of older singles. These Americans are in no danger of starving, but they are unable to visit far-away family members, travel to national parks, purchase tickets for concerts, or do many other things that an affluent society associates with retirement or simply with living life to its fullest.

But income is not the only source of economic security. Accumulated assets can be sold to finance one's retirement. Unfortunately, the data are a bit muddled when one tries to integrate information about income and assets. About half of households with a sixty-five- to seventy-four-year-old have ready retirement savings, half of these households have a defined benefit retirement plan (apart from Social Security), and thirty-six percent own an unmortgaged home. About 62 percent of older Americans who are categorized as poor, on the basis of income, have equity in their homes, and the average equity is $120,000. That does not change the picture much when spread over many years of retirement, but it does rule out serious poverty for a large subset of the elderly whose income alone puts them at or near the poverty line. These homeowners might borrow against their equity, so that their available income is $5,000 to $10,000 more than the $15,000 or $20,000 available from Social Security, depending on life expectancy and imputed interest rates. Many elderly people with low incomes do not live alone or have promised their homes to their children; family members provide support with an understanding that the family home will become theirs upon the death of the older generation. But data about these arrangements are not collected. It is estimated that about 10 percent of the 40 million Americans over age sixty-five fall below the poverty line.

Inequality among the Elderly

If the impoverished elderly comprise just a few percent of the population, why have we not done more for this group? It is well known that older citizens are reliable voters, and that they are fairly well organized through the AARP (the American Association of Retired Persons) and other means. In reforming the healthcare system and in other matters, politicians have seemed sensitive, if not beholden, to the elderly. It might, therefore, seem surprising to find this subgroup of elderly poor among us. There are several reasons why poverty among the elderly persists, and it is useful to understand this state of affairs in order to design solutions that have some chance of success.

The first thing to emphasize is that the mean and even median *wealth* of the elderly is an obstacle to reform. At the high end, we find Warren Buffett and many other older Americans among the very wealthiest. The media pay attention to young billionaires in Silicon Valley, but in fact about two-thirds of the few hundred wealthiest Americans are over sixty, and many are well above eighty. The more important part of the picture, however, captures normal households. There are millions of well-off people who accumulate wealth until retirement, and expect to spend it down or give it away in their retirement years. For the nonpoor, net worth generally increases until retirement, peaking at a median of about $200,000 for sixty-five- to sixty-nine-year-olds. It is about fifty times that for the top 1 percent of the cohort. If we include Social Security benefits (which are treated in the data as income rather than savings or assets), the net worth figures rise considerably for everyone. This wealth distribution, peaking at or soon after the median retirement age, is perfectly predictable once we take into account the pattern of savings for retirement.

It is also no surprise that the wealth gap between the old and the young has been growing. Growing inequality has received a great deal of attention, and so it may seem unsurprising to learn about this increasing gap between age groups. Thirty years ago, households headed by someone sixty-five or older were worth ten times as much as those headed by someone age thirty-five or younger; today this gap has ballooned so that the multiple is fifty. The elderly have become richer, while the younger adult cohorts have become poorer. Older Americans did well for themselves by investing in housing, but they also saved and invested a higher percentage of their earnings than do those who have followed them. Some of these people started out when the economy was booming, but many did not. To be fair, many members of the younger generation will catch up and out-do their parents' and grandparents' generations, because the net worth (and wealth) figures do not take human capital and the value of a college education into account. The younger cohorts started their careers at later ages. Many younger people with low net worth borrowed to finance their education, and the evidence suggests that this will prove to be a good investment. Still, the inescapable fact is that older people are on average significantly better off than are middle-aged and young taxpayers. The elderly might use political muscle to get more benefits, but it will not be on the basis of a moral claim that wealth ought to be redistributed and transferred to the older generation or to the poor among them.

The Problem of the Elderly Poor Will Not Be Solved with Simple Transfers

There are various proposals for transferring wealth to the neediest elderly.[2] Social Security benefits could be made wealth or earnings dependent. One proposal is to pay higher benefits to participants with low lifetime earnings, financed by taxing the Social Security of participants with high lifetime earnings. Another is to allow lower-income participants to retire early with relatively high benefits, but to pay nothing to high-income participants unless they stop working at a significantly older age. The thinking behind this is that high-income people tend to live longer than their low-income counterparts, and often have jobs that are easier to keep and perform past age seventy. Note that these strategies attempt to finance redistribution within Social Security; they aim to "take" money from reasonably well-off elderly citizens in order to redistribute to the elderly poor. The political obstacle is immediately obvious; the financially secure elderly are far more numerous and politically powerful than the elderly poor.

A second strike against the elderly poor is that the rest of the electorate is inclined to favor programs aimed at the young. Social scientists have produced impressive data about the effectiveness of early interventions on behalf of poor children, or even toddlers. Investments in early childhood education, healthcare, and nutrition can have high positive rates of return, perhaps to such an extent that they can be sold to voters as good investments, apart from any redistributive motive. Next in line are investments in retraining and vocational skills for adults with many years ahead in the workforce. Apart from small interventions, such as the provision of flu vaccines to vulnerable subpopulations, it is impossible to make such a case for programs or transfers aimed at the elderly.

There are sensible responses to this argument for making investments in the young rather than the elderly. A society can invest in both groups, so that the choice is not all of one or the other, regardless of budgetary constraints. Investments in the elderly might not pay in terms of future earnings or tax revenues, but they may encourage socially desirable behavior on the part of young and middle-age citizens who will see that they can expect fair treatment when they age. But I trust that readers share the intuition that it is hard to make the case for *investing* in the elderly poor, as opposed to a moral claim for caring for this group. There are superior moral and economic claims when it comes to needy children, and while those arguments and sentiments do not preclude helping the elderly poor, they form a serious barrier in a world with limited resources.

Another reason to expect the elderly poor to continue to struggle is that other citizens, and especially more fortunate senior citizens, often blame them for not saving more during their middle-age years. Children attract empathy because it is hard to fault them. One way to gain a consensus in favor of programs that help children is to show that specific programs are a good investment even from the perspective of taxpayers who simply want to save money that would otherwise be expended later on. No such argument is likely to succeed with respect to the elderly. Optimists will prefer to spend on children, and skeptics will argue that expenditures simply reduce the incentive of the next generation to save for retirement.

There are familiar and obvious liberal and conservative reactions to this comparison. Liberals will think it is heartless to blame poor people for not saving, and they will point to cases where poverty is the product of bad luck, inadequate education, or illness rather than irresponsibility. Conservatives will point to cases where extravagant spending or misbehavior contributed to the decline into poverty. Economists refer to this as a problem of "moral hazard," where the rule or practice itself can exacerbate rather than solve a problem. If people know that in old age they will receive payments only if they are poor, they might save less, invest wildly, or otherwise bring about their own poverty more often. The problem is aggravated if intrafamily transfers are difficult to monitor. People may try to appear poor in order to receive payments that are contingent on poverty—even when they have shared assets with family members or transferred assets to these reliable partners in order to appear poor. This is why traditional means-testing, which would place a cap on benefits based on income and assets, is inadequate. Many people who would never commit outright fraud feel justified in helping younger family members thrive if they know that public funds are available if they qualify as poor once past age sixty-five.

Finally, it is useful to recognize that the data about Social Security, wealth, and poverty do not fully reveal the reality of family life. In many families it is inconceivable to build up savings when another member of the family needs help with a medical problem, a wedding, or even an obligation to repay a loan. The expectation within the family is that resources go to those in immediate need. In many cases the person who parts with resources anticipates receiving help in old age, but of course the family unit may have fewer resources when that need arises, or the family dynamics may change. In some cases this pattern argues against transfers to the elderly. It is, after all, hard to see why the average taxpayer should pay for someone else's retirement needs when that person chose to devote available resources to a large wedding. Some communities have outsized expectations not just about weddings, but also about coming-out parties of various kinds, and there is no reason why the burden of these customs should fall on taxpayers. The popular press is full of stories in which parents and grandparents empty out 401(k) accounts to make these celebrations special, which is to say amazingly expensive.

On the other hand, intergenerational support within families is often triggered by emergencies or needs that would otherwise require government intervention or amount to a good social investment. If, for example, retirement savings are sacrificed to pay for a grandchild's healthcare, then there is often a long-term savings in government or other healthcare expenditures. If private savings are used to buy an automobile so that a family member can get to work, there may be a public benefit in the form of reduced payments for unemployment insurance, or simply increased revenue from taxes on wages. For this reason, some transfers to the elderly poor are a good investment. Rather than encouraging irresponsibility or discouraging savings, the expectation of a safety net may encourage people with savings to spend wisely in the event that family members face emergencies. Some intrafamilial transfers benefit taxpayers. In other contexts, law tries to separate true emergencies from mere consumption. Thus, there is a substantial tax penalty for early withdrawals from a tax-favored retirement account, but the penalty is removed if the withdrawal is used to pay qualified medical expenses, or educational expenses, or if the recipient is over fifty-five and becomes unemployed. Similarly, it is not entirely fanciful to imagine that redistribution to the elderly could be contingent on a showing that when funds were transferred within a family, it was for close family members' medical emergencies.

Many of these considerations figure in recent plans for Social Security reform, but a good solution ought to recognize that the four million elderly poor are only a small part of the larger, long-term problem. We have a relatively small group of elderly poor because they are part of a generation that worked hard, saved, and enjoyed rising real-estate values. The generation that follows has saved much less. It is likely that we will face a future with a much higher percentage of elderly poor, and a good solution to the present problem should plan for the larger problem ahead. But before turning to this bigger problem and its solution, let us expand the problem to think about intergenerational inequality.

Intergenerational Inequality: From Social Security to Wars and to Climate Change

This discussion of the plight of the elderly poor will seem cold-hearted to many readers. I have suggested that the problem has an intergenerational component because of a widespread inclination to care more about needy children than poor grandparents. There is also an in-generation issue because the grandparents' generation as a whole, though politically powerful, has no special feeling for the really poor among them.

In the case of Social Security benefits and taxes, it is apparent that interventions aimed at mitigating inequality can drive a wedge between the old and the young, unless benefits are deferred long into the future. For example, paid parental leave and increases in the minimum wage emerged as responses to concern about income and wealth inequality. But a retired person who is at the low end of the wealth distribution is likely to be worse off with these programs. Parental leave and the minimum wage both target workers; retirees will get no benefit from these programs and will be burdened by the higher consumer prices that inevitably follow these employer mandates. In rare cases, paid leave might enable a worker to care for his or her elderly parents, just as higher earnings might be shared with aging family members, but it is plain that these important initiatives are not in the interest of most elderly poor.

Redistribution in favor of the aging poor comes mostly from programs that benefit the aging cohort more generally. Voters over age sixty-five might at various points succeed in gaining tax advantages, increases in Social Security, and more generous healthcare benefits at the expense of other voters, but these benefits are limited by their enormous cost—which in turn can be traced to the fact that the benefit must be sufficiently attractive to motivate older voters in general, rather than those with low income and wealth. Ironically, the broader and more expensive programs are often easier to put into place than the targeted and less expensive ones.

Intergenerational conflict is most visible when retirement communities seek to exclude children, mostly to avoid the expense of providing local schools, and when communities with school-age children resent their older neighbors who are perceived as voting against the bond issues or higher taxes that are sought in order to improve public schools. In principle, better schools should cause an increase in property values, and this ought to benefit older citizens who can sell or borrow against their appreciating homes. In practice, the increase in property values is modest, and no school bond issue or tax increase is ever embraced by childless homeowners as a good financial investment. One "solution" is age segregation, though this does nothing for the elderly poor, who are unlikely to be mobile enough and able to afford to migrate to age-segregated communities. A more palatable solution is a kind of social compact in which schools are maintained over time, with the aging population recognizing that it once enjoyed the support of the previous generation.

Other large public expenditures present more difficult and often unrecognized problems of intergenerational equity. Who should have paid for World War II or the Second Persian Gulf War (2003–11), the governments that entered the war or succeeding generations that benefited? The resolution of such a question has a dramatic impact on intergenerational wealth inequality, and inequality ought to be measured both horizontally and over time.

Climate change policy is another potential source of intergenerational conflict and inequality. It is one of the most important issues of our time, and even more complicated than war; in war an enemy often pushes the problem upon us, but environmental catastrophes are usually more gradual and a society can choose when to take precautions. From a purely economic perspective, there might be an optimal moment to shut down a carbon dioxide-emitting coal plant, but as a political matter it will be tempting to delay in order to push costs into the future, with the hope that superior future technology will save the day. In principle it will seem that the best strategy is to take the precaution now, but borrow from the future in order to keep the burden of the precaution from falling on people today. One way to think of this is as a contract; the future generation would willingly pay the current generation to shut down the coal plant. But another way to think about it is that it is wrong for the current generation to contribute to global warming, knowing that future generations will suffer as a result.

Climate change policy is about aging in the sense that questions of intergenerational equity can pit aging citizens against younger ones. The disasters that are projected by climate change models are by and large things that someone now in his or her sixties will not experience. It is no wonder that schoolchildren care much more about the topic than do members of their grandparents' generation. Government debt is usually dangerous because it encourages spending on inefficient projects while pushing costs to the future. But here government debt may be appropriate; if we can identify precautions that are cost effective, then long-term debt to finance these projects may help the present generation see that it ought to evaluate these investments from the perspective of future inhabitants of the globe.

A Problem We Can Solve: The Elderly Poor of the Future

It is useful to think about the problem of the elderly poor in the same forward-looking way we think of climate change. Many people who are now older than seventy are struggling and would benefit from a dramatic expansion of Social Security or other programs. But a rescue of today's elderly poor is unlikely because their generation as a whole is economically better off than those that follow. Meanwhile, there is a bigger—and yet more manageable—problem: the enormous number of middle-age Americans who have inadequate savings. We try to educate and nudge (and provide tax incentives) in order to encourage more savings, but our efforts have not yielded much. When this generation is too old to work, real trouble will set in. Horizontal inequality will be rather extreme, and those who have saved will be disinclined to bail out their peers who did not. About half of our middle-age citizens have no savings, and there is every reason to think that these nonsavers will continue to spend all that they earn in the years ahead. The politically astute among them may be counting on some kind of bailout when old age arrives.

We who are aging ahead of this huge group of nonsavers can help them. We should favor a program of forced savings, attached to Social Security. In the past, most increases in Social Security benefits have come at the expense of the young, because higher benefits take effect immediately, and are then paid for by future taxes. But consider instead a proposal to raise both Social Security taxes and benefits, but with a lag. Social Security taxes are now 6.2 percent (plus another 6.2 percent paid by the employer) on the first $118,500 of income. Imagine increasing the individual's 6.2 percent tax by 1 percent a year for six years, or even 0.5 percent a year for twelve years, with benefits increased across the board by $500 per year beginning in ten years and then continuing for twenty years. The idea is to add a large dose of forced savings to Social Security in order to produce a "livable benefit." Benefits might be capped at $40,000 per year, thus introducing a modest, redistributive feature. In the long run, middle-income workers will pay 6 percent more in taxes, but this money will form the equivalent of an individual retirement fund, with an annuity component, yielding $10,000 more in annual benefits for the median household. In the intervening years, taxes, or forced savings, will rise gradually, as will benefits. Someone making $50,000 per year will be forced to save $500 at first, in addition to current Social Security taxes, and eventually $3,000 per year. But upon retirement after forty years, this person would have amassed about $173,000 new dollars, enough to pay $10,000 per year for life.[3] These amounts do not include cost-of-living increases, which have been embedded in Social Security since 1975. In present-dollar terms the average benefit for an individual would rise from about $16,000 to $26,000 (and $6,000 more for a couple with one worker).

The idea is to merge Social Security with a forced savings system, and to do so in a way that would be popular if only because the savings, like Social Security "premiums," earn interest-free income. Citizens between eighteen and fifty might well vote for such forced savings because half these people have no savings, and must be worried about their standard of living in old age, while the other half should worry that they will be called upon to redistribute toward the nonsavers. These voters are not being asked to raise benefits for those who are already retired or close to retirement. Even if many of these young and middle-age voters do not see that they need help, their elders can help by voting for this change. Some older voters might need an inducement to vote for this dramatic change, and that can be provided by the modest annual increase in benefits that would begin ten years from now. This benefit can be made just attractive enough (given projected small tax increases) to bring these voters along.

This is as good a place as any to observe that Social Security benefits are linked to formal participation in the workforce, and past contributions of Social Security taxes. This is plainly unhelpful to people, disproportionately women, who worked in their own homes and did not pay taxes. For the most part, these women and their families are enormously *benefited* by the current structure of Social Security, because a married couple with one earner receives 150 percent of normal benefits. In fact, a couple with one earner who makes $70,000 per year is better off than a family unit with two earners who make $35,000 each. More generally, the internal rate of return for "investments" (taxes paid) in Social Security is much greater for one-earner couples than two-earner couples, though the gap has narrowed in recent years, as survivor benefits have been capped.[4] It is a feature that should change as women's labor force participation rate continues to increase, and as the legislative focus inevitably turns to single-parent households instead of reflecting a bias in favor of marriage or special sympathy for widows.

Returning to the problem of the elderly poor, and the proposal to use Social Security to provide livable benefits, the essential idea is to force more savings in order to avoid a future inequality crisis. In the best of all worlds, each individual decides what to do and how to live life, and the state intervenes only when these decisions harm others. But in the real world we know that, when misfortune hits, most of us cannot and do not want to sit by while others suffer. Knowing that it will be called upon to bail out victims of flooding, for example, a sensible government will put some limits on the ability of people to build houses in flood plains or, at the very least, require them to carry flood insurance. Similarly, the prospect of bailing out truly poor elderly citizens should encourage the government to require retirement savings. One easy way to do this is to increase benefits so that virtually all households will have livable benefits after retirement. In turn, this requires funding with higher taxes, though they might more accurately be labeled as premiums or mandatory savings.

If we succeed in raising Social Security benefits as proposed here, there will be a group of elderly poor that did not or could not work the ten years needed to qualify for benefits. It is much harder to force this group to save for retirement. This group will also contain late-arriving immigrants, who will not qualify and who must rely on family members or work until very late in life. Fortunately, many members of this group will be able to find work because there is no strict mandatory retirement age, as explained in chapter 2; indeed, they may take up jobs vacated by full-time workers who retire a bit earlier because of the increase in Social Security benefits. But the major proposal in this chapter does not do much for this subgroup and it is, as in the past, likely to be politically weak and unsympathetic.

THIS CHAPTER BEGAN with a description of the scale of poverty among the elderly. The title of the chapter suggested that inequality—a topic popularized by academics, Bernie Sanders, and the Occupy movement—is at the root of the problem. But the suggestion made here is that it is quite plausible that low income (and low net worth) rather than inequality is the problem for most people. Most of us are not so envious that we want to destroy Bill Gates's wealth. So long as we have enough to live on, to enjoy our families, and perhaps to retire at a reasonable age, we are not made worse off by some neighbor having much more. The current problem is that there are several million elderly who cannot afford things that the rest of us take for granted. But the bigger problem is that there are many more millions behind them who have not saved and who have little equity in homes. It is these people that we can help by voting for an expanded Social Security system that guarantees a reasonable retirement for all who worked the requisite number of years. For many of us it is unnatural to think of a bigger government program as the solution to a problem. But in this case the alternative is a long and fierce battle over the amount and kind of redistribution to the growing ranks of the elderly poor. Forced savings is a better choice.

Notes

1. For an overview of the problem and some data about the elderly poor, see Ellen O'Brien, Ke Bin Wu, and David Baer, *Older Americans in Poverty: A Snapshot* (Washington, DC: AARP, 2010).
2. Ann Alstott's *A New Deal for Old Age: Toward a Progressive Retirement* (Cambridge, MA: Harvard University Press, 2016) discusses some of these strategies. Alstott advances the idea that retirement benefits ought to be a function of job type,

because less affluent seniors often have more strenuous jobs. This is probably not politically feasible, and in any event would encourage wasteful and intense political lobbying as groups tried to get the extra benefits.

3. These amounts reflect a conservative interest rate of 2.3 percent.

4. https://www.ssa.gov/oact/NOTES/ran5/an2004-5.html (internal rates of return to Social Security); https://www.ssa.gov/policy/docs/ssb/v70n3/v70n3p89.html (widows and Social Security).

Aging and Human Capabilities

Martha

Age and Inequality

Aging, as we've emphasized, offers many pleasures and opportunities. But it also contains many challenges, and these challenges are much more difficult when one is poor. Most of our essays focus on relatively affluent seniors, but we must now confront the ways in which economic inequality shapes this segment of life. Saul's essay discusses the extent of economic inequality among the elderly and proposes measures to address it, particularly an expansion of Social Security. In this essay I turn to my own normative political approach, known as the "capabilities approach," to see what it tells us about this part of the life cycle. I think it tells us a lot; it identifies defects of current US policies and pinpoints areas for change.

Capabilities, Disability, Security

The capabilities approach (CA), in my version, proposes basic political principles that could be protected as constitutional rights or secured by legislation.[1] It claims, first, that the right thing to look at is not simply a nation's average opulence, but, instead, the actual opportunities people have to choose activities that they value. And it then claims, second, that a society has failed to be even minimally just unless it secures to all its citizens a threshold level of certain specific opportunities set forth in my capabilities list. These, then, are essential entitlements inherent in the very idea of a just society, in other words basic human rights.[2] The reason for using the word "capabilities" is to emphasize choice and agency: what people have a right to not just passive satisfaction, but a set of opportunities for choice.

The CA is not a comprehensive account of the meaning or value of life. It is narrow in extent, as any list of constitutional rights is narrow, focusing on core political entitlements and leaving a lot of room for citizens to choose other activities in accordance with their own views of life. Even with respect to what is on the list, what's protected is an area of choice, and people may choose one way or another. (For example, having access to nutritious food does not prevent a person from fasting; the freedom of religion does not force a nonreligious person to go to church.)

With respect to what is on the list, however, the understanding is that the opportunities are to be secured in an ongoing way, promoting security about the future.[3] That is one reason why the approach is closely linked to constitutional law. Placing the core requirements beyond the whims of majoritarianism is a way, though not the only way, of giving citizens security about them.

I've argued elsewhere that the CA's merits as an approach to basic justice become especially clear when we focus on the entitlements of people with disabilities.[4] Since disability and aging overlap considerably, the reasons for my conclusion are pertinent here. One issue is that of equal respect and inclusion. By contrast with approaches based on the idea of a social contract for mutual advantage, the CA starts from the basic idea that policies about core entitlements must respect the equal human dignity of all citizens, regardless of their current economic productivity, and thus regardless of whether it is economically advantageous to cooperate with them. We too easily marginalize or discard people when we believe they do not "pay their way."

A second issue is that of sensitivity to variations in need. Many approaches—and Saul's appears to be like this—think of entitlements in terms of some basic all-purpose resources, such as income and wealth. But people vary in their need for resources if they are to attain the same level of capability to function: a person with severe disabilities may need more money in order to be fully mobile than a person with so-called normal mobility. Moreover, a lot of what this person needs involves not just disposable income but also social transformation: wheelchair access in buildings and on buses, for example. If we focus on the goal of making each person *capable* of a certain level of physical mobility, we have a much richer picture of what will need to be done to include people with disabilities as fully equal citizens. The same holds true when we think about aging. Seniors exhibit huge variety in their needs, and their needs are also not the same as those of the "average" citizen. So let's put the accent where it belongs, on what people can actually do and be.

Aging and the Capabilities List

What, then, does recognizing the fully equal dignity of aging people involve, when we focus on core entitlements to a threshold level of capability (opportunity)? And how might basic political principles adequately recognize, and grapple with, the diverse needs and problems in aging lives? A good set of policies must, first of all, recognize the *variety and nonhomogeneity* of lives that aging people lead. This, as I've said, is a hallmark of the CA. A good set of policies, second, must *combat damaging stereotypes* and not fall into the trap of underrating the capacities of aging adults for choices and activities of many types—while also being prepared to think about varied and flexible forms of guardianship and surrogacy where these seem called for. The CA has already shown it can address these issues for people with disabilities. Finally, a good set of policies must *support and protect agency*, seeing aging people as choosers and makers of their lives (at times in a network of care with others), not as passive recipients of benefits.

A good way to get started, I think, is to work through my list of ten central capabilities, asking, "What protections, what policies, do we need for ourselves and others, as we age? What could a reasonable baseline of adequacy be, in an affluent country such as the United States?" Such reflections will provide an outline or list of topics that can then be filled in later by further work and political argument.

The list is intentionally abstract, and it lacks an account of the minimum threshold of each capability, the idea being that this sketch can be filled in differently by different nations in accordance with their histories and resources. What I think we'll see is that Saul's proposal to beef up Social Security, while a good idea, is not specific enough to address many of the capability failures that afflict poorer seniors. Policies that specifically target problem areas are also required.

> 1. *Life.* Being able to live to the end of a human life of normal length; not dying prematurely, or before one's life is so reduced as to be not worth living.

Aging poses a number of important questions in this area, and many of them are questions of inequality. Of course there is the urgent question of who gets to be aged at all. Our society contains great inequalities in health and exposure to various risks, many resulting in premature death. But let us bracket that larger inequality issue, to focus on what becomes of people who do live into their later years.

First, then, we must consider the just allocation of medical resources. Current allocations give some aging people longer lives than others. Affluent people purchase extra years of life, in effect, by purchasing better medical care, and we need to think well about these inequalities, as medical costs rapidly increase. Some form of rationing, already accepted in Europe, seems inevitable, but goes very much against the American grain: the scare image of "death panels" causes such alarm that rational debate on this question does not occur. Meanwhile, we can perhaps at least agree to respect decisions made earlier in life not to use extraordinary measures to extend life.

A second question is posed by the phrase "not worth living." Aging people have often demanded access to physician-assisted suicide as part of death with dignity. Such policies are already in force in five states (Oregon, Vermont, Washington, California, and, with some restrictions, Montana), so there is regional inequality here rather than class inequality (although affluent people often have an easier time getting doctors to offer surreptitious help). The drawback of such policies is the very real possibility that this autonomy-enhancing capability could be used to coerce and bully older people into opting for death out of fear of being a burden. My tentative conclusion is that the option of assisted suicide is an inherent part of dignity for terminally ill people of all ages, but that this right should not be extended to non-terminally ill people, and can be overridden, even for the terminally ill, by evidence of cognitive disability. Moreover we must do everything in our power to make sure that failure to treat depression does not lead to the choice of suicide, for terminal and nonterminal patients alike.

Another issue of dignity is hospice care, which can be a way of easing terminal illness and respecting both individual dignity and family affiliations. Training medical personnel to provide such care in a compassionate manner is an urgent goal for our healthcare system. Such care seems to be a basic right for all, but it is far from available to all.

But how should a threshold level of a basic right be set? Because social and economic rights are not constitutionalized in the United States, legal scholarship in our country has not addressed this question fully, but it is a growing area of inquiry. Nations such as Canada and South Africa have begun to map out forms of collaboration between legislatures and the judiciary, in which the judiciary urges the legislature to come up with support for a roughly articulated level of provision, which must then be made more precise, and funds appropriated, by the legislature. Some state governments in the United States have long constitutionalized rights that cost a lot, such as education and, increasingly, health. So we are learning more, as time goes on, about how this can be done. Judge Diane Wood of the Seventh Circuit Court of Appeals has argued that the capabilities list can help judges figure out how to play their appropriate part.[5]

2. *Bodily health.* Being able to have good health, including reproductive health; to be adequately nourished; to have adequate shelter.

Once again, the key issue here is how to ration care in a way that respects equality but also respects physician choice and the right of aging people, up to a point, to choose to use their hard-earned money to buy extra healthcare. Countries that totally forbid the private purchase of care (Norway, for example) probably go too far. But the United States clearly errs in the opposite direction. As Saul says, Medicare and Medicaid don't do enough to give decent coverage. And many fine doctors simply don't accept those forms of payment. But the option to purchase extra care should also be protected, up to some reasonable limit, which we have yet to agree on.

One issue that must be confronted: Costs of many routine screenings in the United States are excessive because hospitals have been allowed to pile on extra requirements, such as a hospital setting for a routine colonoscopy, the presence of anesthesiologists even when the procedure does not require anesthesia, and so on. Our costs for that particular procedure are double those in Europe, as I discuss in my essay on stigma. A thorny issue in the entire health area is the endogeneity of costs to policies. Hospitals and pharmaceutical companies are profit-making entities, and their charges reflect this. They can provide the same drug or service more cheaply, but they want profits, part of which are targeted for research and development. But when the political branches tell them to make something affordable, they can usually do so: thus the same medications for HIV/AIDS are available at far lower cost in Africa than in the United States, as a result of the politics of the Bush administration. So costs can be lowered, when need is great and basic rights are at stake; and yet profits are in part socially beneficial, so there should be a well-informed and flexible dialogue between the political branches and the healthcare and pharmaceutical industries, in which we need greater than current frankness about what something "really" costs.

Health insurance never includes basic dental care, which typically becomes more expensive as people age, and dental insurance plans are usually very bad. In-home nursing care is also not covered, so people may have to purchase separate insurance to cover that. Some European countries do better.

But health in aging is not all about sickness. It is about nutrition, recreation, exercise, and "wellness" care, by which I mean things such as physical therapy for athletic injuries, advice from professionals about nutrition and lifestyle, and so forth. Our country has become far more oriented to "wellness" by now, as active baby boomers press their demands, and there are far more individual doctors who will routinely raise such issues. But still, our nation is not well designed for wellness, and inequalities abound. Access to nutritious fresh food is very unequally distributed, as is access to exercise and recreational facilities. That's a problem for everyone, not just the aging: people who live in large cities usually can find plenty of places to walk, and can usually get to a gym of some sort. But in many other places the car rules supreme, there aren't even any sidewalks, and all exercise facilities require driving. For people who no longer drive, America is a hard place to be healthy. Recognizing aging as an active time of life means recognizing that we have a large access problem: people who don't drive need to be able to get around somehow! Many people who would do better living at home move to retirement communities or even nursing homes because they can't drive, and their lives have become impossible. This is an inequality issue because the affluent can afford taxis and limos.

Retirement communities flourish for this reason, and Saul has talked about some of these. But it's not clear that they are the best way to solve the simple problem of living a healthy lifestyle without a car. In most of Europe it is perfectly possible to access markets, recreational facilities, parks, gyms, and cultural attractions by public transportation. We have strong environmental reasons to expand public transportation and decrease reliance on the car, so let's press those twin issues to make progress. But let's also cheer for driverless cars: they offer major benefits for seniors, and may in due course remove the whole problem of access.

3. *Bodily integrity.* Being able to move freely from place to place; to be secure against violent assault, including sexual assault and domestic violence; having opportunities for sexual satisfaction and for choice in matters of reproduction.

People with disabilities used to be unable to access public facilities even when they could get there, and the requirements for accessibility imposed by the ADA (Americans with Disabilities Act) have been an enormous boon for seniors as well. US law is in a pretty good state today with regard to basic building and transport accessibility, although we need to keep insisting on more retrofitting of existing facilities.

Violence is a constant issue for aging people, as indeed for all people. Seniors are much less likely to be victims of homicide than younger people: the FBI's homicide data for the year 2011 show that the peak age for becoming a homicide victim is twenty to twenty-four, after which the numbers drop off rapidly, becoming very low indeed by age sixty-five to sixty-nine. So this is really much more a youth problem than an age problem. Still, aging people who feel weaker than before may also be confined in their movements and choices by a fear of violence, and this is one of the long list of reasons we already have to work to make public spaces such as parks, streets, and shopping centers safer. This is an inequality issue in part, since affluent people can afford to live in safer neighborhoods and in buildings with security guards.

Elder abuse is a common form of domestic violence, alas, and like all forms of domestic violence it needs far more zealous policing—including prompt response to complaints of abuse in nursing homes or caregiving contexts. All forms of domestic violence cripple agency, making people afraid to reach out for help and inhibiting them in their chosen life-activities. Unfortunately, affluent seniors too are vulnerable to violence at home, but at least they are less likely to be forced into subpar nursing facilities.

As for sex and consent: this is a huge topic, barely beginning to be explored. Aging people want and need sex. Stereotypes that portray aging people as sexless create social obstacles, and often induce shame in aging people themselves, who may not acknowledge their needs. But people who are not healthy or fully competent face additional problems. This area is explored by the creative scholarship of Alexander Boni-Saenz about the United States and of Don Kulick about Sweden and Denmark.[6] Recognizing the danger of sexual exploitation, on the one hand, and the fact of sexual desire on the other, Boni-Saenz proposes two minimum requirements for sexual consent in elderly people with some cognitive decline: first, enough cognitive capacity that a person can make his or choice evident; in other words, sufficient agency; and, second, the presence of a surrounding social network of some type (family, friends, caregivers, in some combination) who can interpret the person's wishes and prevent exploitation. Right now society is just beginning to acknowledge that aging people with some dementia have a right to sexual pleasure. So this is an area affecting the core of selfhood concerning which our world is still in a primitive state. As Kulick shows, even nations that look superficially similar, Sweden and Denmark, may adopt extremely different policies (Denmark's more permissive, Sweden's more puritanical).

This is not primarily an inequality issue, since affluent seniors are as likely to have repressive families as nonaffluent people. It is, however, an issue that needs to be addressed. Kulick and Boni-Saenz both use the capabilities approach to argue for active government planning to facilitate choice. Boni-Saenz notes that one strength of the CA is that "it does not dictate specific policies in all domains, which allows countries to vary the ways in which they try to ensure fundamental human capabilities."[7]

I have focused on connection, but we must also consider the issue of privacy. One of the horrible things about most institutional facilities for seniors is the almost total surrender of solitude. Seniors are infantilized by caregivers, and the minute they are unable to do some specific thing for themselves, for example walk, it is simply assumed that they are infants and have no life of their own.

> 4. *Senses, imagination, and thought.* Being able to use the senses, to imagine, think, and reason—and to do these things in a "truly human" way, a way informed and cultivated by an adequate education, including, but by no means limited to, literacy and basic mathematical and scientific training. Being able to use imagination and thought in connection with experiencing and producing works and events of one's own choice, religious, literary, musical, and so forth. Being able to use one's mind in ways protected by guarantees of freedom of expression with respect to both political and artistic speech, and freedom of religious exercise. Being able to have pleasurable experiences and to avoid nonbeneficial pain.

Aging people need, and don't always get, access to cultural and sporting events and continuing education, and yet the evidence is that they flock to these things when they can. Museums, musical organizations, local sports teams, and movie theaters are aware of this market, and typically offer senior discounts as incentives. These discounts should probably be general rather than means-tested because of the intrusiveness and stigma of demonstrating need at the door, but the affluent senior can always make an extra donation to balance the ledger. Universities already make money from continuing education, a lot of it for seniors, but there remains an inequality issue, and those that provide exciting programming free of charge are to be commended.

Once again, in the United States the dominance of the car is a large equality problem. Seniors who do not live near adequate public transportation and do not have drivers simply cannot get to cultural events, to libraries and bookstores, and often even to church, temple, or mosque. Driverless cars can change this, but let's hope that they will not constitute another source of inequality.

> 5. *Emotions.* Being able to have attachments to things and people outside ourselves; to love those who love and care for us, to grieve at their absence; in general, to love, to grieve, to experience longing, gratitude, and justified anger. Not having one's emotional development blighted by fear and anxiety. (Supporting this capability means supporting forms of human association that can be shown to be crucial in their development.)

Aging brings surprises, and many of those are difficult to handle. That's true at all times, but perhaps there are more and more traumatic surprises as one ages. Wise policy cannot prevent life's accidents from being occasions of fear and grief, but respectful treatment from medical personnel, caregivers, and other people with whom seniors routinely interact could go a long way to removing crippling fear and anxiety—for example, by explaining medical issues in a calm and explicit way rather than cooing to the senior as to an infant. I believe that this is to at least some extent an inequality issue, since in American society the trappings of wealth command respect. If one arrives wearing nice clothes, or if, having disrobed for a medical exam, one nonetheless speaks like an educated professional, one is a lot more likely to get decent treatment. Respectful treatment also removes unnecessary incentives to anger, an emotion that I now would like to remove from the capabilities list![8] Doctors need more emotional intelligence, and some medical schools are beginning to focus on this issue. Compassion, of course, is very different from condescending pity, of which doctors display all too much.

An emotional issue that needs urgent thought is loneliness. In both the United States and Europe, a high proportion of aging people live alone. Studies of many types link feelings of loneliness not only to depression but also to decline in general cognitive functioning, physical health, and physical mobility.[9] The British innovation of the "Silver Line," a phone line where aging people can simply talk about their lives to a responsive listener, is a tiny step in the right direction, but addressing isolation—beyond my usual suggestion of better transportation—needs much more. I've long favored mandatory national service, and this would be one area in which such a program would reap rich rewards, promoting the capabilities of both aging and younger people by bringing them together.

> 6. *Practical reason.* Being able to form a conception of the good and to engage in critical reflection about the planning of one's life. (This entails protection for the liberty of conscience and religious observance.)

Privacy, sexual choice, access to healthcare, access to culture, all these are ways of exercising practical reason. Central, however, is being seen and respected as a full person, one who really is a center of agency and choice, and that is something that even healthy and competent seniors have to struggle to achieve, particularly if, being poor, they cannot command respect through signs of affluence.

One area in which respect for practical reason has been successfully implemented for all is informed consent. Doctors used to decide based on their own view of a patient's interests, but they now understand the distinction between interests and rights, and they respect patient's wishes and advanced directives.

This is a good place to begin talking about guardianship and surrogate decision-making. Respect for practical reason doesn't stop being an important issue when cognitive decline sets in. There are many areas of life in which, through partnership with a suitable guardian or extended-care network, cognitively diminished seniors can still exercise choice: in will making, sexual consent, political participation (to be discussed later). As with lifelong disability, so here: surrogate decision-making should be flexibly instituted, specific to the function in question, and no more than is necessary. This is an inequality issue to some degree, since affluent seniors can typically win respect from their guardians (although many are also exploited and abused by them). Poorer seniors who can't hire a network of lawyers, caregivers, and other employees have a far harder time making assisted decisions, and will much more easily be treated as mere objects.

7. *Affiliation.* (A) Being able to live with and toward others, to recognize and show concern for other human beings, to engage in
various forms of social interaction; to be able to imagine the situation of another. (Protecting this capability means protecting
institutions that constitute and nourish such forms of affiliation,
and also protecting the freedom of assembly and political speech.)
(B) Having the social bases of self-respect and nonhumiliation;
being able to be treated as a dignified being whose worth is equal
to that of others. This entails provisions of nondiscrimination on
the basis of race, sex, sexual orientation, ethnicity, caste, religion,
national origin.

Friendship and love, we've said, are central to a happy life as people age. Here's another place where national service could add to other
already-mentioned strategies, promoting valuable new friendships.
Similarly, recreation centers should not simply focus on creating this
or that program for seniors only. Seniors do want to interact with other
seniors. But for those who no longer work, one great loss is cross-
generational friendships, and these too should be encouraged—not only
within the family network.

One striking attempt to solve problems of social isolation is the seniors-
only retirement community, which both Saul and I discuss elsewhere.
These communities, however, usually cater to relatively affluent seniors.

The capabilities list speaks of nondiscrimination, but (formulated a
long time ago) it did not mention age discrimination, a great evil (see
my essay on retirement). Here the CA was shortsighted, and ought to be
changed!

8. *Other species.* Being able to live with concern for and in relation to
animals, plants, and the world of nature.

9. *Play.* Being able to laugh, to play, to enjoy recreational activities.

I'll treat numbers 8 and 9 together, since both are serious areas of inequality among seniors, in related ways. With money, seniors can take fulfilling trips to sites of beauty and access other recreational activities. Poorer
seniors may not even be able to get to the local city park, if transportation is inadequate. Companion animals are a tremendous asset to many
seniors' lives, and one reason why continuing to live in one's own home
as long as possible is usually desirable.

10. *Control over one's environment.* (A) *Political.* Being able to participate effectively in political choices that govern one's life; having
the right of political participation, protections of free speech and
association. (B) *Material.* Being able to hold property (both land and
movable goods), and having property rights on an equal basis with
others; having the right to seek employment on an equal basis with
others; having the freedom from unwarranted search and seizure.
In work, being able to work as a human being, exercising practical
reason and entering into meaningful relationships of mutual recognition with other workers.

There are many topics here, but let's focus on political affiliation.
Seniors are a very active political group. The AARP is among the nation's
most successful lobbying organizations, and in every election at all levels,
seniors are unusually well represented as voters. And the usual transportation issue does not even impede participation, since that is one time
when rides and special busses are sure to be available. Cognitive assistance is a different matter. The Help America Vote Act guarantees people
with both physical and cognitive disabilities access to the polling place,
special assistance explaining the ballot, and wheelchair access, but these
requirements are not always observed.[10] Nor do they go far enough: here
again, a place for surrogate decision-making is crucial, if seniors are to
be counted as one person with one vote, and their interests taken fully
seriously. Seniors usually are able to vote through absentee ballot, even
though a surrogate may actually fill out the ballot, but surrogates should
be encouraged to take up that role.

THIS TOUR THROUGH the capabilities list has raised only a few of the
issues that ought to be discussed, but these examples should give a sense
of what the capabilities perspective offers for policy about aging and
inequality.

How is the United States doing by comparison to other affluent
countries? The capabilities list exposes some serious issues for the
aging poor. One issue on which the United States does worse than
most affluent nations is public transportation, so crucial to many of
the central capabilities. Countries with well-developed public transportation even in rural areas (for example, Germany, Finland) are more
favorable to seniors. Still, our geographical situation is very different. Extending public transportation should be a long-term goal. My
suggestion of mandatory national service could also greatly empower

seniors who either don't want to depend on their family for transport or can't. Another highly appealing and perhaps more important goal is to encourage urban living for seniors (and others as well). Far from being the dirty, crime-infested horrors that many people imagine, America's cities are rich in both cultural and human opportunity. As economist Ed Glaeser shows with rigorous analysis, cities offer distinct advantages for human flourishing.[11] These advantages are all the greater for seniors, who increasingly (as longevity increases) face the risk of isolation and loneliness.

More generally, US seniors, like seniors in other nations, typically face large issues of capability security if they are not rich. The Finnish welfare system has often been praised as superior to that of the United States, for its assurance that seniors may remain in their own home for as long as possible, using in-home nursing care and other free or low-cost government assistance (housecleaning, shopping). Such arrangements, it is plausibly claimed, alleviate stress on family relationships.[12] All such arrangements, however excellent, are fragile in times of economic stress. The very features of the Finnish system that have been widely praised, for example, have recently been greatly curtailed.[13] Many hospitals and retirement homes are being closed, putting the burden back on families. Increasingly, Finns encounter a two-tier system, where, according to philosopher Sara Heinämaa, people with high pensions and large properties do well and others live in poverty.

Capabilities theory is a useful supplement to Saul's focus on Social Security. By delving more concretely into the varied parts of a meaningful life, it helps us identify weak points in modern societies, and it leads to specific policy proposals that a simple increase in Social Security would not achieve. The philosopher's focus on aspiration complements the economist's realism!

All nations, however, need to forge a social consensus about what types of care for aging seniors are central enough to count as basic entitlements, to be abridged only in the most dire emergency. Since no nation has deliberated well about the rights of the aging, there is no such secure understanding. Aging thoughtfully means, then, group solidarity and a spirit of protest that may, over time, create a consensus about basic rights. It is this idea of basic entitlements that is central to the capabilities approach. As time goes on, its ideas can guide public thinking—but only if there is public thinking and debate in the first place! The pervasive feeling that capability losses in aging are just "natural" is a huge impediment to the debate we badly need.

Notes

1. I develop my own version of the CA in three books: *Women and Human Development: The Capabilities Approach* (Cambridge: Cambridge University Press, 2000); *Frontiers of Justice: Disability, Nationality, Species Membership* (Cambridge, MA: Harvard University Press, 2006); and *Creating Capabilities: The Human Development Approach* (Cambridge, MA: Harvard University Press, 2012). The last of these contains, as well, a discussion of differences between my version of the approach and Amartya Sen's, and a comprehensive bibliography.

2. On rights and capabilities, see Nussbaum, "Capabilities, Entitlements, Rights: Supplementation and Critique," *Journal of Human Development and Capabilities* 12 (2011), 23–38.

3. See Jonathan Wolff and Avner De-Shalit, *Disadvantage* (New York: Oxford University Press, 2007), and my approving use of their work in *Creating Capabilities*.

4. See Nussbaum, *Frontiers of Justice* (Cambridge, MA: Harvard University Press, 2006).

5. See Diane Wood, "Constitutions and Capabilities: A (Necessarily) Pragmatic Approach," *Chicago Journal of International Law* 2 (2010), article 3.

6. Alexander Boni-Saenz, "Sexuality and Incapacity," *Ohio State Law Journal* 75 (2015), 1201–53; Don Kulick and Jens Rydström, *Loneliness and Its Opposite: Sex, Disability, and the Ethics of Engagement* (Durham, NC: Duke University Press, 2015), and "A Right to Sex?," the review by Boni-Saenz in *New Rambler*, April 18, 2015, http://newramblerreview.com/book-reviews/gender-sexuality-studies/a-right-to-sex.

7. Boni-Saenz, "A Right to Sex?"

8. See my *Anger and Forgiveness* (New York: Oxford University Press, 2016).

9. Summarized in http://www.nytimes.com/2016/09/06/health/lonliness-aging-health-effects.html?_r=0.

10. See my "The Capabilities of People with Cognitive Disabilities," *Metaphilosophy* 40 (2009), 331–51, reprinted in *Cognitive Disability and Its Challenge to Moral Philosophy*, ed. Eva Kittay and Licia Carlson (Malden, MA: Wiley-Blackwell, 2010), 75–96.

11. Ed Glaeser, *Triumph of the City: How Our Greatest Invention Makes Us Richer, Smarter, Greener, Healthier, and Happier* (New York: Penguin, 2012).

12. Anu Partanen, *The Nordic Theory of Everything: In Search of a Better Life* (New York: HarperCollins, 2016).

13. Correspondence with philosopher Sara Heinämaa.

Chapter 8

Giving It Away

WHAT ARE GOOD ways of perpetuating oneself? Is there "option value" in waiting before giving money away? How should we give wealth away if our children and grandchildren are in disparate financial circumstances? How should we think about different kinds of legacies and altruism? Can we learn to be good, or is it too late?

Paradoxes of Giving (Solutions Included)

Saul

IMAGINE THAT YOU are fortunate enough to be aging affluently. It is unlikely you will spend all the money you have earned or otherwise acquired, and saved. Your major remaining financial anxiety probably derives from the fact that you do not know your lifespan, or the condition you will be in during your later years. You might purchase an annuity in order to have a guaranteed income if you live a longer than expected life, but for most affluent people the uncertainty falls on their children or favorite charities. Most people who are financially secure prepare for old age and even for the possible expense of a debilitating illness. Most affluent people "oversave"; unless death comes at an extremely old age, they leave wealth to their spouses, children, and favorite charities.

If you are fortunate to be healthy, then even without wealth you are likely to have more free time as you age. Retirement brings the opportunity to spend more time with family and to volunteer for various causes. Time is money, after all. I will end with some important differences between time and money, but for now it is sufficient to recognize that one can give both money and time, and the discussion of money here applies as well to time. Planning is as important for nonfinancial assets as it is for financial assets, though planning with respect to the latter is easier, because money, unlike time, can earn interest and be easily divided.

This chapter develops two ideas about transmissions of assets from well-meaning affluent people to their relatives or to philanthropies. These ideas are best understood by exploring two "paradoxes of giving." The first concerns the strategy of deferring gifts to gain information, and moves to the paradoxical question of how this deferral strategy ever gives way to rational gift-giving. Put more practically, the idea is to reach some conclusion about when one ought to part with resources. The second paradox begins with the current social norm, discussed in chapter 1's essay on *King Lear*, of egalitarian distribution. Unless one has a child with special needs, most people today believe rather firmly that they should treat their children equally, especially when it comes to inheritance. This equality norm might have evolved to reduce competition among siblings, but let's just accept that it has become deeply ingrained. Equal treatment does not require much defending. The discussion will show that this egalitarian mindset leads people to withhold money from beneficiaries they really want to favor. The paradox is revealed when, on our own, we fail to redistribute in the very way we wish the government would do. This, in turn, suggests a strategy some readers may want to adopt with respect to their own estate plans.

The first paradox is a bit theoretical and requires some basic arguments about deferral and options. Economists assume or simply observe that most people need to be paid in order to defer consumption. If Elon wants a new car, he'd probably prefer to have it now rather than in two years. On the other hand, if a bank will pay him a rate of interest higher than the expected increase in the cost of new cars, then he might save his money, buy the new car in two years, and have some money left over to spend elsewhere. Economists say that the future is *discounted*, though certainly more by some people than by others. There are exceptions to this pattern, but let's turn to philanthropy with the assumption that immediate enjoyment is preferred over delayed gratification.

Elon can give money to a good cause now or he can defer, invest the money himself, and be charitable later. Discounting suggests two reasons why he ought to give now rather than later. First, to the extent that he will get pleasure from helping others, or even from expressions of gratitude, he will get that satisfaction sooner rather than later. Elon may also benefit from a charitable deduction on his income tax return, which is worth more the sooner he takes it; in the long run he may also reduce his estate taxes by making gifts before death,[1] which can come at any time. Second, the eventual recipient whom he helps will get the benefit sooner rather than later. On the other hand, the same tools, taken to the next level, can rationalize deferral. If Elon defers giving, but eventually gives away that principal amount plus all that he earns from investing it, then he will be doing more good later than he can do now. Some recipient will be better off if he gives it now, but another lucky future recipient could get yet more help if Elon defers. From this perspective, a donor should be indifferent between giving now and giving later—unless the donor is eager to enjoy the pleasure of making gifts in the present and observing the benefits gained by intended beneficiaries. The same might be true for time; someone can volunteer for a cause now or, with good planning, work more hours to earn money now in order to afford early retirement and give away more time later on.

Elon has some choice in the matter if the charitable entity he has in mind uses current income as well as endowment income to finance its work. If he wishes to support student scholarships at a university, for instance, then he surely knows that the university has an endowment and is unlikely to spend every dollar it receives in a given year from tuition-paying students and donors. The university earns a higher rate of return on investments than most donors, both because the university benefits from the large size of its investment fund and because it is a tax-exempt entity. In any event, the question is whether the donor's money grows more in the charity's hands than in the donor's. I recall a conversation in Shanghai in the early 2000s, when I was soliciting a large gift for my university from a prospective donor. He took me to several factories that he had built. I learned that under his management these factories had returned 40 percent a year for several years. My putative donor had invited me to come see him, but now he asked whether my university could also make money grow by 40 percent. If not, he said, were we not all better off if he held off endowing something at the university inasmuch as he could then give us much more later on? At the time I responded with a claim that if he gave us the money for student scholarships and research, the rate of return from his investment in us might indeed be much higher than 40 percent because of all the good our graduates and faculty would do. I was only partly successful on this fundraising trip, in large part because the donor and I both knew that it is hard to beat a 40 percent investment opportunity. The university would have invested the bulk of the gift and earned less than it was earning in the donor's hands.

It is tempting to say that one reason to give now rather than later is that we should encourage philanthropy—and later might turn into never for many people. One who is inclined to be generous with time or money might really invest now and then give more later on, but it often happens that preferences or perceptions change. My friend in China might well have earned 40 percent a year and then given us $26 million five years after our conversation. That would have made me happy that he did not part with $5 million when I first asked. But it is quite likely that other nonprofit organizations, business ventures, or family projects would capture his interest during the period in which he earned money, and waited before making a major gift. To be sure, he might see what a great job our university does in the interim and be inclined to give even more than he first suggested, but a donor who defers giving might instead become disenchanted in the intervening years and then donate to a different cause.

This reason for delay is best described as *option value*. The donor is like the holder of an option who gains by waiting because over time he gets more information about alternative investments. In this case the option value probably dominates any argument for immediate giving; there is a benefit to waiting in order to learn more, and also a benefit because the donor can earn a higher rate of return than the university. The only cost is that he postpones the pleasure of doing some good. Universities are happy to take care of this problem by accepting and celebrating pledges of future gifts, but a formal pledge reduces or eliminates the option value to the donor.

It is apparent that there is something of a paradox here. If it makes sense to defer giving in order to learn more about one's choices, then one ought to defer in every time period until the next, until deferral is indefinite and one never parts with resources.[2] The paradox rests on the fact that it is costly to revise one's last will and testament or other transfer formalities. It is not as if one can defer until the moment before death and then, with as much information as one will ever have, decide among charities. Once you defer giving, it can be hard ever to make the gift. A truly charitable and generous person had better not overthink the problem.

Before exploring this *paradox of giving* any further, it is worth observing that options seem to be more highly valued by young people today than by their predecessors. I sometimes call this millennial set "Generation O," where "O" is for options. Two provocative examples are the rising age of marriage and the younger generation's disinclination to respond definitively to social invitations. Where dating and marriage are concerned, the option may simply be more valuable than it was twenty years ago because mobility and technological change have made it easier to search and experience new partners. Tinder and other apps on smartphones make it easy to meet people, superficially at first, but then in face-to-face encounters that resemble the dates of yesteryear. These dates are often cursory or purely flirtatious and recreational, perhaps because any commitment gets in the way of the option, or possibility, of meeting someone "better" on a later date. When I was twenty-five, the option value of putting off a marriage decision for a year was that someone could date or otherwise meet five or ten new people during the year. Today the number can easily be five times that, so that the value of the delay is much greater.[3]

But Generation O is not just a product of smartphones. A widely observed phenomenon, and one that appears rude to elders, is that people resist responding to invitations, except with a "Thanks, maybe I'll be there." Young recipients behave as if any firm commitment will block some extraordinary conflicting opportunity that could come their way at any moment. Even response rates to wedding invitations are much lower than a generation or two ago. Social conventions have evolved in the direction of casual get-togethers with little need to plan around a set number of guests.

Aging people, in contrast, find options less valuable, even apart from technological and other changes. The fundamental tenet of option theory is that an option increases in value with the length of time during which it can be exercised, as well as with the volatility of the value of the underlying asset or opportunity that one can acquire with it. An option is a deferred choice, and this deferral is more valuable the more the alternatives will diverge in the future and the longer the period during which one can watch all this happen before making a decision. Older people have less time and less certainty about health, and so we put a lower value on options as we age.

Options come into play in thinking about our legacies and how to do good in the world. It is natural for older people to want to leave a mark. Young people may care more about the future but, almost paradoxically, older people are more likely (especially if they are affluent) to do something about it because their time is limited.

Let us return to the paradox of giving. It seems reasonable to postpone gift-making—but the underlying logic has no stopping point. Is this paradox solved if we assume the world will improve, so that philanthropy is needed now more than it will be needed in the future? Not really, because it might then be irrational to endow anything at all; all charitable giving should be directed to the present where it is most needed. More accurately, benefactors should calculate the rate at which famines disappear, or the standard of living among the poor generally improves, and then allocate funds (or time) accordingly, more to what seem like the neediest periods, but much more than zero to the slightly less dire eras. One way out of this bind, or calculation nightmare, is to think of the incentives of philanthropic organizations, and the need to monitor them. It is plausible that organizations will undervalue their own options about how to do good, because those who run them will look better the more they get immediate results.

Endowments can function as a means of control over these organizations, even as they offer a means for benefactors to experience a sense of immortality, because their gifts will do good in apparent perpetuity. In other words, one way to think about charities is that we entrust them to solve the problem of allocating money across time and disasters. They will be around long after we are gone, and they can exercise the options that we would if we were fully informed. For this delegation to be effective, one must trust these organizations or encourage their executives to have the values and preferences of the benefactors. Most large donors to universities show great faith in the universities they endow, but not so much as to permit the universities to allocate freely across time. The university's own rules—meant to appeal to donors—determine a slow and steady rate of spending out of endowment. Endowed gifts are meant to last forever; this encourages the donor's sense of immortality through philanthropy and also controls the university's officials who may be inclined to overspend during their careers. It does nothing to resolve the problem of spending more money when the need or rate of return is greatest. That is accomplished by eliciting new gifts in these periods; if a cure for a kind of cancer were just around the corner, we can be certain that donors would open their wallets. Put in option terms, with reliable information about such an investment in medical research even my friend in Shanghai would think that funding the research would be a better investment than his very profitable factories.

Another escape from this paradox of giving is to recognize that the option value of deferral privileges a benefactor's later preferences. Perhaps Elon should recognize that his charitable inclinations are likely to change over time, and it is not necessarily the case that the later Elon is wiser than his present self. One reason to give sooner rather than later is to preempt the later, regretful self. Economists and philosophers wrestle with this problem of unfixed preferences, but rather than entering that fray, the point here is simply that it is easier to give some money to charities one believes in at age sixty—or at least to pledge the money even if one insists on investing at a higher rate of return and actually transferring the resources later on—than it is to hold on to it all until age ninety, and then wrestle with the philosophical question of allocating some gifts to causes the previous self favored.

The paradox of giving can also come into play when one contemplates gifts or bequests to people, rather than to philanthropic causes. Chapter 1 touched on reasons we might want to hang on to our savings until death, even when we have children or others whom we are eager to support or spoil. A critical reason is that one rarely knows how many years of life remain, and it is often better to be self-supporting during life and then generous at death, rather than to give assets away and then rely on others for support.

But let us say that a donor, Amy, has set aside more than enough to support herself; she anticipates Social Security benefits and has enough savings to meet any eventuality including longevity. Philanthropy aside, Amy has decided to give a substantial amount of her savings to her children. Should she give annual gifts to them (taking advantage of the gift tax exclusion if that matters) and encourage their self-sufficiency by holding back major transfers until her death? Or should she do the reverse and give large gifts now because her beneficiaries would prefer to get money sooner rather than later? If they will choose to invest the money, there is no difference whether she or they do so, unless one generation makes better investment decisions than the other. But the money might reduce stress in their lives or give them options they do not otherwise enjoy. A present-day large gift might allow one of Amy's children to buy a house, switch to a more meaningful job, or buy a business—and these things would not be possible without the resources Amy can provide. In chapter 1, while learning from *Lear*, we examined the interaction between these gifts and filial gratitude. If Amy makes sizable gifts sooner rather than later, she must be prepared to find out how companionable she really is or how she is loved for her money.

Other things equal, it is apparent that a gift to a loved one should be given sooner rather than later. If one has more than enough for oneself, then why wait, when delay makes the object of affection worse off? The pleasure of giving might also be worth more if done sooner rather than later. It would seem ludicrous to tell a child or adult: "I could give you a birthday present this year, but I decided to save the money and give you a more expensive one next year." It is not just that this logic continues until death, in keeping with the paradox of giving, but also that the recipient discounts the future and gains more utility from a gift received now. An economist would put it a little differently: if the donor gives the recipient money, then the recipient can also choose to save the money and earn interest in order to enjoy a bigger expenditure in the future. Most recipients will calculate that they gain more from immediate consumption than they would gain from interest income. In this regard, children are not like philanthropic organizations. For the most part, we know our children well and do not need more time to help us make informed choices. We do not, however, know their future financial circumstances, and that is an uncertainty to which we now turn.

THE SECOND PARADOX of giving has more to do with family matters and, oddly, the individual's attitude toward the state. Consider first the case where an affluent person has three children in disparate financial circumstances, but with no one in danger of starving or foregoing important medical care. Perhaps Amy has $300,000 to distribute and Amy's three children, Fiona, Jock, and Prince, earned $300,000, $52,000, and $120,000, respectively, during the preceding year. Fiona is in finance, Jock coaches high school sports teams, and Prince is the principal at a private school. Amy is inclined to distribute in egalitarian fashion, though she recognizes that her gift or bequest will change Jock's life much more than it will the others. Her friends encourage the equal treatment pattern with familiar arguments. Amy's children made their own choices about careers and lifestyle, and no child should "lose" money because another chose to be a coach or struggling artist. Amy may admire Prince's career the most, especially if Prince gave up yet more lucrative work in order to work with children, but the strong social convention is not to commodify this approval. Similarly, if Jock married a very wealthy person, it would be strange or even perverse to redirect resources away from him. But what if Jock has ten children and the others have one each, with no wealthy spouses in the picture? Most people in Amy's position would stick to the equal distribution principle. If Amy has particular preferences, she is free to follow those in making consumptive and philanthropic decisions, but when it comes to passing on wealth to her children, society has developed a strong equal treatment norm in order to control parental behavior.

If Amy has $3 million to distribute, it is much more likely that she would distribute some of this money in egalitarian fashion—but directly to her grandchildren. By aiming at her grandchildren, Amy can adhere to the equal treatment norm, albeit by subtly skipping over the generation that she does not truly want to treat equally. Amy does not want to distribute to her own children in unequal fashion, both because they made their own choices and because she fears sibling resentments. On the other hand, perhaps she encouraged Jock to have a big family, or she simply sees no reason why some of her grandchildren should have fewer opportunities in life than the others. She has been encouraged to think she should love all her children equally, but Amy would say the same about her grandchildren—and if so, why not distribute equally to them? If asked, she would probably say that she would feel differently if her wealthiest child, Fiona, had more children than the others; Amy would be unlikely to skip a generation and give equally to her grandchildren if this would favor the branch that is already best situated in financial terms. But given that her low-earning child has been the most procreant, the equal treatment idea can serve a useful purpose.

Making the problem a bit harder, imagine that these grandchildren are all adults and that two of Jock's children are much needier than their siblings, as well as the other grandchildren. Amy recognizes that these two grandchildren cannot look to their father for extra support. Now she is in a bind. If she provides for these two grandchildren, and then divides the balance of her estate among her own three children, the other grandchildren (and their parents) are likely to feel wronged. Indeed, Amy herself will be apt to think that she has violated some fundamental understanding about love and equal treatment. With $300,000 to distribute, if she gives $50,000 to each child, and then divides the balance among the twelve grandchildren, each grandchild will receive $12,500, and that might not be enough to make an appreciable difference in the lives of the two who could most use help. And the same is true if she divides her entire estate equally among her children, and does nothing directly for any grandchild.

A similar problem arises with respect to more distant relatives. Imagine now that Amy's children and grandchildren are all doing fine, but that two of her brother's five children are struggling. If Amy provides for all five of these nephews and nieces, her own children are likely to feel shortchanged and resentful, because five beneficiaries will require a good deal of money. And if she more efficiently singles out the two needy ones, their siblings, and perhaps Amy's own brother, may react negatively. I have seen cases where the benefactor in Amy's position does something subtle in her will, for example, "I leave $100,000 to each of my nieces and nephews who is an ordained minister" or "who lives in the holy land of Israel," or "who works on our family's ancestral farm in South Dakota." The more the benefactor can do this long before death, when the identities of the qualifying beneficiaries are unclear, the more likely this is to avoid hard feelings, but by and large unequal distribution begets trouble. Someone is bound to think that her sibling lobbied the aunt or parent for special treatment, or that the beneficiary exaggerated his impoverishment. It is quite likely that Amy will not want to risk creating ill will among her relatives; she is likely to leave nothing to her nephews and nieces even though she wishes she could help two of them. The outcome is a product of the strength of the equal treatment norm. Note that there are very few families in which siblings would get together in their twenties and agree by contract to share the money they earn—or redistribute everything they inherit toward the least well-off person.

I think of this pattern as paradoxical because if taxes had been higher, and the welfare state much more extensive, it is plausible that the government would have directed public funds to the brother's two struggling children. With a little imagination, we might think of a responsive government as taking Amy's money and redistributing it to these two relatives, albeit as part of a much larger tax-and-redistribution scheme. The paradox or irony is that Amy has better information than the government. Amy is a superior judge of the financial security of her relatives, the reasons some are struggling, and the likelihood that the prospect of a transfer payment (or bequest) will have the perverse effect of reducing the beneficiaries' work effort or somehow cause them to require help in the first place. The government is ill-equipped to learn these things, and for this reason many socially minded citizens disfavor more generous redistributive programs.

We have already seen the explanation of this veridical (as logicians call it) paradox of giving. It is that the party best situated to redistribute, and most motivated by affection for all the involved family members, is also the one most likely to cause resentment and to bring on family discord. The egalitarian norm within the immediate family, and then within familial categories, is strong even when the same people or forces would want the government to bring about more egalitarian outcomes on a larger scale. The result is that neither Amy nor the government redistributes. She does not trust the government to redistribute on her behalf, and she declines to redistribute on her own because she fears familial resentments.

Once the irony in Amy's position is comprehended, it is possible to solve her problem. Some targeted redistribution is desirable, but the problem is that Amy should not herself favor one child or one niece in a group of similarly situated family members. The solution—if Amy wants to use it—is to empower a third party with sufficient emotional distance from the family, and yet with good enough judgment and information to do as Amy would wish. For example, Amy can entrust funds to a close friend and instruct as follows: "Please leave this money invested in the low-fee mutual fund I have designated, but check regularly to see whether my children or my brother's children are struggling. If, for example, one nephew needs help paying tuition or one cannot afford a down payment on a modest home, and in your judgment my children and my other nephews and nieces are significantly better off financially, then give as much as $25,000 to this person. You can tell the family that these were my instructions, and that I wanted to leave a rainy-day fund to help with just such a crisis. If there is money remaining in this crisis fund ten years after my death, then please divide it among my children." Amy might need a lawyer to draft these instructions in order to reassure her friend that she will not be held personally liable for her decisions.

I do not mean that everyone in Amy's position ought to set up such a third-party decision-maker. But the more one's mindset is inclined toward redistribution, the more one can redistribute at the micro level, in homemade fashion, by engaging a friend or other intermediary. Another way to think about the solution offered here is that it increases the option value of Amy's resources. Through a third party, Amy can extend her option period even beyond death, so that no decision about redistribution needs to be made before there is sufficient information about various family members' financial circumstances.

PHILANTHROPY NEED NOT be agonizing. Just as most investors ought to find a low-fee indexed mutual fund in which to invest, most people with charitable impulses can rely on relatively efficient large charities as intermediaries to choose among causes and distribute for them. But many of us are more inclined to be charitable the more we are involved in, and knowledgeable about, the causes we support. This chapter has explained how a hyperrational person might endlessly defer giving away money and even time, and in the end deny oneself the pleasure of helping others. If we are fortunate enough to be secure in our retirement years, even though we do not know their number, then the option value of holding on to excess resources declines. It is time to think not only about our descendants but also about philanthropic causes. This might be our best opportunity to leave the world a little better off than we found it. An easy escape from the first paradox of giving is to assume that the social rate of return on thoughtful philanthropy is higher than the return available from investments. In turn, the second paradox of giving suggests that in leaving money to one's family members, it is also sensible to give before the very end, although in some situations it may be wise to set money aside and ask an outsider to distribute those funds when a loved one faces a crisis.

And as for time, rather than money, most people are able to identify causes and give of themselves, especially after retiring from full-time work. Their surplus resources are time, labor, and enthusiasm, in addition to or instead of accumulated wealth. Retirement affords more time for friendships and hobbies—and also more time to volunteer in ways that will help others. If time cannot easily be shifted across years, then some of the first paradox discussed here melts away. The second paradox may also disappear when the volunteering is directed at family members. If Amy, once retired, helps Jock by caring for his small children, Fiona and Prince are unlikely to feel cheated. Whether this is because the gift of time almost always comes with strings attached, so that the two siblings may not want Amy's time, or because it is apparent that Amy cannot simply save and shift her expenditures of time, it seems plain that unequal gifts of time are less likely to generate resentments than are unequal gifts of money.

It is apparent that people who are fortunate enough to be philanthropists take great pleasure in helping others. Similarly, most people who volunteer for good causes report this activity to be among the most satisfying of their life experiences. We should also think of them as philanthropists, acknowledging the value of the time they contribute. Like time spent with grandchildren, the experience is valuable for both donor and beneficiary—and often free of the paradoxes of giving.

Notes

1. If this statement alters your estate planning, please consult a lawyer. If I have assets that have gone up in value, I am often better off *not* selling or giving those away because at my death the income tax system essentially forgives tax on the appreciation.
2. With time it is a bit more complicated. Deferral might continue until the donor thinks that there is only as much time left as he or she plans to give away.
3. Cutting in the other direction is the idea that searching for a partner is easier in the modern world. If the marriage age were falling, we might say that is because one can meet many people and then decide. But the fact that the age of marriage is rising suggests that perceived opportunities matter more than optimal search.

Aging and Altruism

Martha

In this manner every mortal being preserves itself: not by remaining altogether the same forever like divine beings, but by leaving behind another new being similar to itself, when it grows old and departs.

—PLATO, *Symposium 208A*

IN PLATO'S *SYMPOSIUM*, the wise priestess Diotima offers young Socrates an account of human altruism and creativity. She traces these virtues to our awareness of mortality. We realize at some point that we are going to die, so we strive to leave behind us something that would be like us, so that in some manner, at least, we remain in the world after our death. This strategy requires thinking about who one is and what one stands for, even if not with elaborate conscious deliberation. Some people—and she views these as the least imaginative—figure that only physical children could replace them, so they get to work creating children. (In ancient Greek culture, where women's bodies were strongly devalued, the fact that this strategy required heterosexual reproduction counted for Plato as a strong point against it.)[1] Others aspire higher. Some focus on education of the young, trying to mold souls in accordance with what they value. This strategy is better, she thinks, but it has the disadvantage of requiring face-to-face contact, so it doesn't reach very far ahead in time. Wiser types, therefore, try to embody their vision in systems of science, or political governance, or philosophy, thus creating structures that could well survive for an extremely long time—as Plato's ideas actually have. The bottom line, however, is that the world derives many benefits from our awareness of our own death, benefits that might not arrive in any other way.

One might immediately have many skeptical questions about Diotima's picture. Is physical childbearing really such an inadequate way to perpetuate oneself in the world? More generally, doesn't her strategy focus on the outstanding individual who can incorporate a distinctive personal vision in a complete system of some sort, neglecting corporate activities in which the individual's role is nothing without the contributions of others? (We might recall that this same question was raised to Simone de Beauvoir by Sartre in my first essay, though his own conclusion that only communal activities are good vehicles for identity seemed narrow in its own way.) But above all, one might ask, where is real altruism? The person Diotima imagines seems to do good for others only incidentally, as the result of a selfish project. Isn't there more we should be striving for, as we age?

We might also ask whether Diotima isn't one-sided in mentioning only the benefits of our awareness of mortality. Isn't there any problem we might need to try to avoid?

In this essay I set out some alternatives and ponder them. First, I distinguish several types of altruism, situating Diotima's proposal among them. Next I discuss the potential downside of our awareness of death, discussing the impediment to altruism supplied by fear, which typically escalates as we age, and which is, I think, more destructive than creative. (Here I turn to Plato's adversary Epicurus, who argues that the fear of death is responsible for many of life's great evils.) Next, I discuss altruism in personal relationships, asking how aging people ought to relate to others whom they know, as time goes on. Finally, I return to Diotima's theme, asking about how, as we age, we ought to think about our contribution to the ongoing life of the world.

Varieties of Altruism

Many people do good for the world more or less accidentally, while focusing on an essentially selfish goal. Sociologist Kristen Monroe calls such people "entrepreneurs," because a typical instance is a person who is trying to become wealthy or influential, and admits that this is her primary motive, but whose work or discoveries have a socially beneficial effect.[2] There are complexities even here: some entrepreneurs would veto any pursuit that seemed likely to have morally pernicious effects; some think it a strong plus that effects are likely to be good. Still, the primary motive is personal gain.

In a second group, "philanthropists," we can, with Monroe, place those who benefit a cause or causes, often with a real appreciation of their inherent value, but also expecting some type of personal gain. (In all categories we should define the type of altruism in terms of the rationally expected dividend, not in terms of what actually happens, which lies in the realm of chance.) This personal gain might be simply a good reputation during life; it might be reciprocating favors from those whom one has benefited. It might be a feeling of personal satisfaction connected with the thought that one is doing good. Or it might be the type of good described by Diotima, surrogate immortality. (Note that immortality can itself take different forms: for Diotima the actual creation of something valuable is required, but some might, instead, want primarily an immortal reputation. Poets frequently allude to the latter motive, although, being human, they probably assume that their works are inherently valuable.)

The most influential contemporary accounts of altruistic behavior derive from economics, and according to standard economic accounts all altruism is either entrepreneurial or philanthropic. In a variety of ways, these accounts attempt to explain altruism as consistent with the model of the person as a rationally self-interested actor, maximizing his or her expected utility. Personal utility is taken to be the real goal of the altruistic act; the act is seen as an instrumental means to that goal. Such accounts have not gone undisputed within economics itself. Amartya Sen's famous paper "Rational Fools," for example, argued in 1977 that such accounts could not explain the behavior of many people who, out of sympathy or commitment, sacrifice their own personal well-being.[3] Introducing a more complex account of human motivation into economics, he argues, would have far-reaching consequences for many economic models. More recently, empirical research in behavioral economics has offered strong support to Sen's claim: people really do behave altruistically even when no reward is in the offing.

What is this further type of altruism? Monroe focuses on people who do good for others even though faced not only with a strong possibility of death but also with bad results for reputation and family. Her central exhibits are rescuers of Jews during World War II. The rescuers were part of a culture that disparaged their acts. They risked death and loss of family reputation, incurring great risk when they might have remained safe. Nor did they seek after-life religious rewards. They did so, Monroe concludes, because they just felt it was the right thing. The results of Monroe's study dovetail with the more extensive empirical study of rescuers conducted by Samuel and Pearl Oliner.[4]

Rescuers are unusual individuals, although one of the unusual things about them is that they don't see themselves as special. Repeatedly, they say it was just what they felt they had to do. The case is analytically valuable, because only in such extreme cases can we see clearly the distinction between "philanthropists" and more selfless altruists, people who do good because of the inherent value of the good deed and its recipients. But we should expect (and the behavioral literature suggests) that selfless altruism is often a mundane matter, encompassing the standard behavior of many loving parents, friends, and fellow citizens.

There is, however, one further distinction to be drawn. There are really two distinct varieties of selfless altruism. In the first type, the person does the good deed because it is a good deed—so the act is selfless in that sense—but it's still important to the person that she is the one doing that good deed. Putting on my Aristotelian hat, I might say that she chooses it as a constituent part of a flourishing human life. Thus, she really wants to promote social justice for its own sake, but it is important to her that she be the one who promotes social justice. She wants to do what will promote the flourishing of her children, but she wants them to flourish as a result of her excellent care. This sort of altruism is genuinely selfless: the person doesn't seek reputation or satisfaction or even posthumous survival, she just wants to do the good action. But she wants to do it herself: we can't describe what she wants without putting in the "I."

The second type is subtly different. The person still wants the good for its own sake, but her concern for her own involvement in producing it drops away. As philosopher Bernard Williams puts it, her desires are "non-I desires."[5] As Williams notes, these cases often arise in testamentary decisions: a person wants her child to be comfortable and well-off— and it is only incidental that her own actions contribute to that result. Or she wants a particular painting to be well displayed—and again, her own causal role is incidental. Testamentary cases, however, are ambiguous, since in fact it is the person's own act that promotes the desired result. It's very hard to distinguish "non-I altruism" from selfless but "I-mentioning" altruism—and even from the more selfish philanthropic version, in which one seeks posthumous satisfaction of a current selfish desire (for vicarious immortality, say). But we can at least see that there is a distinction, and that, for example, many environmentalists really want to stop global warming as a good in itself, even if they themselves can contribute little or nothing to that end.

So we have four possibilities:

(1) A selfish act, undertaken for selfish ends, in fact does good to others.
(2) An act undertaken for a mixture of selfish and unselfish ends is reasonably expected to do good for others.[6]

(3) An act, undertaken for the sake of others (or some impersonal value), is reasonably expected to benefit others, and the person sees her own participation in the act as important.

(4) An act or project or wish is undertaken for the sake of others (or some impersonal value), and the person does not see her own participation as important.

Both (3) and (4) are robust forms of altruism. But (2), the form of altruism lauded by Plato, is not so bad either. Mixed motives are not a bad thing, if they work to incentivize good projects that might otherwise not occur. Plato's form seems very close, indeed, to the purer altruism of (3), in that the projects undertaken are chosen because the person values them and for that reason thinks them suitable vehicles for her posthumous life. (He ignores cases where people might foster quirky and nonvaluable projects just because they feel close to them.) It seems to me that Plato is right: people are often led to altruism by some idea of leaving their imprint on the world, and such desires do encourage selfless behavior, even if it isn't entirely free of ego.

Fear's Narrowing Influence

Plato suggests that the awareness of mortality leads primarily to good things. Even if the people who have children are not his favorites, those people, at the bottom of Plato's ladder, are still caring about the world and its future and doing something to improve it. He talks about awareness of mortality, but he doesn't really talk about fear. But fear poses problems for his sunny view of the ways in which awareness of death influences behavior.

The fear of death was hardly unknown to ancient Greek culture. Epicurus, a philosopher writing just after Plato's death, thought that the fear of death was the central problem in human life. Calling death "the most terrifying of evils," he argued that this fear makes human beings subservient to religious superstition—which, in turn, creates incentives for very bad behavior. His Roman pupil Lucretius begins his marvelous poem *On the Way Things Are* by depicting Agamemnon's slaughter of Iphigenia, ordered by the priests. The Epicureans' basic idea is that we are so terrified of death that we give organized religion too much power in our lives and agree to do whatever priests tell us, without thinking for ourselves.

We also do other irrational things to stave off death, Lucretius argues in a later part of his poem. We amass money in miserly fashion, thinking somehow that riches make us immortal—but riches only make us obsessive, and greedy for more. We go to war with other nations, believing irrationally that conquest of territory protects us from death—but violence only breeds further violence, escalating in a gory crescendo.[7] At the climax of this section of the poem, Lucretius imagines that people get the idea that using lions and tigers in combat will help them win battles—and then those beasts turn on their "masters" and devour them. You get the point: the fear of death breeds pointless, self-destructive acts that are bad for the world as a whole—not Diotima's happy world of creative altruism. Of Plato's idea of the "beautiful," central to his picture of creativity, Epicurus is said to have remarked: "I have spat upon the beautiful."

Who is right? To go deeper we need to think about fear. What Epicurus and Lucretius suggest is that fear, and especially the fear of death, is a particularly strong and nondeliberative passion, capable of eclipsing rational thought and producing obsessive and even bizarre behavior. Plato just doesn't register this problem. The way he sees it, people are pretty calm about death, and are surely capable of reasoned planning in the face of it. We have to say that much of the time Plato seems to be right: we go about our business, aware that we are mortal, and that, though it simmers in the background, does not stop us from doing useful things. On the other hand, we also know that there are times when fear breaks through: times of illness, for example, or the loss of a spouse or even parent, and we are brought to the brink of the abyss, so to speak. Epicurus understands this. A dialogue falsely attributed to Plato, but really produced by a pupil of Epicurus, imagines an elderly pupil of Socrates, who used to be very calm, suddenly encountering the imminent prospect of his own death. Axiochus is devastated, and rolls around on the ground in agony. When "Socrates" asks him what happened to all the arguments he learned from him (really, of course, Plato), Axiochus confesses: "Now that I am right up against the fearful thing, all my fine and clever arguments sneak away and breathe their last."[8]

Epicurus is sparring with Plato, and he makes a good point. When fear grips the mind, it becomes narrow, and people tend to forget their high commitments and fine arguments. Modern biology confirms this insight. Neuroscientific research into the roots of fear show us that it is an unusually primitive emotion, which responds, often, to subrational hardwired prompts, rather than to rational deliberation.[9] It is the only emotion, very likely, that all animals share, and the fear of a rat caught in a trap is not as different from human fear as we like to imagine, exalting our species.

Le Doux does not claim that his evolutionary story gives us a complete account of the roles played by fear in human life. In many cases, clearly, fear is more cognitively mediated, driven by dangers that we learn to believe in or are persuaded to think serious—the reason why Aristotle devotes so much attention to fear in the *Rhetoric*, giving instructions to orators about how to whip it up or take it away. But particularly in the context of death and pain, the primitive self-centeredness of fear does take center stage. Descriptions of battle frequently draw attention to the way in which danger narrows the minds of soldiers, making them keenly aware of their own bodies and their immediate surroundings, and not much beyond that.[10] In such a state of mind, morality is likely to suffer—a reason why soldiers are trained so obsessively in the duty to rescue their comrades, and to identify their own bodies with theirs, their selfhood with the unit as a whole. The fact that this training often works does not show that fear is not a threat to altruism: the very fact that it is required shows the immense danger fear creates. When such rigorous training is absent, fear often engenders total solipsism.

Philosopher Adam Smith makes the point vivid by imagining a generous-spirited person in Europe who hears about an earthquake in China. At first he is very upset, grieving for the suffering people. Probably he would be ready to donate to an Internet charity to help them, if such options were before him. But then, Smith imagines, he learns that his own finger will have to be amputated the following day. Immediately all his generous and humane sentiments vanish. He can't sleep. And "the destruction of that immense multitude seems plainly an object less interesting to him, than this paltry misfortune of his own."[11] Fear contracts the mind, riveting it to the preoccupations of the ego. As novelist Iris Murdoch wrote in her novel *The Black Prince*, "Anxiety most of all characterizes the human animal. . . . Fortunate are they who are even sufficiently aware of this problem to make the smallest efforts to check this dimming preoccupation."

We have two views of the fear of death before us. Plato says that it is amenable to moral guidance, and that it generally leads people to invest energy in improving the world of the future. Epicurus says that it is far more primitive and ungovernable than that: it dims the sight, leading people to do destructive things to others in the misguided belief that they will somehow prevail over death. Both appear to be right part of the time. Plato is right that people do fine things in search of a surrogate immortality—but he greatly underrates the paralyzing and disorienting power of fear, which Epicurus gets right. Epicurus is right about the danger of fear, though he simply ignores the possibility of happier cases. How might we promote Platonic altruism and discourage Epicurean destructiveness?

One way that seems unpromising is the way chosen by Epicurus himself. He thinks that if people clearly understand that the person ends at death and can never come back again, the fear of death will simply vanish—so he devotes most of his career to cosmological and physical arguments allegedly proving this point. Although a profound psychologist about many things, here he simply fails to understand what people really fear, all his subtle metaphysical arguments notwithstanding. A better direction is suggested by my discussion of battlefield altruism. It is evidently possible so to habituate people to altruistic behavior that they will disregard the promptings of terror and behave well to their comrades. In all times and places, producing this sort of committed and deeply habituated cohesion has been a major goal of any successful military enterprise.

We might be able to generalize this by thinking about the type of habituation in virtue that extends throughout life. If people are brought up to honor certain goals and ideals, to love other people, and to love good causes, and if those commitments are somehow implanted in them at a deep level by teaching, habituation, and parental love, then virtue may be able to overcome terror, producing Platonic rather than Epicurean results.

This strategy gives bad news to the aging: it basically says that it's too late for you. Either you are a good person or you aren't, and the seeds of good or bad character have been sown early. Ancient Greek views of character, however, exaggerate the extent of our psychological immobility. Some Christian views exaggerate in the other direction, suggesting that it is always possible to begin anew and become someone else. But more subtle Christian views (along with related views in other religions) do not represent this recommitment as an easy process: they suggest a patient effort to divest oneself of self-centeredness and greed, which may require constant watchfulness and meditation. So if aging people want to be ready for terror when it strikes, that is the sort of self-work they ought to be doing.

A complementary strategy is "precommitment." Odysseus asked to be lashed to the mast so that he could hear the Sirens' song but would not be led by it to run his ship aground. Economists have generalized from this case and created the category of precommitments, ways of making ourselves do things that we might not want to do in the moment.[12] Having a certain amount automatically deducted from one's paycheck for a retirement account is a typical example: in the moment we might consume impulsively, but if it's too much trouble to change the wise strategy, we will stick with it. A central example of precommitment is, of course, making a will. Wills are good things anyway, since intestacy is usually disadvantageous to all the people one cares about, but they are above all a way to make sure that one's values and commitments prevail, and can't be easily led aground by momentary terror. Wills can be changed, but that takes work, so wills are a way of not being hijacked by the moment.

But wills, of course, can favor good causes and bad. They can reward kin fairly or unfairly. They can result from careful deliberation or they can embody resentments and grudges stored up over a lifetime. So we won't get much out of this general strategy unless we have much more to say about the way we should try to face the future, forming good habits and solidifying ethical commitments, both in our intimate circle and toward the wider world.

Altruism in Close Relationships

Altruism in close relationships means not being manipulative, not using people as mere means, but trying hard to see them, and to benefit them, for their own sake, as people whose well-being is of intrinsic importance. Well, of course that's a good way to treat people at any age. What's special about getting older that makes this type of altruism a challenge?

As people age, they continue to need and love friends and family members; as time goes on they may become asymmetrically dependent on others. Even if aging people are not in the egocentric state of terror I've already depicted, they can become self-preoccupied as a result of daily irritations, lesser pains, difficulties of mobility, fears of faltering competence. They may be irritable, difficult to be with; they may also fear that they are unacceptable because they are not who they used to be. And the very fact of needing the help of others is often felt as a diminution of agency and selfhood.

To some extent these worries can be addressed by promoting ongoing mobility and independence through wise public policy. Family relationships are eased by sensible policy interventions (good and extensive public transportation, in-home nursing care) that make it possible for people not to demand so much care from their families. To some extent, too, the workplace needs to adjust to allow working adults more flexible schedules when they do have caregiving responsibilities, thus removing strain at the other end. But there is still much to be pondered about the relationships themselves, and the sorts of virtues that make it possible for aging adults to be unselfish and generous to their loved ones.

In thinking about altruism here, we have the same four possibilities that I identified in my general discussion of altruism. (1) An aging person might treat loved ones well for the sake of some self-centered end: say, to manipulate them into offering more service and care. That, as I've said, is not real altruism, and I won't discuss it further. (2) Then there are some aging people who, like Plato's married couples, are primarily focused on their own lasting mark on the world through children and grandchildren, and in the service of that immortality they promote their children's well-being. Finally, there are my two types of pure altruism. Since my theme is forming habits of good behavior in interacting with loved ones, I shall focus on what I've called type (3): aging people treat their loved ones well because they are committed to the value of that way of acting, and because they love the people for their own sake.

Altruism is partly financial, and I have little to add to Saul's discussion of those aspects. But it is also a much more mundane matter of promoting the happiness of loved ones. What traits or habits make that possible?

The first point to be made is that one should prepare for loss of control long before it happens, by not emulating King Lear, addicted as he is to controlling everything and everyone, as we saw in chapter 1. Interdependence is a feature of all human life, frequently a delightful one; by valuing and learning to enjoy it people prepare for the greater dependency that may come with age.

Second, aging people should also focus on emotional self-control. Honesty has value, but honesty doesn't mean blurting out every fear, annoyance, and complaint. Our culture, addicted to self-revelation, has to some extent forgotten the obvious fact that a statement of one's emotions is far from neutral. It makes demands on others. Altruism toward loved ones crucially involves sparing them a lot of the negative emotions one feels. People who do not show their every emotion are sometimes regarded as cold in American culture, as if they didn't have deep emotions and weren't vulnerable to deep need, longing, and fear. However, often the deeper love is the love that does not proclaim itself all the time or make demands associated with such proclamations. Reticence is grace.

Third, trying hard to imagine the perspective of one's loved ones is just as crucial here as in the rest of life, but it can be especially difficult as one ages on account of the narrowing influence of anxiety, which can rivet us to our own perspective. Trying to remember how one's children and grandchildren and younger and older friends feel and what they want is an exercise that one ought to perform every day. Keeping a journal—not of one's own feelings but of other people's—can assist this process, but people all too rarely keep such journals, whether in notebooks or on blogs, preferring to let the ego take over.

It's a cliché that one can view a glass as half empty or as half full, but this old idea is true and offers useful guidance. We all know people, aging or not, who find reason for complaint or sadness in everything around them. They are always unhappy, and they drive people away. It is far better to get accustomed to seeing the positive side. But it's harder as one ages, since there are some really bad things, ill health, pain, and the prospect of death, to contend with. Still, focusing on the good parts is a great way of both being happier and making others happier.

Perhaps the greatest asset to altruism as one ages is a sense of humor. (Here we get no help from either Plato or Epicurus.) One might think that this is something that cannot be cultivated, but of course it can and should, in a lifelong way, simply by forming habits of looking at the comical or absurd side of things and finding something hilariously delightful that might otherwise seem awkward, or disgusting, or grim. Refining one's sense of the ridiculous through films, TV, and novels is a great preparation for the tragicomedy of age.

How We Survive in the Future of the World

Altruism, however, is not just about how we treat those we love. As Plato wisely notes, we want to be involved in the future of the world in some way, leaving some mark, some difference that our life has made. This is a perpetual theme in philosophy, and it is usually treated very badly. Namely, from Plato to Simone de Beauvoir (whose views I discuss in chapter 1), philosophers tend to be elitists, and they imagine this mark on the world as a creative contribution made by an outstanding individual. In other words, only a few people can be altruists. Beauvoir even concludes that for this reason only a chosen few can overcome the horror and despair of aging.

This is a very narrow and partial conception of how one contributes to the future of the world. Many valuable contributions are corporate: one takes part in a movement, or an enterprise, which over time bears fruit. The environmental movement, the animal welfare movement, the Civil Rights movement, an army fighting a just war, an arts organization, a religious organization—all these and countless other group efforts are ways of working for the future of the world in which unheralded people may contribute a valuable share. Some excellent contributions, like Plato's writings, are individual products, but many others are more like a medieval cathedral, built up over the ages by the incremental contributions of many people.

Moreover, as I remarked in chapter 1, the Beauvoir/Plato position wrongly denigrates all sorts of contributions nonphilosophers make to the future of the world: by having and raising children, by teaching children or older students, by helping colleagues with their work, and so forth. One can engage in genuine altruism—promoting the good of others as an end in itself—in countless ways, and in whatever walk of life one's talents and circumstances suggest. This is as true during aging as earlier in life.

Most strikingly, this position neglects or denigrates the value of economic activity. I'm sure that both Plato and Beauvoir (for different reasons, Greek elitism in the one case, Marxism in the other) think that making money is base and trivial. But of course they are wrong. No nation or cause or organization can flourish without economic activity. Oskar Schindler saved more Jews by running a business and bribing Nazi officials than others saved by goodwill and pious efforts. It is quite striking to see our nation's current rapturous enthusiasm for the figure of Alexander Hamilton, whose credo was that a good cause needed a strong financial system and a centralized bank. Hamilton was correct, and the people who helped create the economic structure of the United States, or who operated within it, deserve great credit. Some such people are those entrepreneurs with individual profit as their goal; their contribution to others is an incidental byproduct. But it is obviously possible to practice economic activity as a mode of genuine altruism. One might focus on the way one's product, or business, or innovation enhances the world—a form of Platonic altruism. Or one might more simply focus on the good of one's employees, as did Schindler, or on the good of one's fellow employees if one is not a manager, and see a well-run decent business, which treats people decently

and also contributes to economic growth, as a way of contributing positively to the world.

Such thoughts are rarely thought within philosophy, which spurns the
mere moneymaker as a low, base type of person. For this reason, philosophers of the past have had a very incomplete picture of altruism.

ALTRUISM IS ALWAYS a difficult challenge, since human beings are basically selfish, and reach out to others, in infancy, only as means to gratify
their needs. As children grow older, if they are loved and well brought up,
they learn how to love others as ends in themselves. If their education is
really good, they learn how to care about people beyond their immediate
familial and friendly circle, and about general causes, forming a range of
valuable commitments. But aging does risk bringing us all to a second
childhood, in which the imperious demands of the ego, and of immediate
bodily need, get in the way of the good habits one has formed, cutting us
off from the larger world of value. We all need to be aware of this moral
risk, in order to fight against it as well as we can—preferably with grace,
humor, and humility.

Notes

1. Plato's strong preference for male-male love was widespread in the culture.
   Many males married and reproduced while reserving intense romantic relationships for males, but Plato does not recommend this alternative: in the *Phaedrus*
   he proposes that pairs of males will spend their entire lives together.
2. See Kristen Renwick Monroe, *The Heart of Altruism* (Princeton, NJ: Princeton
   University Press, 1996), reviewed by Nussbaum in the *New Republic*, October
   28, 1996, 36–42; the review is reprinted in Nussbaum, *Philosophical Interventions*
   (New York: Oxford University Press, 2012).
3. Amartya Sen, "Rational Fools: A Critique of the Behavioral Foundations of
   Economic Theory," *Philosophy and Public Affairs* 6 (1977), 317–44, reprinted in
   Sen, *Choice, Welfare and Measurement* (Oxford: Blackwell, 1982), 84–106.
4. Samuel P. Oliner and Pearl M. Oliner, *The Altruistic Personality: Rescuers of Jews in
   Nazi Europe* (New York: Free Press, 1988).
5. Bernard Williams, "Egoism and Altruism," in Williams, *Problems of the Self*
   (Cambridge: Cambridge University Press, 1973).
6. "Reasonably expected" is important here, because, unlike the first case, this is a
   case of intelligent aiming at the good; I don't want to label as nonaltruistic a person who is simply mistaken.

7. See my detailed discussion of these passages in *The Therapy of Desire: Theory and Practice in Hellenistic Ethics* (Princeton, NJ: Princeton University Press, 1994), chapter 8.

8. Pseudo-Plato, *Axiochus.*

9. See Joseph Le Doux, *The Emotional Brain* (New York: Simon and Schuster, 1996). I discuss his work further in *The New Religious Intolerance: Overcoming the Politics of Fear in an Anxious Age* (Cambridge, MA: Harvard University Press, 2011), chapter 2.

10. For one classic example, see *The New Religious Intolerance,* 28.

11. Smith, *The Theory of Moral Sentiments.* See Ronald Coase, "Adam Smith's View of Man," *Journal of Law and Economics* 19 (1976), 529–46.

12. See Jon Elster, *Ulysses and the Sirens* (Cambridge: Cambridge University Press, 1979).

Index